# The Changeling

## ARDEN EARLY MODERN DRAMA GUIDES

Series Editors:

Andrew Hiscock, University of Wales, Bangor, UK and
Lisa Hopkins, Sheffield Hallam University, UK

*Arden Early Modern Drama Guides* offer practical and accessible introductions to the critical and performative contexts of key Elizabethan and Jacobean plays. Each guide introduces the text's critical and performance history, but also provides students with an invaluable insight into the landscape of current scholarly research, through a keynote essay on the state of the art and newly commissioned essays of fresh research from different critical perspectives.

*A Midsummer Night's Dream* edited by Regina Buccola
*Doctor Faustus* edited by Sarah Munson Deats
*King Lear* edited by Andrew Hiscock and Lisa Hopkins
*Henry IV, Part 1* edited by Stephen Longstaffe
*'Tis Pity She's a Whore* edited by Lisa Hopkins
*Women Beware Women* edited by Andrew Hiscock
*Volpone* edited by Matthew Steggle
*The Duchess of Malfi* edited by Christina Luckyj
*The Alchemist* edited by Erin Julian and Helen Ostovich
*The Jew of Malta* edited by Robert A. Logan
*Macbeth* edited by John Drakakis and Dale Townshend
*Richard III* edited by Annaliese Connolly
*Twelfth Night* edited by Alison Findlay and Liz Oakley-Brown
*The Tempest* edited by Alden T. Vaughan and
Virginia Mason Vaughan
*Romeo and Juliet* edited by Julia Reinhard Lupton
*Julius Caesar* edited by Andrew James Hartley
*The Revenger's Tragedy* edited by Brian Walsh
*The White Devil* edited by Paul Frazer and Adam Hansen
*Much Ado About Nothing* edited by Deborah Cartmell and
Peter J. Smith
*King Henry V* edited by Karen Britland and Line Cottegnies

Further titles are in preparation

# The Changeling

*A Critical Reader*

*Edited by*
*Mark Hutchings*

THE ARDEN SHAKESPEARE
LONDON • NEW YORK • OXFORD • NEW DELHI • SYDNEY

THE ARDEN SHAKESPEARE
Bloomsbury Publishing Plc
50 Bedford Square, London, WC1B 3DP, UK
1385 Broadway, New York, NY 10018, USA

BLOOMSBURY, THE ARDEN SHAKESPEARE and the Arden Shakespeare logo
are trademarks of Bloomsbury Publishing Plc

First published in Great Britain 2019
This paperback edition published in 2021

Copyright © Mark Hutchings and contributors, 2019

Mark Hutchings and contributors have asserted their rights under the Copyright,
Designs and Patents Act, 1988, to be identified as authors of this work.

Cover image taken from the 1615 title page of *The Spanish Tragedy* by Thomas Kyd

All rights reserved. No part of this publication may be reproduced or transmitted
in any form or by any means, electronic or mechanical, including photocopying,
recording, or any information storage or retrieval system, without prior
permission in writing from the publishers.

Bloomsbury Publishing Plc does not have any control over, or responsibility for,
any third-party websites referred to or in this book. All internet addresses given
in this book were correct at the time of going to press. The author and publisher
regret any inconvenience caused if addresses have changed or sites have
ceased to exist, but can accept no responsibility for any such changes.

A catalogue record for this book is available from the British Library.

Library of Congress Control Number: 2019941516

ISBN:  HB:    978-1-3500-1140-3
       PB:    978-1-3501-9757-2
       ePDF:  978-1-3500-1138-0
       eBook: 978-1-3500-1139-7

Series: Arden Early Modern Drama Guides

Typeset by RefineCatch Limited, Bungay, Suffolk

To find out more about our authors and books visit www.bloomsbury.com
and sign up for our newsletters.

# CONTENTS

*Series Introduction* vii
*Notes on Contributors* viii
*Timeline* xi

   Introduction 1
   *Mark Hutchings*

1 The Critical Backstory 15
   *Sara D. Luttfring*

2 A Performance History 35
   *Jennifer Panek*

3 State of the Art 67
   *Patricia A. Cahill*

4 New Directions: Embodied Theatre in *The Changeling* 93
   *Peter Womack*

5 New Directions: Doubles and Falsehoods: *The Changeling*'s Spanish Undertexts 121
   *Berta Cano-Echevarría*

6 New Directions: Performing *The Changeling*: 2006–2015 143
   *Sarah Dustagheer*

7 New Directions: Loving and Loathing: Horror in *The Changeling* from Text to Screen  165
*Nathalie Vienne-Guerrin*

8 Resources  187
*Nora J. Williams*

*Notes*  211
*Select Bibliography*  263
*Index*  269

# SERIES INTRODUCTION

The drama of Shakespeare and his contemporaries has remained at the very heart of English curricula internationally and the pedagogic needs surrounding this body of literature have grown increasingly complex as more sophisticated resources become available to scholars, tutors and students. This series aims to offer a clear picture of the critical and performative contexts of a range of chosen texts. In addition, each volume furnishes readers with invaluable insights into the landscape of current scholarly research as well as including new pieces of research by leading critics.

This series is designed to respond to the clearly identified needs of scholars, tutors and students for volumes which will bridge the gap between accounts of previous critical developments and performance history and an acquaintance with new research initiatives related to the chosen plays. Thus, our ambition is to offer innovative and challenging guides that will provide practical, accessible and thought-provoking analyses of early modern drama. Each volume is organized according to a progressive reading strategy involving introductory discussion, critical review and cutting-edge scholarly debate. It has been an enormous pleasure to work with so many dedicated scholars of early modern drama and we are sure that this series will encourage you to read 400-year-old play texts with fresh eyes.

Andrew Hiscock and Lisa Hopkins

# NOTES ON CONTRIBUTORS

**Patricia A. Cahill** is Associate Professor of English at Emory University. She is the author of *Unto the Breach: Martial Formations, Historical Trauma, and the Early Modern Stage* (2008) and is currently completing a book project that explores affect and animal skins on the early modern stage.

**Berta Cano-Echevarría** is Associate Professor of English Literature and Culture at the University of Valladolid, Spain. Her research interests focus both on cultural and literary exchanges and textual transmission. She has published a number of articles and book chapters on the literature of the exiles in the English College at Valladolid, on the work of Philip Sidney and on the cultural manifestations of the Anglo-Spanish peace of 1604–5. She has been editor of *Sederi*, and is currently serving as Head of Department at the University of Valladolid.

**Sarah Dustagheer** is Senior Lecturer in Early Modern Literature at the University of Kent, and a member of Shakespeare's Globe's Architecture Research Group. She is the author of *Shakespeare's Two Playhouses: Repertory and Theatre Space at the Globe and Blackfriars, 1599–1613* (2017), which has been shortlisted for Shakespeare's Globe Book Award 2018, co-author of *Shakespeare in London* (Bloomsbury, 2014) and co-editor (with Gillian Woods) of *Stage Directions and the Shakespearean Stage* (Bloomsbury, 2017). Her essays on early modern playwriting and theatre space and contemporary Shakespearean performance have appeared in *Shakespeare Jahrbuch, Literature Compass, Cahiers Élisabéthains* and *Shakespeare Bulletin*.

**Mark Hutchings** teaches at the University of Reading, where he specializes in early modern theatre and performance. He has published widely on Thomas Middleton, including (with A.A. Bromham) *Middleton and His Collaborators* (2008); *Turks, Repertories, and the Early Modern English Stage* was published in 2017.

**Sara D. Luttfring** is an Associate Professor of English at Penn State Behrend. She is the author of *Bodies, Speech, and Reproductive Knowledge in Early Modern England* (2016). Her current research focuses on the gendering of readers and print markets in early modern publication histories.

**Jennifer Panek** is an Associate Professor of English at the University of Ottawa. She is the author of *Widows and Suitors in Early Modern English Comedy* (2004), and editor of the Norton Critical Edition of *The Roaring Girl*. Her essays have appeared in *ELR*, *ELH*, *Renaissance Drama*, *Journal for Early Modern Cultural Studies*, *Studies in English Literature 1500–1900*, and elsewhere. She is currently working on a book about sexual shame in early modern drama.

**Nathalie Vienne-Guerrin** is Professor in Shakespeare Studies at the Université Paul-Valéry Montpellier 3 and director of the 'Institut de Recherche sur la Renaissance, l'âge Classique et les Lumières' (IRCL, UMR 5186 CNRS). She is co-editor-in-chief of *Cahiers Élisabéthains* and co-director (with Patricia Dorval) of the *Shakespeare on Screen in Francophonia Database* (shakscreen.org). She is co-editor, with Sarah Hatchuel, of the *Shakespeare on Screen* series, and author of *The Unruly Tongue in Early Modern England, Three Treatises* (2012) and *Shakespeare's Insults: A Pragmatic Dictionary* (2016). She is currently working on a monograph, *The Anatomy of Insults in Shakespeare's World* (Arden Shakespeare).

**Nora J. Williams** is Lecturer in Shakespeare and Early Modern Drama and Literature at the University of Essex. Her previous work on *The Changeling* had been published in *Shakespeare Bulletin*, *Early Modern Literary Studies*, and in *Contemporary Approaches to Adaptation in Theatre & Performance*, edited by Kara Reilly. Current projects include a monograph on Shakespeare and Twitter, and a practice-as-research project that uses *Measure for Measure* to facilitate discussions regarding rape culture and instigate policy change in educational institutions.

**Peter Womack** is a professor of literature and drama at the University of East Anglia; his more recent books are *English Renaissance Drama* (2006) and *Dialogue* (2011).

# TIMELINE

| | |
|---|---|
| 1580 | Thomas Middleton is born in London, and baptized in St Lawrence Jewry. |
| 1585 | Conjectural date for the birth of William Rowley, probably in London; whether he had any familial connection with fellow actor and playwright Samuel Rowley (?–1624) is unknown, but there is no record of their having worked together. |
| 1588 | Spanish Armada launched against England by Philip II. |
| 1596 | Sack of Cadiz by English forces. |
| 1598 | Middleton begins his studies at Queen's College, Oxford.<br>Death of Philip II and accession of Philip III to the Habsburg throne. |
| 1599 | In June, Middleton's recently-published poem, *Microcynicon: Six Snarling Satires*, is among ten works ordered to be publicly burned by the archbishop of Canterbury and bishop of London. |
| 1600 | Middleton's poem *The Ghost of Lucrece* is published. |
| 1601 | Earliest record of Middleton's association with the London theatre, Middleton having apparently left Oxford before completing his degree (which was not unusual for gentlemen). |
| 1602 | The first-known mention of Middleton as a playwright, recorded in Philip Henslowe's *Diary* as receiving payment (along with Anthony Munday, Michael Drayton, and John Webster) for a now lost play, *Caesar's Fall*, for the Admiral's Men. Over the |

|  |  |
|---|---|
|  | next five years Middleton writes predominantly for the children's companies, notably Paul's Boys. |
| 1603 | Death of Elizabeth I and accession of James VI of Scotland to the throne of England. |
| 1604 | Peace negotiated with Spain at the Treaty of London. |
| 1605 | Ratification of the Treaty of London in Valladolid; the returning English embassy brings Spanish books into England, most notably Cervantes' *Don Quixote* (Book I), published in Spain earlier in the year. |
|  | Middleton collaborates with Shakespeare on *Timon of Athens* for the King's Men. |
| 1606 | Middleton writes *The Revenger's Tragedy* for the King's Men. |
| 1607 | Rowley's earliest-known association with playmaking: he is named along with George Wilkins and John Day as co-authors of *The Travails of the Three English Brothers* for Queen Anne's Men. Rowley may have written and acted the role of William Kemp, based on the famous Shakespearean clown who had died several years previously. |
|  | Rowley and Thomas Heywood write *Fortune by Land and Sea* for Queen Anne's Men. |
|  | The Dutch navy defeats Spanish forces at the Battle of Gibraltar. |
| 1609 | Earliest firm record of Rowley as an actor, with the Duke of York's Men (later renamed, after the death of Prince Henry in 1612, Prince Charles's Men). |
|  | Treaty of Antwerp signed, providing for a cessation of hostilities between Spain and Holland, for a period of twelve years. |
| 1611–15 | Rowley's first-known sole-authored play, *A New Wonder*, written for Prince Charles's Men. |
| 1612 | Death of Prince Henry, heir to the throne of England. |

| | |
|---|---|
| 1613 | Middleton and Rowley collaborate for the first time, on *Wit at Several Weapons*, for Prince Charles's Men.
Middleton writes, *The Triumps of Truth*, the first of several entertainments he is commissioned to provide for the inauguration of the Lord Mayor, performed on 29 October.
Marriage of Princess Elizabeth to Frederick V, count palatine of the Rhine and elector of the Holy Roman Empire.
Spanish diplomat Don Diego Sarmiento de Acuña (later Count Gondomar, widely believed to be the principal architect of the 'Spanish Match', the plan for a dynastic marriage between the Habsburg and Stuart houses and satirized in Middleton's *A Game at Chess* a decade later) arrives in England to serve as Spain's ambassador; a period of convalescence in Spain in 1618–20 aside, he is ambassador until 1622.
In May Frances Howard, countess of Essex, petitions for the annulment of her marriage to the earl of Essex on the grounds of non-consumation, which following a medical examination in June by a committee widely believed to have been influenced by the king himself is granted in September, the same month in which Sir Thomas Overbury, who opposed Howard and Carr's marriage plans and had been imprisoned in the Tower for displeasing King James, dies; in December Howard marries Carr, recently created earl of Somerset. |
| 1615 | In October Frances Howard and Robert Carr are arrested on suspicion of murdering Overbury, amid rumours of witchcraft. |
| c.1616 | Middleton writes *The Witch* and revises Shakespeare's *Macbeth* (1606) for the King's Men. |
| 1616 | Middleton and Rowley write *A Fair Quarrel* for Prince Charles's Men; as with *The Changeling* |

Rowley provides the subplot and also contributes other elements of the play.

Howard and Carr are indicted in January for the murder by poisoning of Sir Thomas Overbury and in May Howard confesses and is sentenced to hang; Carr, protesting his innocence, is also sentenced to death: both are imprisoned in the Tower; their accomplices had been executed, following earlier trials, while the Somersets received pardons, though the earl not until 1624.

**1618** Middleton and Rowley (perhaps with Thomas Heywood) write *The Old Law* for Prince Charles's Men.

Outbreak of the Thirty Years' War; Frederick and Elizabeth exiled to Holland.

**1618–20** Rowley writes *All's Lost by Lust* for Prince Charles's Men and, probably for the same company and around this time, *A Shoemaker a Gentleman*.

**1619** Death of Anna of Denmark, Queen of England.

Death of Philip III and accession of Philip IV to the Habsburg throne.

**1620** Middleton and Rowley write *The World Tossed at Tennis* for Prince Charles's Men.

Middleton appointed City Chronologer for London.

**1621** John Reynolds' *The Triumphs of God's Revenge* published. Its popularity is attested to by its printing history: it is reissued thirteen times during the seventeenth century, including in 1622, 1623 and 1624.

Rowley, Dekker and Ford write *The Witch of Edmonton* for Prince Charles's Men.

Middleton's *Women Beware Women* was most likely written this year, probably for the King's Men.

Middleton revises *Measure for Measure* for the King's Men.

| | |
|---|---|
| | Expiration of the terms of the 1609 Treaty of Antwerp between Spain and Holland. |
| 1622 | In January Frances Howard and Robert Carr are released from the Tower. |
| | Leonard Digges' translation of *Gerardo the Unfortunate Spaniard* is entered in the Stationers' Register on 11 March. |
| | *The Changeling* is licensed by the Master of the Revels, on 7 May for Lady Elizabeth's Men. |
| | Rowley writes *The Birth of Merlin* for Prince Charles's Men. |
| | Earliest possible date for the staging of *The Changeling* at the Phoenix indoor playhouse. |
| 1623 | Middleton and Rowley, together with Dekker and Ford, write *The Spanish Gypsy* for Lady Elizabeth's Men. |
| | By this date Rowley has joined the King's Men. |
| | Rowley and Fletcher write *The Maid in the Mill* for the King's Men. |
| | Prince Charles and the Duke of Buckingham travel incognito to Madrid for what proves to be an abortive mission to Madrid to secure a 'Spanish Match' with the Infanta. |
| | Publication of the Shakespeare First Folio, which includes the Shakespeare-Middleton collaboration *Timon of Athens* and Middleton's revisions of *Macbeth* and *Measure for Measure*. |
| 1623–4 | *The Changeling* is one of a number of plays performed at court, following Charles's return from Spain; records indicate the prince attended the performance on 4 January 1624. |
| 1624 | In August Middleton's *A Game at Chess* is staged by the King's Men at the Globe, before being banned by order of the Privy Council, following the Spanish ambassador's complaint to James; subsequently the play circulates in manuscript. Rowley plays the part of Fat Bishop. |

|  |  |
|---|---|
|  | Rowley, Heywood and Webster write *A Cure for a Cuckold* for Prince Charles's Men. |
|  | Rowley, Dekker, Ford and Webster write *Keep the Widow Waking* (lost) for Prince Charles's Men. |
| 1625 | Death of James I and accession of Charles I; Middleton is commissioned to write the accession pageant but it is not performed, due to an outbreak of plague. |
|  | *A Game at Chess* is printed, three times (Q1–3). |
|  | Outbreak of war with Spain, in September. |
| 1626 | William Rowley dies and is buried in St James's, Clerkenwell. |
| 1627 | Thomas Middleton dies and is buried in Newington Butts, Southwark. |
| c.1629 | It is probable that *The Changeling* is staged at the Salisbury Court indoor playhouse. |
| 1630 | Anglo-Spanish hostilities are brought to an end with the Treaty of Madrid. |
| 1639 | *The Changeling* is one of a group of plays confirmed by the Lord Chamberlain as belonging to William Beeston, following the death of his father, Christopher Beeston, impresario at the Phoenix. |
| 1642 | Public theatricals are banned by order of Parliament. |
|  | Outbreak of the first English Civil War. |
| 1645 | William Robbins, almost certainly the actor who had played the 'changeling' (Antonio) to acclaim, prior to the closure of the theatres, dies in a clash during the Civil War. |
| 1646 | End of first Civil War. |
| 1647 | The Beaumont and Fletcher folio, which includes several plays now attributed to Middleton, is published by Humphrey Moseley. |
| 1648 | Outbreak of second English Civil War. |
|  | End of Thirty Years' War. |
| 1649 | End of second English Civil War. |
|  | Execution of Charles I. |

|   | Commonwealth of England established. |
|---|---|
|   | Outbreak of third English Civil War. |
| 1651 | End of third English Civil War. Charles I's son, later Charles II, along with many of his supporters, goes into exile. |
| 1653 | Protectorate under Oliver Cromwell replaces the Commonwealth. |
|   | *The Changeling* is first printed, in quarto for Humphrey Moseley (publisher) by Thomas Newcomb (printer). |
| 1658 | Death of Oliver Cromwell. |
| 1659 | According to John Downes (writing early in the eighteenth century), a troupe led by John Rhodes revives *The Changeling* at the Phoenix Theatre. |
| 1660 | Charles II is restored to the throne. |
| 1661 | Samuel Pepys sees a performance of *The Changeling* at the Duke of York's theatre by Sir William Davenant's company. |
| 1668 | *The Changeling* is performed at court, and reprinted, for 'AM', probably Anne Moseley (her father, printer of the 1653 quarto, having died in 1661). |
| 1784 | Publication of William Hayley's *Marcella*, a play inspired by *The Changeling*. |
| 1789 | A production of *Marcella* in Drury Lane is poorly received. |
| 1815 | C.W. Dilke includes *The Changeling* in Volume 4 of *Old Plays; Being a Continuation of Dodsley's Collection*; this is the first printing of the play since 1668. |
| 1840 | *The Changeling* is included in Alexander Dyce's five-volume *The Works of Thomas Middleton*, the first attempt to bring Middleton's sole-authored and collaborative plays together under one roof. |
| 1885–6 | A.H. Bullen's eight-volume edition, based on Dyce's and which includes *The Changeling*, is published. |

# TIMELINE

**1886** — *The Changeling* is included in Algernon Charles Swinburne and Havelock Ellis's two-volume, ten-play collection for the Mermaids series.

**1927** — T.S. Eliot's essay 'Thomas Middleton' published in the *Times Literary Supplement*, and subsequently reprinted in Eliot's collections of essays on early modern dramatists.

**1935** — Publication of William Empson's *Some Versions of Pastoral* and M.C. Bradbrook's *Themes and Conventions of Elizabethan Tragedy*, both of which discuss *The Changeling* and in particular explore the significance of the subplot.

**1938** — *The Changeling* is staged by the Birkbeck College Literary Society.

**1949** — *The Changeling* is staged by the Magdalen Players, Oxford.

**1956** — The first modern profesional production of *The Changeling* in the United States is mounted, directed by Joseph Papp for the New York Shakespeare Festival.

**1958** — Publication of N.W. Bawcutt's edition of *The Changeling* for the Revels series.

**1960** — Publication of Christopher Ricks' seminal essay, 'The Moral and Poetic Structure of *The Changeling*'.

**1961** — The first modern profesional production of the play in England, directed by Tony Richardson, is staged at the Royal Court.

**1964** — *The Changeling* is performed at the Lincoln Center's Repertory Theater, New York; directed by Elia Kazan, it receives poor reviews.

**1974** — A BBC TV production of *The Changeling* is broadcast, directed by Anthony Page.

**1980** — The publication of Margot Heinemann's *Puritanism and Theatre: Thomas Middleton and Opposition Drama under the Early Stuarts*, which advances the influential view that Middleton is notable as a politically-engaged writer.

| | |
|---|---|
| **1994** | A BBC TV production of *The Changeling* is broadcast, directed by Simon Curtis. |
| **1998** | *Middleton's Changeling*, a film directed by Marcus Thompson, is released. |
| **2004** | Roberta Barker and David Nicol's study of theatre productions and reviews, 'Does Beatrice Joanna Have a Subtext?: *The Changeling* on the London Stage', is published. |
| **2007** | *Thomas Middleton: The Collected Works* is published by Oxford University Press. |
| | *The Changeling*, a film directed by Jay Sterns, is released in New York. |
| **2009** | *Compulsion*, an ITV television drama adaptation of *The Changeling*, directed by Sarah Harding, is broadcast. |
| **2015** | *The Changeling* is directed by Dominic Dromgoole in the Sam Wanamaker Playhouse at Shakespeare's Globe, London. |

# Introduction

## Mark Hutchings

T.S. Eliot's evaluation of Thomas Middleton and William Rowley's 1622 collaboration – that it 'stands above every tragic play of its time' – has long found endorsement in the academy, the modern theatre repertory, school and university curricula, and latterly on the screen; indeed, for many who encounter it *The Changeling* challenges Eliot's rather predictable rider, 'except those of Shakespeare'.[1] In its own time, for which inevitably records are incomplete, all the indications are that it was popular. Featuring at court in 1624 (usually taken as an indication of previous stage success), it seems it appeared frequently up to the banning of public theatricals in 1642; it received its first printing during the Interregnum, and it was revived and reprinted in the Restoration, staged by Sir William Davenant's company, the Duke of York's, at Lincoln Inn Fields, as well as at the court of Charles II.[2] If thereafter, for the long eighteenth century at least, it disappeared almost entirely from view, it played no small part nonetheless in contributing to Middleton's (if not Rowley's) modern reputation – especially since, unlike Shakespeare, Jonson, and Beaumont and Fletcher, Middleton had not been collected and memorialized in folio, and so did not benefit from the canonization such literary monuments fostered.[3] Rather than being remembered textually in his own time, Middleton, like Rowley, was *dis*membered, several plays being re-attributed through their inclusion in the Shakespeare and Beaumont–Fletcher folios, others scattered to the four winds. Today, however, their masterpiece is regarded as one of the finest achievements in English drama – by any writer.

Eliot's much-reprinted essay anticipated and contributed significantly to the critical appreciation the play has enjoyed over nearly a century since; it also built on the Enlightenment rediscovery – one is tempted to call it a second Renaissance – of early modern English drama (which is to say, *non-Shakespearean* plays) that began with the efforts of Robert Dodsley. His twelve-volume *Select Collection of Old Plays*, first published in 1744, laid the foundations for the modern interest in the drama of this period, if principally in the study rather than on the boards. As it happens, although Dodsley's collection (reprinted in 1780 and reappearing in third and fourth editions in 1825–7 and 1874–6) did include several Middleton-attributed plays and collaborations, *The Changeling* was not among them.[4] Not until C.W. Dilke oversaw the publication of the six-volume *Old Plays; Being a Continuation of Dodsley's Collection* (1814–16), which added a further twenty-four plays to the sixty-one Dodsley had first compiled, was the play made available to potential readers (for the vast majority of whom surviving copies of the 1653 and 1668 quartos must have been inaccessible) – for the first time in more than 150 years.[5] Thereafter the play became central to what we now regard as the *Middleton* canon, his collaborator's contribution often ignored, as is the case in Eliot's essay. Over the course of two centuries, then, *The Changeling* has come to assume a position of some prominence, not only as the most highly regarded of all the plays associated with Middleton and Rowley, but also as one of the most esteemed examples of early modern drama – more visible, indeed, than some of Shakespeare's plays. This collection of essays charts that trajectory and explores the enduring interest of this canonical play, on stage, page and screen, up to the present time.

Prior to their earliest known work together, in 1613, it is unarguable that Middleton had established himself as the more accomplished dramatist, not only in terms of output but because Rowley was primarily a collaborative writer: the older man had already written plays that are highly regarded today, while the younger had proved himself an able contributor.[6] The sole-authored *Michaelmas Term* (1604), *A Trick to Catch the Old One* and *A Mad World, My Masters* (both 1605, all for the Children of Paul's), and *The Revenger's Tragedy* (1606, for the King's Men) – to cite only four of the plays we now associate with Middleton up to 1613 – demonstrate his range across genres and his facility for writing for both children's troupes and adult companies. But unlike Rowley, Middleton was not an actor, and the younger man had an aptitude for writing and performing clown scenes that would become his trademark. As Tony Bromham points out, 'that as accomplished a dramatist as Middleton worked quite extensively with Rowley and probably wrote parts for him (Plumporridge in *The Inner Temple Masque* [1619] and the Fat Bishop in *A Game at Chess* [1624]) suggests respect for the man as a writer and an actor'.[7] That these two plays were written by Middleton alone indicates that their collaboration was not confined to writing, and indeed points to a much broader partnership; as David Nicol remarks, *A Game at Chess* 'could be regarded as Middleton and Rowley's last collaboration', since the role of the Fat Bishop seems to have been conceived late in the composition process.[8] However, the accepted division of their respective contributions to *The Changeling* both demonstrates and qualifies assumptions that are traditionally made about their respective strengths – the one expert in tragedy, the other adept at comedy. Rowley did write the three subplot scenes, consisting of comic material set in a hospital or madhouse, yet he also wrote the opening and closing scenes of the play, setting up and concluding the main plot, the central tragedy. And yet even this broad-brush summary oversimplifies matters: as

Douglas Bruster points out, 'readers have [now] moved toward a model of collaboration *within* scenes'.[9] The consensus, then, is that this was a very close collaboration, and scholars readily recognize that identifying their respective contributions runs the risk of simplifying and perhaps misrepresenting the nature of their working practices, as well as undervaluing the subplot and its function.[10]

In any case, the recent resurgence of interest in collaboration as a standard theatre practice in this period – it is worth remembering that as many as two-thirds of the plays recorded in Philip Henslowe's account book were of this type[11] – has not only urged that collaborations were neither inferior to nor deviations from what might be considered, inappropriately for this theatre culture, the 'norm' of sole authorship traditionally more highly valued by critics, but that correspondingly plays such as *The Changeling* were successful not in spite of but *because* they were the work of more than one hand. For all that critics like Eliot think of the play as epitomizing *Middleton's* talent (echoed as recently as 1998 in the film-title *Middleton's Changeling*), Rowley's contribution is now widely regarded as crucial, although some modern directors have found the subplot a considerable challenge and indeed on occasion somewhat puzzling, as we shall see. But placed in the context of Middleton and Rowley's professional relationship the structure of *The Changeling* fits a pattern. Their first joint venture, *Wit at Several Weapons* (1613), drew on Middleton's skill in city comedy, R.H. Barker noting echoes of earlier Middleton plays (such as *A Trick to Catch the Old One* and *A Mad World, My Masters*).[12] As with their subsequent collaborations, *A Fair Quarrel* (1616) and *The Old Law* (1618, with Thomas Heywood), this play capitalizes on Rowley's distinctive skill in writing clowns, figures who typically feature in subplots. Some scholars have seen in this arrangement the possibility of creative tension, rather than harmony, between the two dramatists.[13] Indeed, the function of the clown is to disrupt, to subvert the main plot narrative. (It is a nice question, if Rowley did indeed play Lollio, whether he acted extempore as well, as clowns were wont to do.)[14] It may also be that this pattern of working helped speed up the process of composition. As Michael E. Mooney has demonstrated, there are close similarities in structure between their second collaboration, *A Fair Quarrel*, and *The Changeling*.[15] For the latter it would seem they had to work quickly, because one of their main sources, Leonard Digges' translation *Gerardo the Unfortunate Spaniard*, was only entered in the Stationers' Register on 7 March 1622, a matter of weeks before the Master of the Revels licensed *The Changeling* for performance.

*The Changeling* and *The Spanish Gypsy* (co-written with Thomas Dekker and John Ford, 1623) saw the two dramatists commenting directly and indirectly on a topical and (for many) troubling matter: the Stuart court's relationship with Spain.[16] This later play daringly alludes to the Prince of Wales and the Duke of Buckingham's reckless mission to Madrid to woo the Spanish Infanta, appearing *in medias res* in the summer of 1623, and both plays have received attention for their oblique commentary on international politics that would find a fuller and more open expression in the remarkable allegory *A Game at Chess*, a play that was allowed (for reasons that are still a matter of debate), then banned, following the Spanish ambassador's complaint to James.[17] Implicitly – though covertly – critical of James's foreign policy, these plays registered a climate of concern over domestic as well as international matters, for widespread, popular fears that the monarch and his Catholic queen were pursuing a pro-Rome policy were rooted in perceptions of the Jacobean court.

*The Changeling* alludes to the greatest scandal of the first Stuart reign, one which led directly to the king himself. Scholars have mapped the play's articulation of Beatrice-Joanna's – and Alsemero's – anxiety over bridal virginity onto the arranged marriage between Frances Howard and Robert Devereux which Howard subsequently claimed had not been consummated, her aim being to annul the marriage so that she could marry Robert Carr, the king's favourite and long believed at court to be her lover. The virginity test and bed-trick in Middleton and Rowley's play presents a suggestive parallel (especially for those who saw the play at court, in January 1624) to the physical examination Howard underwent to determine her claim that Devereux was impotent, overseen by a jury widely believed to have been influenced by the king, while Howard herself was rumoured – as Beatrice-Joanna does in the play – to have sent a virginal substitute in her place. But the scandal took a further twist when Howard and Carr were accused of poisoning Sir Thomas Overbury, who was strongly opposed to their proposed union; while their non-aristocratic accomplices were convicted and executed, they were tried and found guilty, but instead of being hanged they were pardoned, their punishment confinement in the Tower. Modern commentators have decoded Alemero's remark towards the end of the opening scene, 'How shall I dare venture in his castle, / When he discharges murderers at the gate?' (1.1.215–16), as alluding to their release in January 1622, and further glances at the scandal have been detected to support this.[18] Framed thus, the play has been seen to offer a double vision, explicitly of contemporary Spain, and implicitly of the Stuart court.[19]

For all that *The Changeling* evokes Jacobean domestic and international politics, however, its appeal today – certainly beyond the academy – lies principally in its literary richness, linguistic dexterity, and enduring dramatic power. Inevitably, a tension inheres in the performance of early modern drama in the present, particularly where, as here, the text blends what is taken to be strikingly modern with material that – bound as it is to the conventions of an early modern theatre aesthetic – appears obscure and dated. As numerous commentators note, Beatrice-Joanna's complex psychology appears modern, which is to say, 'realistic'; rather less so the virginity test and bedtrick, which today – particularly in a theatre that inclines towards realism rather than symbolism – seem implausible, not to say absurd. The bed-trick, a theatre convention drawing on examples in the Bible and folklore and typically employed in comedies to resolve crises but also, as here, for more sinister purposes, may well have evoked the Frances Howard–Robert

Carr scandal, but for modern theatregoers such historical echoes have no purchase today. Similarly, while the tragic main plot 'translates' effectively in modern terms, the subplot has generally fared less well. This 'problem' is worth dwelling on.

Playgoers today do not always appreciate that the multiple plot was the mainstay of early modern theatre practice. Not only did it facilitate the doubling of roles (and costume change), but it presented the illusion of time passing – or, rather, it gave the impression that while the *onstage* plot was progressing, other action was continuing, *offstage*.[20] But for some modern critics the most significant objection to *The Changeling*'s subplot is that its comic material jars with the serious nature of events in the castle, and this ahistorical concern with genre harmony can hamper understanding of its function. A careful reader of the play may readily perceive parallels between the two plots, characters, and situations. Isabella and Beatrice-Joanna are besieged by suitors and by over-attentive servants; Alibius and Alsemero are anxious about the honesty of their wives, neither appreciating the danger posed by the trusted Lollio and De Flores respectively; Antonio and De Flores are both gentlemen who go under other guises; Alsemero, Antonio, and Franciscus are all outsiders admitted to a privileged enclosed space which, far from offering security, harbours danger. At only three scenes it might appear that the subplot is indeed marginal to the action, and might be dispensed with; but these scenes are amongst the longest (in terms of lines) of the play, and amount to almost one-third of the total.[21] Moreover, they have a structural function, appearing at pivotal moments: the first (1.2), follows on from De Flores' soliloquy in which he declares his intention to 'have my will' (1.1.230); the second (3.2) follows De Flores' removal of the corpse of Alonzo, and thus similarly provides a period of suspense before (as the audience anticipates) Beatrice-Joanna is presented with the ring, finger, and De Flores' demands – indeed, Lollio's attempt on Isabella foreshadows what happens in the next scene; and the third (4.3) follows the bride's successful negotiation of the virginity test (following her discovery of

Alsemero's closet in 4.1) and gives way to the wedding night itself, as Beatrice-Joanna agonizes over Diaphanta's prolonging of the bed-trick. In each case there is a clear rationale for the design and placement of these scenes, and for their content.

The play's central conceit, many commentators agree, is to oppose the apparently sane inhabitants of the castle to the inmates of the madhouse, and yet over the course of the play that very opposition is deconstructed. It is worth pointing out, too, that although the plots appear separate, it is not only thematic parallels that link them. We learn in 3.3 that Vermandero has commissioned Alibius to put on a show of his fools and madmen – 'a frightful pleasure' (3.3.251) – in the castle to entertain the wedding guests, and 4.3 closes with the rehearsal, in the madhouse. We do find the subplot characters, Alibius, Isabella, Franciscus and Antonio, in the castle in 5.3, but no madmen dancing – and no Lollio. Antonio, Franciscus and Alibius confess their faults, Isabella pointing out her husband's; perhaps the playwrights simply decided to omit Lollio from the parade of confessants, but otherwise the only practical explanation is that the actor playing him also doubled as Tomazo.[22] An alternative possibility is that the planned dance, to 'make the fag / Of all the revels' (3.3.248–9), did indeed feature at the fag end of *The Changeling* – after Alsemero's epilogue (5.3.219–26). Although jigs were associated with outdoor playhouses, Lollio's clown function makes this an attractive possibility, and would accord with the popularity of the subplot in the seventeenth century: whether originally so conceived, or added subsequently, this form of closure would have made sense for playmakers and audiences alike.

Nevertheless, it must be admitted that what may be dissected on the page calls for clever design in modern productions if the subplot is to work, as several of the essays in this volume point out. That said, early modern plays such as *The Changeling* which become canonical, not only in the academy but in the theatre, produce by accretion a 'workshopping' of interpretative ideas: it is not, then, that early modern 'context' is opposed to modern expectations, but that performance history, cumulatively, together with critical evaluation, explores cultural/theatrical difference between then and now, and reworks or remakes past conventions for present purposes. The rich performance history of *The Changeling*, and how this might inform critical evaluation of the play, is correspondingly prominent in the essays that follow.

If there are discernible shifts in cultural and critical tastes over nearly four centuries of reception – and there are – there are also continuities, as Sara D. Luttfring charts in the opening essay. Tracing responses to the play up to the end of the last century, she finds confirmation of one of the oddities in the critical fortunes of this play: that while the surviving evidence indicates that in the seventeenth century it was the subplot that was markedly popular, when the play was rediscovered in the nineteenth century it was the main plot that was praised; the upshot of this is not only that Rowley comes to be regarded as the lesser writer, but that even though critics were disturbed by the virginity test and bed-trick there was no corresponding denigration of Middleton. As she demonstrates, this pattern continues long into the twentieth century, as critics focused their attention on the relationship between De Flores and Beatrice-Joanna, for which Rowley receives little credit. Only much later would Muriel Bradbrook's and William Empson's understanding of the structural and thematic function of the madhouse scenes gain general support – though only (like Rowley) as supporting actor to the main event. In the theatre the three madhouse scenes have sometimes suffered a similar fate, though examples of productions where they are omitted altogether are the exception rather than representative of the play's performance history, as Jennifer Panek's account makes clear. Indeed, for a time, in the 1960s, it became fashionable to subvert or even invert the main plot/subplot hierarchy. Certain parallels with Luttfring's findings stand out, notably Beatrice-Joanna as an immature and/or spoilt girl, which, while evading the implications of sexual politics, later segues into precisely that, though it is only relatively recently that the dominant 'Freudian' reading, which proposes that she is unconsciously attracted to De Flores, has given way to consideration of the play's sexual violence. Canonical early modern drama poses interesting questions about the relationship between theatrical revival and scholarship. As Roberta Barker and David Nicol have pointed out, modern stage productions (or professional reviewers, at any rate) have lagged behind their academic counterparts, clinging doggedly to a Freudian interpretation which for scholars has fallen from favour, though as Panek shows there have been exceptions to this trend.[23] Where academics and directors do seem to be mostly in accord, however, is in recognizing that the subplot is – and can be shown to be – an integral part of the play. Partly as a consequence of the accumulation of performance-based analysis resulting from the sheer number of revivals of plays such as *The Changeling*, and in part because performance studies is now established as a field in its own right, an important recent trend in scholarship is the general recognition that stage-related approaches can feed back into scholarly work, as Panek demonstrates.

With such a rich critical heritage it might be thought that there is little new to say about *The Changeling*. In her review of recent and ongoing developments, however, Patricia A. Cahill shows this is manifestly not the case. She identifies six areas in *Changeling* scholarship for consideration: authorship and collaboration; space and place; sexual coercion and consent; body narratives; service and exchange economies; and science and nature. This essay brings together the latest, state-of-the-art approaches to the play from a range of angles which illustrate, once again, both change and continuity. As these subheadings indicate, even the debate over Middleton and Rowley's respective contributions to the play, and the nature of the process, has received fresh impetus recently. Perhaps unsurprisingly and no less urgently, the sexual politics of the play has received considerable attention, on several planes, including the logic of space in theatrical performance and – re-siting the play in the context of the Howard/Carr scandal – as a dissection of the body in early modern thought.

Attention has turned, too, towards the social make-up of the play and its representation of servants, Diaphanta as well as De Flores. As this essay demonstrates, *The Changeling* continues to offer a rich resource for historical excavation, as well as demonstrate its continuing relevance today.

Several of the themes Cahill identifies are brought into dialogue in Peter Womack's contribution, 'Embodied Theatre in *The Changeling*'. This essay reminds us that early modern playwrights wrote for specific theatre conditions, and sometimes for particular playhouses. He points out that much of the action of the play takes place offstage – that it is implied, not staged; it has already happened, or is happening off, but we do not see it, only hear of it through the characters onstage. In a series of moves he ponders whether this onstage/offstage binarism might suggest by analogy the working of the unconscious, and then considers the historical coordinates of such an investigation. This does not mean that for all its modern appeal the critic must think in psychoanalytic terms, however; rather, Womack shows that the issues the play raises lie at the heart of the Christian tradition, so that the embodiment of flesh on the stage situates the play in specific cultural circumstances, for all that Beatrice-Joanna's predicament appears recognizably (and perhaps reassuringly) modern.

Another kind of offstage presence lurks behind (or beneath) *The Changeling* in Berta Cano-Echevarría's excavation of its Spanish subtexts. The puritan tradition underpinning John Reynolds' tale no doubt appealed to the playwrights' beliefs, as Peter Womack remarks, and numerous scholars have noted that, given the political and cultural circumstances domestically, the play offered confirmation of playgoers' anti-Spanish and anti-Catholic prejudices. But in re-examining the importance of Reynolds and refocusing attention on Middleton and Rowley's less-discussed source, Cano-Echevarría argues that not only was *Gerardo the Unfortunate Spaniard* a greater influence on the play than is sometimes recognized but that it served as a means of activating tropes that were prominent in Golden Age literature. Approached in this way, *The Changeling* is more than simply 'about' Spain; moreover, these undertexts invite re-examination of the play's deployment of rape and the bed-trick, which we might otherwise understand as operating purely in terms of English playhouse tradition.

Returning to recent productions of the play, Sarah Dustagheer picks up where Jennifer Panek left off, returning our attention to *The Changeling* in performance, specifically four productions staged this century (2006–15). Her focus is on how the conventions of early modern theatre operate today, an issue that is pertinent, in different ways, to the three modern theatre spaces she considers and the Sam Wanamaker Playhouse at Shakespeare's Globe, a new venue designed to replicate (or represent) an indoor theatre space from the period. Each of these productions affords an opportunity to examine in detail how directors treat the two plots, and practices that do not easily translate into the modern theatre environment, such as asides. While the play's canonicity ensures that it is regularly produced, every director is faced with key questions. As Panek's essay illustrates, one significant development in the revival of early modern drama is the onstage representation of what previously it had only been possible to imply. De Flores' price for the killing of Alonzo is Beatrice-Joanna's virginity. Middleton and Rowley did not *choose* not to show the act: since they could not show it onstage, the play must imply it, offstage, during the interval between 3.3. and 4.1. Act 4 begins with the wedding, presented in dumb show, after which Beatrice-Joanna says, 'This fellow has undone me endlessly' (4.1.1): the audience has been invited to imagine what ensues at the end of 3.3, when De Flores and Beatrice-Joanna exit together, and the beginning of Act 4 confirms what has happened in the interim. The interval, a convention in indoor playmaking because the candles had to be mended or changed, since they could not last throughout an entire performance, could be incorporated, as here, into the play narrative.[24] As Dustagheer shows, the modern theatre, liberated from such restraints, has often shown the act on the stage. But what, precisely, do such representations signify? Since quite what befalls Beatrice-Joanna remains a much-contested issue among critics, when directors choose to stage it such decisions are significant interventions.[25]

To date *The Changeling* has attracted writers for both the small and large screen. Indeed, a clear sign of its absorption into the mainstream was its adaptation for a television drama, *Compulsion*, in 2008. Here a modern tale of arranged marriage is loosely moored to Middleton and Rowley's play. While most of the names are changed to reflect its British-Asian setting, and Anjika ('Beatrice-Joanna') survives to marry Alex ('Alsemero'), the decision to name the chauffeur 'Don Flowers', who commits suicide at the end, signals the film's indebtedness to the Jacobean play; if, in other respects, it resembles the BBC's 'ShakespeaRe-Told' series broadcast earlier in the century, where the plot is re-scripted for a modern television audience, *Compulsion* is a sign of the play's canonicity, a topic to which the final chapter in this collection returns. The focus of Nathalie Vienne-Guerrin's essay is Marcus Thompson's 1998 film *Middleton's Changeling*, which (not unlike Alex Cox's film version of Middleton's 1606 play, *Revengers Tragedy* [2002]) does not seek to remake a play for a popular audience, as *Compulsion* does, but reinterprets *Jacobean* horror through the conventions of the modern horror film genre. As her title suggests, the play's exploration of loving and loathing lends itself to a particular kind of filmmaking, one that trades precisely on the discomfited-yet-fascinated viewer, whose expectations are shaped by the horror genre. Vienne-Guerrin anchors her reading of Thompson's film in the text of the play, demonstrating interesting correspondences between early modern terror and the horror film genre. As she shows, *Middleton's Changeling* – in its genre-driven excess, facilitated by the film medium – draws out the terror of the play and forces the audience to participate, vicariously, in a kind of abjection such as that Beatrice-Joanna herself experiences in the play.

In the final essay in the collection, Nora Williams draws together several of the key issues raised in previous chapters and explores how teachers and students might engage with them. Situating *The Changeling* in a broader context of early modern drama in the present, she identifies performance, textual, editorial, historical and formal elements of the play for further exploration in the classroom. As she shows, Middleton and Rowley's play – and its critical and performance history – presents opportunities to debate issues of particular relevance today, such as gender politics, sexual violence and disability. The subplot poses new questions now: in an important intervention she invites us to think about the politics of *performing* disability, which has recently become an issue of some urgency in the theatre and the cinema. This concern returns us to the subplot, and the play's representation of madness. As befitting its subversive potential, perhaps, the subplot continues to pose awkward questions for scholars and theatre practitioners alike. Williams closes her essay with an annotated list of modern editions of the play and a selection of resources to support further study; the selected bibliography offers some additional suggestions for further reading.

# 1

# The Critical Backstory

## Sara D. Luttfring

Following the first publication of Thomas Middleton and William Rowley's *The Changeling* in 1653, one of the earliest and most explicit print references to the play occurs in *The Marrow of Complements* (1655). The title page of this book advertises it as 'A most Methodicall and accurate forme of Instructions for all Variety of Love-Letters, Amorous Discourses, and Complementall Entertainements'. The book contains three unattributed excerpts from *The Changeling*: Jasperino's flirtation with Diaphanta from 1.1.132–45, entitled 'Jasperino, a merry fellow, at first sight thus boards the Joviall Diaphanta'; Alibius's conversation with Lollio from 1.2.1–34, entitled 'A Dialogue betwixt an old jealous Doctor, and his man'; and Antonio's attempt to woo Isabella from 3.2.113–35, entitled 'A Gentleman to obtain the love of his Lady, faignes himself Mad, and thus courts her in his keepers absence'.[1] The play, which most modern readers, audiences and critics think of as centring on the doomed love triangle composed of Beatrice-Joanna, De Flores and Alsemero, seems an incongruous source for romantic bon mots, and indeed, the excerpts singled out for inclusion focus on supporting/subplot characters rather than the main plot's leads. In fact, if all we knew of *The*

*Changeling* was derived from *The Marrow of Complements*, we might assume that this play of merry fellows, jovial maids, old jealous husbands and disguised wooers would bear more resemblance to one of Middleton's city comedies than to a tragedy.

As many of *The Changeling*'s modern editors have noted, the play's popularity in the seventeenth century seems to have been due primarily to the subplot and its titular changeling, Antonio.[2] The focus in *The Marrow of Complements* on the play's more comic characters and moments appears to reflect this trend in its early reception. When the first critical commentary on the play appeared in the early nineteenth century, however, we find this trend reversed. As we will see, early critics bemoaned, derided and/or outright ignored the play's subplot even as they praised the main plot's dark power. Similarly, they celebrated the play's main plot as evidence of Middleton's skill as a writer while lamenting his association with Rowley, to whom they attributed the inferior subplot. Whereas many of the play's earliest audiences seem to have focused on the play's comic elements, nineteenth-century critics insisted that its only merits were to be found in its tragedy. The play's provocative, and at times almost perverse, blend of tones and genre markers would continue to be a source of fascination and frustration throughout the nineteenth and twentieth centuries.

Aside from some seventeenth-century references to the play in performance and an unpopular eighteenth-century rewriting of the play, William Hayley's *Marcella* (1785),[3] the next specific mention of *The Changeling* in print occurred in Walter Scott's edition of the thirteenth-century Middle English verse romance *Sir Tristrem*, first published in 1804. In this version of the Tristan and Iseult legend, Tristrem and Ysonde fall in love and have sex despite the fact that they are en route to England so that Ysonde can marry King Mark. Upon arrival in England, Ysonde marries King Mark as planned. According to Scott's plot summary: '[T]o conceal her guilty intercourse with Sir Tristrem, [Ysonde] substitutes her attendant, Brengwain, in her place, on the first night of her nuptials.' Ysonde then 'becomes fearful lest Brengwain should betray the important secret with which she was entrusted; to prevent which, she hires two ruffians to dispatch her faithful attendant'.[4] Ultimately, Brengwain's life is spared after she proves her loyalty to her mistress. In his notes on this part of the poem, Scott writes, 'The barbarous ingratitude of the queen of Cornwall [i.e. Ysonde] resembles that of the heroine in Middleton's *Changeling*, an old play, which contains some passages horrible striking.'[5] Scott seems clearly to be referencing the bed-trick episode in *The Changeling*, in which Diaphanta takes her mistress's place on her wedding night in order to conceal Beatrice-Joanna's loss of virginity; unlike Brengwain, however, the less fortunate Diaphanta is murdered for her perceived disloyalty. Two things seem of note here. First is the decisively unsympathetic characterization of Beatrice-Joanna as, like Ysonde, 'barbarous'. Second is the characterization of the play itself as both 'horrible' and 'striking'. As we will see, such characterizations of Beatrice-Joanna were commonplace in much early criticism of *The Changeling*. Scott's characterization of the play itself is similarly prescient, as many nineteenth-century critics found the play to be 'horrible' both in its ability to provoke horror and in what they perceived to be the low quality of some of its scenes. Despite the disgust and exasperation with which early commentators viewed the subplot and certain elements of the main plot, however, they also found much in the play that was 'striking' and worthy of serious thought and discussion.

Following the first printing in 1653 and a reissue in 1668, the play did not appear again in print until 1815, when C.W. Dilke included it in his *Old English Plays*. In his prefatory remarks on the play, Dilke (rather astonishingly) compares it unfavourably with Hayley's *Marcella*, noting that while Hayley's heroine is made sympathetic, 'Beatrice can only be regarded with detestation and abhorrence.' Dilke also remarks approvingly on Hayley's omission from the narrative of 'the disgusting scene which passes in Alsemero's closet in the beginning of Act IV'.[6] Presumably he is referencing Beatrice-Joanna's discovery of Alsemero's virginity test, an incident which, along with the bed-trick that Scott apparently found memorable, was a source of frequent critical consternation. The play's next editor, Alexander Dyce, found more to praise in *The Changeling*, arguing that the play showcases 'Middleton's tragic powers'. He is also the first commentator to directly address the question of the play's co-authorship: 'According to the title-page, William Rowley, who was frequently [Middleton's] literary associate, had a share in the composition; but I feel convinced that the terribly impressive passages of this tragedy ... are beyond the ability of Rowley.'[7] Dyce's seeming reluctance to give Rowley equal billing with Middleton is notable and characteristic of much nineteenth-century criticism. Dyce refers to Rowley as Middleton's 'associate', not his co-author or collaborator, and he admits only that Rowley had 'a share' in the play. Clearly this 'share' did not include the play's strongest parts, and Dyce declines to speculate as to what Rowley's contributions were. As we will see, later critics would be more specific about Middleton and Rowley's division of labour, but not necessarily to Rowley's benefit.

In 1843, James Russell Lowell effectively ignored both Rowley and the subplot in his analysis of *The Changeling*. He begins his reading with a brief plot summary, at the end of which he notes: 'The tragedy takes its name from the chief character in an underplot, which, as is usually the case in the old drama, has nothing whatever to do with the action of the piece.'[8] This is Lowell's only reference to the subplot, and Rowley's name is never mentioned. Instead, Lowell focuses on the brilliance of Middleton's characterization of Beatrice-Joanna and De Flores. Despite the fact that Beatrice-Joanna takes the initiative in hiring De Flores to kill Alonzo, Lowell depicts her as a passive victim, comparing her to 'a child talking aloud in the dark to relieve its terrors' and contrasting her 'shrinking dread' with De Flores's 'contemptuous coolness'.[9] Two years later, Leigh Hunt was similarly struck by the forceful characterization of De Flores: 'there is one character of [Middleton's] (De Flores in the "*Changeling*") which, for effect at once tragical, probable, and poetical, surpasses anything I know of in the drama of domestic life'.[10] Whereas Scott and Dilke appear to cast Beatrice-Joanna as the arch villain of the play, Lowell and Hunt depict De Flores as the play's most forceful character, thus presenting the murderous couple in more conventionally gendered ways.

In his 1885 edition of Middleton's works, A.H. Bullen follows Lowell in excluding the subplot entirely from his summary of *The Changeling*. He does, however, acknowledge Rowley's specific contribution to the play, although not favourably: 'The wild extravagance of the madhouse scenes is quite in [Rowley's] manner.' In addition to crediting Rowley with the inferior subplot, Bullen also attributes to him the play's final scene, noting that the 'violence of the language', 'ill-timed comic touches' and 'metrical roughness' differentiate this scene from the rest of the main plot.[11] By contrast, Bullen praises Middleton's work in the main plot, particularly the confrontation between De Flores and Beatrice-Joanna in 3.3.[12] Bullen nervously sidesteps what were widely held as the main plot's most glaring flaws – the virginity test and bed-trick: 'I must be excused for passing over the device by which [Beatrice-Joanna] conceals the loss of her virginity from Alsemero.'[13] Despite this squeamishness, however, Bullen is the first commentator to note the virginity test's possible historical links to Frances Howard and the Essex divorce trial, a connection which would become an important historical referent for many future scholars of the play.[14]

Two years after Bullen's edition, Havelock Ellis edited another collection of Middleton's works. Ellis's introduction to *The Changeling* reviews the play's publication history and source material, but does not give an opinion on the play's merits or failings. Regarding the joint authorship, Ellis notes simply that 'Rowley is probably responsible for the underplot . . . as well as for much in the treatment of the main story'.[15] A.C. Swinburne, who wrote the introduction to the collection as a whole, provides more critical commentary, and like others he disparages the subplot as 'very stupid, rather coarse, and almost vulgar'.[16] Despite this, compared to other critics Swinburne is much more generous in his assessment of Rowley. In addition to the subplot, he attributes the play's first and last scenes to Rowley, and as such must acknowledge Rowley's contribution to the allegedly superior main plot and in particular to 'the perfect and living figure of De Flores', which he, like Hunt, views as one of the play's great achievements: 'To Rowley ... must be assigned the very high credit of introducing and of dismissing with adequate and even triumphant effect the strangely original tragic figure [De Flores].'[17] Writing in 1894, Edmund Gosse takes a much less sympathetic view of the Middleton–Rowley collaboration than does Swinburne: 'The influence of Rowley upon Middleton was an unwholesome one.'[18]

In 1897, Pauline G. Wiggin delved deeply into the authorship controversy with a book-length study of the plays co-written by Middleton and Rowley. Whereas previous critics tended to make judgements based on instinct or opinion when attributing different sections of *The Changeling* to each writer, Wiggin uses the single-author plays of Middleton and Rowley to look for hallmark qualities of plot, diction, style, vocabulary and metre in the co-written plays. Based on this evidence, she concurs with critics such as Swinburne that Rowley wrote the play's first and last scenes in addition to the subplot. Although like many nineteenth-century scholars she is critical of the subplot, Wiggin attempts to place it in context:

> The underplot ... is thin and clumsily connected with the main story, and the introduction of madmen in comedy is repulsive to our modern taste; but it was far from repulsive to an Elizabethan audience, and there are few plays of this period that are not disfigured by equally objectionable underplots.[19]

Wiggin speculates that Rowley actually had a positive, humanizing effect on Middleton, who 'lack[ed] belief in the essential dignity and beauty of human nature, a belief which Rowley possessed and without which sustained tragedy is impossible'.[20] As a result of Rowley's influence, Wiggin argues, readers are able to maintain sympathy for the play's characters (all but De Flores) in spite of their flaws.[21]

By the early twentieth century, many nineteenth-century critical assumptions about the play had been widely, if not universally, accepted. In 1921, Gamaliel Bradford argued that *The Changeling* 'is marred by the introduction of a secondary plot ... of far inferior importance and interest'.[22] Like Lowell, Bradford infantilizes Beatrice-Joanna, characterizing her as a 'giddy schoolgirl' and a 'sweet, foolish devil' with a 'poor, silly, idle brain'.[23] Bradford also concurs with earlier critics in his distaste for the virginity test scene, which he claims is 'very disagreeable, not to say grotesque'.[24] Despite its flaws, however, Bradford concludes that the play is 'one of the most intensely human' of its time, 'full of both truth and power'.[25] Two years later, William Archer strongly disagreed with Bradford's assessment in his scathing analysis of the play. For Archer, *The Changeling* is an example of how 'minor Elizabethans neglected verisimilitude, ignored psychology, and concentrated their whole effort on the elements of lust and horror'.[26] The madhouse scenes are, presumably, beneath his contempt and barely worth acknowledging; in a footnote he says only, 'I have said nothing of the distasteful and tedious underplot, usually ascribed to Rowley.' Ultimately, Archer characterizes the play's failings as typical of the period, and laments that Middleton was a writer born before his proper time; unlike Rowley, Middleton is 'a real dramatist, who, in another environment, would have been capable of working up to higher standards'.[27]

Despite Archer's critique, other commentators during the first half of the twentieth century found much to praise in what they viewed as the play's naturalism and psychological verisimilitude. T.S. Eliot's influential 1927 essay acknowledges that the play could be 'long-winded and tiresome', but argues that its characters 'are real and impelled irresistibly by the fundamental motions of humanity to good or evil'.[28] Despite its 'absurd' plot, *The Changeling* contains a 'stratum of truth permanent in human nature'.[29] Writing in 1935, M.C. Bradbrook, like Eliot, praises the play's psychological realism: 'Compared with the characters of earlier plays, Middleton's are fuller, more natural and human.'[30] Moreover, Bradbrook disagrees with earlier critics who would dismiss the subplot entirely, arguing instead that the two plots are connected by themes of 'change', 'judgement' and 'will' in a way that is 'very carefully worked out'.[31] In a sharp break from critical consensus, Bradbrook does not subordinate the subplot to the main plot, but instead views them as distinct yet equally skillful parts of a gracefully combined whole: 'So firmly does each half of the play retain its own proper atmosphere, and yet so closely are they interwoven with each other.'[32] In his 1935 study, William Empson similarly acknowledges the connection between main plot and subplot, albeit more grudgingly than Bradbrook: 'however disagreeable the comic part may be it is of no use to ignore it; it is woven into the tragic part very thoroughly'.[33] Both he and, a year later, Una Ellis-Fermor align with earlier critics who infantilize Beatrice-Joanna; Empson claims that she is '[m]orally a child', and Ellis-Fermor describes her as a childlike sleep-walker who is forced to mature over the course of the play.[34] Ellis-Fermor, however, disagrees with critics who would argue for the subplot's relevance to the main plot: 'The avowedly comic sub-plot could ... be detached without much damage and the resulting tragedy would stand as one of the most compact and pitiless in this drama.'[35]

In his 1955 study of Middleton's tragedies, Samuel Schoenbaum likewise has little use for the subplot, which he excludes entirely from his summary of the play: 'It is stupid and tedious, and the treatment of insanity is offensive to the modern reader.'[36] He also critiques the 'superfluous sensationalism of the conclusion', which he likewise attributes to the 'third-rate' Rowley.[37] Like Archer, Schoenbaum posits that Middleton struggled against the vulgar conventions of his time: 'Middleton was finding it increasingly difficult – possibly even distasteful – to try to reconcile the sensational melodrama of his age with the psychological drama toward which he aspired.'[38] Schoenbaum locates this psychological realism primarily in the interactions between Beatrice-Joanna and De Flores, and like some earlier critics he views De Flores as the more interesting and complex of the two. While Beatrice-Joanna is 'a pampered, irresponsible child' and 'a moral idiot', De Flores 'is her superior', 'a remarkably subtle and alert intelligence channeled into the pursuit of wholly morbid objectives'.[39]

In his 1958 study of Middleton's plays, Richard Hindry Barker agrees with Schoenbaum that De Flores 'is the more complex' of the pair.[40] Barker goes even further, however, depicting De Flores as a dashing leading man: 'At first ostensibly a weakling, [De Flores] develops into a really masterful figure who not only wins a mistress despite almost insuperable obstacles but afterwards protects her with a remarkable display of competence.'[41] According to Barker, Beatrice-Joanna is unable to resist De Flores's mastery and reciprocates his desire for her without realizing it: 'it is perfectly clear that [Beatrice-Joanna] does love [De Flores], that unconsciously her feelings toward him have undergone a profound change'.[42] In Barker's analysis, the relationship between Beatrice-Joanna and De Flores plays out like a twisted version of those between Beatrice and Benedict or Katharina and Petruchio: two characters who begin the play at odds fall inevitably in love. These achievements in psychological complexity come about in spite, not because, of Rowley's contributions to the play. Opposing the work of scholars such as Bradbrook and Empson, Barker insists that 'no real unity can be expected from a play in which the tragedy is as brilliant and the comedy as completely contemptible as in this one'.[43]

Published in the same year as Barker's study, N.W. Bawcutt's Revels edition of *The Changeling* mounts an important and detailed defence against those who would dismiss the subplot entirely. Bawcutt concedes that the subplot is 'much inferior to the main plot', but he insists that the two plots are linked through shared themes of sexual intrigue, blackmail, deceptive appearances and madness.[44] This doubling is important,

Bawcutt argues, because the subplot 'enable[s] the audience to grasp the essential themes of the main plot . . . by isolating and enlarging them to the point of literalness'.[45] The overall effect, suggests Bawcutt, is deeply ironic, since the characters in the madhouse plot are revealed to be more sane than those in the 'normal' world of the main plot. Bawcutt's formalist approach to the play, although not entirely unprecedented, marks an important moment in *The Changeling*'s critical history. During the second half of the twentieth century, critics gradually stopped feeling obligated to critique or apologize for the subplot, and instead begin to analyse seriously its contributions to the play as a whole.

In a seminal 1960 article, Christopher Ricks uses detailed close readings of the double meanings of specific words (service, blood, will, act, deed) to examine the play's 'moral and poetic structure'.[46] Ultimately, he argues that 'the verbal structure . . . provides the moral structure of the play': just as the double meanings of certain words combine sex and violence inextricably, so do the actions and interactions of Beatrice-Joanna and De Flores.[47] Ricks sidesteps the question of collaboration by focusing primarily on the parts of the play believed to have been written by Middleton, but he does note that the subplot reinforces the importance of sexual innuendo in the main plot.[48] Ricks also expands on Barker's argument regarding De Flores and Beatrice-Joanna's mutual attraction, suggesting (albeit rather tentatively) that Beatrice-Joanna's 'initial loathing for [De Flores is] sexual in origin'.[49] In other words, Beatrice-Joanna doesn't just grow to love De Flores, but desires him from the beginning, and so her use of certain sexually charged words amounts to Freudian slips.

Like Ricks and Bawcutt, T.B. Tomlinson focuses on the overarching unity of *The Changeling*'s structure which, he argues, is achieved through the 'single dominating image' of Vermandero's castle.[50] In Tomlinson's 1964 analysis, the castle projects reason and intellect on the outside, but inside it is a labyrinth of sex and passion. The image helps to portray 'the ironic balance of the appearance of reason against the reality of lust' and 'the gap between intellect and the passions'.[51] Tomlinson argues that the subplot contributes to the play's structural unity; like the labyrinth at the heart of the castle, the madhouse contrasts with the castle's controlled, rational exterior, helping to develop the play's governing images and metaphors. In fact, Tomlinson asserts that *The Changeling* 'is obviously richer in texture, more imaginative in outline than any other of Middleton's, and indeed this may be Rowley's doing in part'.[52] Robert Jordan's 1970 article also analyses *The Changeling*'s structure, but he argues that it is governed by 'a mythic and poetic pattern' rather than the psychology of the characters.[53] According to Jordan, the relationship between De Flores and Beatrice-Joanna 'hover[s] on the verge of one of the more potent of mythic confrontations, that of beauty and the beast, the princess and the frog'.[54] In such tales, as well as in the motif of the wild man and the maiden that these tales stem from, the beautiful woman can 'tame' the wild man/ beast man. As Jordan notes, however, the play adds a twist: 'Instead of the beast being revealed as a prince, the process of this story is to reveal that the princess is in fact a beast.'[55] One year later, Richard Levin similarly noted 'the discrepancy between Beatrice's appearance and her inner self', arguing that this plays into *The Changeling*'s larger theme of disguise.[56] Levin argues that the main plot's major themes, such as disguise and madness, are literalized in the subplot; thus, although the subplot's 'execution leaves much to be desired', there is nevertheless a 'very rich and meaningful formal relationship' between the two parts of the play.[57]

In her 1973 study of Middleton's realism, Dorothy M. Farr also wades into the double-plot debate, carefully threading the needle to argue for the play's inherent unity while also celebrating the individual brilliance of Middleton: 'Clearly the sub-plot is an integral part of the author's design, but whatever the correct distribution of the text may be it seems likely that the play's overall conception was the work of one mind.'[58] This singular mind is, presumably, Middleton's, although Farr does give Rowley credit for the play's more excitingly theatrical moments:

> As an actor-dramatist Rowley was a theatre man in a sense in which Middleton was not, and his instinct for quickening the action with noise and bustle just when the tempo requires it is of some importance in *The Changeling*.... Undeniably it was in association with Rowley that Middleton found his proper bent in the popular theatre and it was with Rowley that he began to formulate a new kind of tragedy.[59]

Although Farr seems to envision Middleton as the lead innovator with Rowley playing a supporting role, her argument nevertheless marks a break from earlier critics who disparaged Rowley as unworthy of collaborating with Middleton.

Farr argues that in *The Changeling*, 'Middleton had employed the methods and to some extent the matter of comedy to broaden the scope of tragedy'.[60] Raymond J. Pentzell's 1975 article similarly (but more emphatically) calls the play 'a tonal thrill-show' that alternates between artificiality and psychological realism as well as between comedy and tragedy.[61] He disagrees, however, with previous critics' assessments of the structural links between the main plot and the subplot: 'The madhouse story is just not similar enough in plot and character to the major plot for us to regard it merely as a comic version of the same action.'[62] Rather than arguing for a logical structure binding the two plots, Pentzell argues that the play's formal and tonal illogic *is* its structure: 'The patterned juxtaposition of one kind of stage reality with another and one range of mood with another is constantly in flux, continuously unpredictable, yet by means of those very qualities the primary unifying dynamic of the play.'[63]

Like earlier critics, both Farr and Levin tend to infantilize Beatrice-Joanna. Levin characterizes her as a 'child who is certain the world revolves around her' and a 'pampered coquette', while Farr similarly notes Beatrice-Joanna's 'childishness' and 'adolescent naivety'.[64] In her 1973 study of women in Middleton's plays, Caroline Lockett Cherry delves more deeply into the social milieu that formed Beatrice-Joanna into the childish, amoral woman that critics had long claimed her to be. Cherry argues that Beatrice-Joanna's flaws are not innate, but are the 'result of limited education and restricting social conventions. She is seen by her father, though he is loving and even somewhat indulgent, as both a possession and a toy; he never questions his right to marry her off as he pleases'.[65] Beatrice-Joanna's crimes are, therefore, not merely the result of juvenile immorality or sexual promiscuity; her rejection of Alonzo in favour of Alsemero is her way of 'rebelling against parental authority and assuming control over her own fate'.[66] In doing so, she threatens not just familial hierarchies, but broader political structures as well: 'Beatrice ... is the poison corrupting the commonwealth, the bad blood that must be purged from her father, representing the state, in order to restore him to health.'[67]

Roger Stilling similarly notes the danger that Beatrice-Joanna, as a sexually rebellious woman, poses to the patriarchal society of the play. His 1976 study asserts that Middleton's tragedies follow a predictable pattern: 'to set up some situation of romantic love tragedy and then subvert it by means of determinedly antiromantic analysis of the nature of woman and the nature of love'.[68] In following this pattern, Stilling argues that the play is clear when it comes to assigning blame: 'there is no room in Middleton for ... moral ambiguity ... about the role of woman in all this evil doing... [W]ith Beatrice-Joanna there is no question where the blame lies'.[69] De Flores, by contrast, comes off as a kind of anti-hero: 'cool, lucid, witty, precise', 'he dies without recantation or breast-beating'.[70] Moreover, Stilling argues that De Flores's influence has a salutary effect on Beatrice-Joanna: 'under his tutelage Beatrice-Joanna comes to know herself better'.[71]

A year later, Paula Johnson similarly characterized the relationship between De Flores and Beatrice-Joanna as one of dominance on his side and pleasurable submission and dependency on hers. She argues that their confrontation in 3.3, which leads to the consummation of their relationship, 'is a rape-fantasy objectified, enacting the covert wish of men and women alike for pleasure without blame because without consent'.[72] Of course, in the play the lack of consent is entirely the woman's; De Flores, in contrast, is empowered to a state of 'increased dignity'.[73] Once they become sexually involved, Johnson argues, Beatrice-Joanna and De Flores assume conventional gender roles: 'Their dependency inverts: the woman relinquishes her unnatural tyranny; the man escapes his unnatural servitude.'[74] In a 1979 study, Nicholas Brooke conceives of the relationship between Beatrice-Joanna and De Flores as one of 'mutual' pleasure and dependence, but he nevertheless, like Johnson, understands Beatrice-Joanna's feelings toward De Flores to be on some level non-consensual: 'she has been forced to love him, and she does'.[75]

For Johnson and Brooke, as well as for a long string of critics preceding them, *The Changeling*'s psychological realism (or lack thereof) is the most important object of scholarly inquiry. In 1980, J.L. Simmons identified a critical split between those who saw Middleton as a 'historical moralist' and those who saw him as a 'modern psychological realist'.[76] Simmons's goal is to bridge the gap between what he sees as two different approaches to the same fundamental truth: 'I hope to establish a meeting ground between our [modern] preoccupation with the psychological in sexual matters and the Jacobean preoccupation, in such matters, with the demonic.'[77] Simmons argues that the relationship between Beatrice-Joanna and De Flores has the hallmarks of a 'demonic pact', with De Flores as a 'satyr or incubus' to Beatrice-Joanna's 'nymphomaniac'.[78] Moreover, in providing historical context for his reading of the play's interest in demonology, Simmons is one of the first critics to take up Bullen's 1885 suggestion regarding the connections between the play and the Essex divorce/Overbury murder trials, noting that Frances Howard's crimes were also allegedly 'abetted by a literally demonic force'.[79]

Margot Heinemann's important study, also published in 1980, similarly notes *The Changeling*'s references to Frances Howard, but whereas Simmons explores what he calls the play's 'diabolical realism', Heinemann is more interested in its social realism. According to Heinemann, '[t]he realism of [Middleton's] late tragedies includes a very subtle and precise placing of the characters socially', and this social commentary is influenced by what Heinemann argues is the 'decidedly plebeian, citizen note' of Middleton's Puritan outlook.[80] In this reading, Beatrice-Joanna is the 'spoiled and sheltered child of a noble family' who views murder as 'a commodity, like anything else one buys', and her 'moral blindness' is coupled with a 'conviction that her superior rank enables her to use inferior people [such as De Flores and Diaphanta] as tools'.[81] Michael Scott's 1982 Marxist reading is similarly interested in the play's class dynamics. His analysis depicts De Flores as 'in conflict with a society from which by class, position and physical disfigurement he is totally alienated'.[82] As a wealthy member of this society, Beatrice-Joanna 'thinks only in terms of markets, uses and creatures. For her life is a matter of buying and selling'. As Scott notes, however, Beatrice-Joanna is objectified by this same system when Alsemero uses the virginity test 'to test the fidelity of his bargain as a smith might try the temper of his gold'.[83] In his 1984 study of 'radical tragedy', Jonathan Dollimore likewise argues that *The Changeling* promotes 'the dissociation of social rank from innate superiority', and that Beatrice-Joanna's 'act of transgression and its consequences actually disclose "blood" and "birth" to be myths in the service of historical and social forms of power'.[84]

Peter Morrison's 1983 essay offers a similarly radical reading of *The Changeling*, but his focus is more on sexual repression than on repressive class hierarchies, noting 'the hollow, brooding tension between [the play's] own frightening dispassion and the blunt release of primordial violence, madness, and sexuality within an impotent, repressive, wedding-cake civilization'.[85] According to Morrison, Beatrice-Joanna and De Flores operate in a world populated by 'zombies' like Alsemero, who is 'incapable of seeing women as anything other than virgins or whores'.[86] Beatrice-Joanna is consequently 'terrified of her sexual identity', and '[i]t is only De Flores who genuinely understands her'.[87] Sara Eaton also examines the sexually restrictive nature of the play's society, but in her reading Beatrice-Joanna is subjected to repressive stereotypes by *both* Alsemero, who idealizes her, and De Flores, who degrades her.[88] The play's male characters use the virgin–whore rhetoric of courtly love to exert control over Beatrice-Joanna's body and sexuality, representing her 'as an object to be claimed and possessed'.[89] Dale B.J. Randall is also interested in the play's depiction of Beatrice-Joanna's sexuality, but rather than analysing the play's sexual politics, he revisits the play's virginity test, using an historical lens to argue for the seriousness of an episode that previous critics tended to dismiss as ridiculous.[90]

In addition to new approaches by Marxist, feminist and new historicist critics of the play, the 1980s also produced more traditional formalist/moralist readings. In 1986, T. McAlindon argued that the play's formal symmetry reveals the 'astonishingly close' collaboration between Middleton and Rowley: the polarity in Beatrice-Joanna's own nature is externalized in her relationship with De Flores, which is in turn 'figured in the antithetical but confused relationship between castle and Bedlam'.[91] Over the course of the play, Beatrice-Joanna is 'robb[ed] … of her moral and aesthetic sense, her very soul' by De Flores, although her dying confession redeems her.[92] Published the same year, Leo Salingar's book on dramatic form similarly focuses on *The Changeling*'s moralism: 'Middleton's realism is a quality of moral judgement'.[93] While he does note the play's 'social as well as psychological insight', which makes it 'a study in class-consciousness', Salingar also views the play as 'a character-portrait of a perverse young woman'.[94] In his 1988 formalist reading of the play as a study of folly and madness, Joost Daalder similarly analyses the (often abnormal) psychology of the characters, particularly Beatrice-Joanna, whom he deems 'dangerously unaware' of her sexual attraction to De Flores, and therefore, 'psychotic'.[95] While Daalder argues that the relationship between main plot and subplot is 'vital', McAlindon and Salinger follow earlier critics in commenting on the subplot's aesthetic inferiority, even as they acknowledge its formal and thematic contributions to the play as a whole.[96]

The 1990s saw a wave of scholarship that focused on the play's relationship to politics, both the state politics of the Jacobean period and the politics of gender and/or class. In 1990, A.A. Bromham and Zara Bruzzi published a book-length study analysing the play's encoded commentary on issues including the trials of Frances Howard, foreign policy and the perceived threat of Catholicism, domestic regulation of freedom of speech and allegiance to the monarch, and controversies surrounding Arminianism.[97] The same year, Cristina Malcolmson's article on politics and gender in *The Changeling* argued that the play 'appealed to Parliamentary opposition to Stuart policy by objecting to James's plans for a Spanish marriage'.[98] However, Malcolmson notes that this challenge to monarchal power is couched in terms of a woman's rebellion against patriarchal power, a rebellion that the play ultimately quells. In another 1990 article, Sharon Stockton similarly argues that the play's scapegoating of Beatrice-Joanna allows Middleton and Rowley to uphold patriarchal norms by 're-establish[ing] the moral purity and ideological necessity of patrilineal succession'.[99] Although Stockton, Malcolmson, and Bromham and Bruzzi note the play's potential for radical socio-political critique, they also argue that this critique must be concealed, suppressed and contained.

Even studies of *The Changeling* published in the 1990s that are not primarily concerned with sexual politics frequently incorporate readings of the play's gender hierarchies into their analysis. Michael Neill's 1991 article focuses on tracking 'the shaping metaphor' that governs the play, which he argues is 'the penetration and display of hidden secrets'.[100] Vermandero, as protector of the castle and its secrets, represents 'patriarchal authority and reason'.[101] The secret he is supposed to protect, 'at once a source of mysterious power and the cause of fearful weakness[,] . . . reflects the ambiguous nature of female sexuality'.[102] Published the same year, Martin Wiggins's analysis of the play's moral emptiness notes Beatrice-Joanna's thoughtless, naïve obedience to patriarchal norms: 'Elopement and adultery are unthinkable . . . because they would involve her defying patriarchal authority', whereas 'murder is a remote, nebulous sin that seems less real . . . than disobeying Daddy.'[103]

Two articles that focus on the virginity test follow Randall's shift away from earlier criticism that viewed this episode as vulgar and unrealistic, although they read the significance of the test in opposing ways. In his 1993 study, Arthur L. Little, Jr argues that the effects of the test place women in a double bind, forcing them to enact madness in order to confirm their sexual purity. In an ironic show of social sanity, Beatrice-Joanna fakes the hysteria demanded by the virginity test 'not because she is evil . . . but because she wishes to protect the patriarchal validation of her virginal self'.[104] The following year, Marjorie Garber's Freudian reading of the test argued that its effects are not those of hysteria *or* virginity, but rather of orgasm.[105] The test is designed to be 'a fantasy projection of the lover's power' to give the virgin sexual pleasure, but Beatrice-Joanna 'fakes it'.[106] Beatrice-Joanna is thus not in thrall to patriarchal expectations, but in control of them. According to Garber, it is only with De Flores that she finds 'the frisson of involuntary response', 'a relationship in which loathing and desire are intertwined and finally beyond her control'.[107]

Garber, like others before her, argues that Beatrice-Joanna's erotic/romantic feelings toward De Flores are repressed and involuntary. Both her alleged desire/love for De Flores and her sexual intercourse with him are to an extent non-consensual and coerced. Joost Daalder and Anthony Telford Moore similarly argue that 'Beatrice's visible, conscious loathing is in some way a manifestation of unconscious love': 'The strength of [De Flores's] appeal is the greater precisely because it *is* unconscious: in Freudian terms, [Beatrice-Joanna] "represses" it, but it cannot go away, and overwhelms her with the more force.'[108] Despite Beatrice-Joanna's alleged desire for De Flores, she must be 'unconscious' to it, 'overwhelmed' with 'force' that is 'involuntary' and 'beyond her control'. This sounds, of course, very much like rape, and in a 1995 article Deborah G. Burks confronts and contextualizes this aspect of De Flores and Beatrice-Joanna's relationship. In her analysis of early modern rape law, she notes that 'English law treated ravishment as a crime targeted at propertied men, through a piece of their property, women'.[109] The law was concerned not simply that men might sexually abuse women, but that 'women might lack the sense to conduct themselves appropriately' and might actually be complicit with their rapists.[110] The play depicts Beatrice-Joanna as 'an active participant in her rape', 'an archetype of the woman-driven-by desire' and this is how many critics have read her.[111] Burks, however, notes the misogynist legal theories underpinning this representation: 'Middleton and Rowley have designed a heroine who confirms the law's paternalistic concern for women's weakness.'[112]

In 1996, Swapan Chakravorty added social class to the discussion of gender politics, arguing that De Flores's insistence on his 'moral solidarity' with Beatrice-Joanna 'is a powerful reminder of the shared subservience of servant and woman'.[113] De Flores, however, is able to turn '"service" into sexual mastery and "servitude" into social revenge' by having sex with his mistress.[114] Beatrice-Joanna, although she shares De Flores's subservience, does not share in his revenge against supposed social superiors; instead, the servant's triumph is predicated on making the woman a scapegoat: 'By showing [Beatrice-Joanna's] beauty to be morally foul, De Flores destroys the ethical pretext of class privilege.'[115] The same year, Lisa Jardine advanced a similar argument, although she asserts that the threat to traditional hierarchies based on dynastic marriage is not De Flores, but (surprisingly) Alsemero: 'the social imperative for hierarchical organisation of family and inheritance is endangered by the self-centered plans of a well-born fortune hunter'.[116] Alsemero's plan to undermine Vermandero's marriage arrangements for his daughter is socially disruptive, but as in Chakravorty's analysis, Beatrice-Joanna is made the scapegoat: the plot 'shifts the epicentre of blame for the disruption of traditional family alliance from the fortune-seeking man who is ultimately the cause to the woman whose fortune he seeks'.[117] A 1997 article by Lisa Hopkins argues that it is Beatrice-Joanna herself, not De Flores or Alsemero, who challenges social power structures by entering Alsemero's closet and reading his Book of Secrets.[118] However, at the end of the play Beatrice-Joanna undergoes a kind of self-scapegoating when she 'internalize[s] ... assumptions about her own status as a whore and villainess', 'resum[ing] her designated position as the objectified other of demonization'.[119]

It may seem that late-twentieth-century criticism of *The Changeling* returns to where it began in the early nineteenth century, with Walter Scott declaring Beatrice-Joanna to be 'barbarous'. Over the course of the twentieth century, however, criticism shifted from viewing Beatrice-Joanna and De Flores's crimes as the result of moral failure to depicting them as the consequence of restrictive social and sexual hierarchies. Similarly, criticism shifted from viewing the double-plot structure as an artistic failure to challenging the hierarchization of main plot over subplot, tragedy over comedy, and Middleton over Rowley. Instead, scholars have looked for ways to understand how the two parts of the play work together to create an effect that is still, for many readers, 'horrible striking'.

# 2

# A Performance History

## Jennifer Panek

All the evidence points to *The Changeling* having been a theatrical success in its day, though only a single specific record of performance survives. Sir Henry Herbert, Master of the Revels, licensed the tragedy on 7 May 1622, 'to be acted by Lady Elizabeth's servants at the Phoenix'; in all likelihood, it was indeed acted at Christopher Beeston's recently rebuilt indoor theatre in Drury Lane, also called the Cockpit, before the first performance listed in Herbert's records: 'Upon the Sonday after, beinge the 4 of January, 1624, by the Queene of Bohemia's company, The Changelinge, the prince only being there. Att Whitehall.'[1] Beeston's company changed names, players and even Beestons, when William took over after his father Christopher's death in 1638, but it kept *The Changeling* in its repertory and out of the hands of printers for as long as the theatres stayed open: it appears, along with forty-four other plays, in a document issued by the Lord Chamberlain in 1639, legally declaring them all to be Beeston's 'propriety' and ordering 'all other Companies of Actors herby concernable: that they are not in any wayes to intermeddle with or Act any of th'above mentioned Playes'.[2] The forty-five titles were 'probably the younger Beeston's checklist of the best playbooks he had inherited from his father'.³ Years later, long after playing had been prohibited, Beeston likely relinquished his claim to *The Changeling* in dire financial circumstances, as in 1651 he found himself imprisoned for debt, obliged to sell and pawn 'his most necessary goods' and to '[take] up money upon ill conditions': in 1653, Humphrey Moseley published the now thirty-year-old play, the title-page declaring it had been 'Acted (with great applause) at the Privat house in Drury-Lane and Salisbury Court' and '*never printed before*'.⁴

The only pre-Restoration theatregoer to make (extant) note of going to see *The Changeling* was John Greene, a Lincoln's Inn barrister, who recorded the fact – but no impressions of the play – in his diary for March 1635.⁵ Chances are that Greene found the madhouse subplot more memorably entertaining than the tragedy of Beatrice-Joanna and De Flores, for the few contemporary references to the play consist of praise for the comic role of Antonio, the 'changeling' who feigns idiocy to court Isabella. Fond memories of Antonio as played by Timothy Reade, the lead comic actor for Queen Henrietta's Men, are assigned to a citizen and a country landlord in the 1638 'Praeludium' to Thomas Goffe's *The Careless Shepherdess*: 'I heard a fellow / Once on this Stage cry *Doodle, Doodle, Dooe,* / Beyond compare', recalls the landlord; 'I'de give the other shilling to see him act the Changling once again.' Thrift, the citizen, agrees:

> And so would I, his part has all the wit,
> For none speaks Craps and Quibbles besides him:
> I'd rather see him leap, laugh, or cry,
> Then hear the gravest Speeche in all the *Play*.
> I never saw Rheade peeping through the Curtain,
> But ravishing joy entered my heart.⁶

Reade's practice of poking his head through the tiring-house curtains to pull faces – the landlord remembers it making him 'laugh . . . Untill [he] cry'd again' – was a bit of comic business dating back to Tarlton.⁷ And while such tastes may have been mocked as unfashionable in the late 1630s, by 1648 some were nostalgic for the now-banned actors: 'indeed, we need not any more *Stage-playes*', runs a sarcastic (and wisely anonymous) screed against the Puritans in parliament; 'we thanke them for suppressing them, they save us money; for Ile undertake we can laugh as heartily at *Foxley*, *Peters*, and others of their godly Ministers, as ever we did at *Cane* at the *Red Bull*, *Tom Pollard* in the humorous Lieutenant, *Robins* the Changeling, or any humorist of them all.' William Robbins preceded Reade in the role of Antonio before transferring to the King's Men; sadly, the start of the Civil War cost him not only his career but his life.[8]

When the playhouses reopened, *The Changeling* was among the earliest plays revived, first staged at some point between 1659, the year John Downes gives in his 1708 memoir of the Restoration theatre, and 23 February 1661, when Samuel Pepys enjoyed a birthday outing to Salisbury Court. Either Pepys was speaking loosely when he described the performance as 'the first time it hath been acted these twenty years', or Downes was hazy on the events of nearly fifty years past when he listed *The Changeling* among the plays performed when 'Mr. *Rhodes* ... fitted up a House then for Acting call'd the *Cock Pit* in *Drury Lane*', but whatever the exact date of the revival, it went memorably well. 'It takes exceedingly', was Pepys' brief but enthusiastic review, much better (in his appraisal) than Middleton's *The Widow*, only 'indifferent good', or his 'very silly' collaboration *The Spanish Gypsy*.[9] Downes recalls the audience's pleasure at being able to laugh at Antonio once more – 'Mr. *Sheppy* Perform'd ... several other Parts very well; But above all the Changling, with general Satisfaction' – and for the first time, De Flores earns a mention, if only because the actor who played him went on to greatness:

> Mr. *Betterton*, being then but 22 Years Old, was highly Applauded for his Acting in all these Plays, but especially, For the Loyal Subject; the Mad Lover; *Pericles*; The Bondman: *Deflores*, in the *Changling*; his Voice being then

as Audibly strong, full and Articulate, as in the Prime of his Acting.

Thomas Betterton might possibly have been paired with a Beatrice-Joanna played by the teenaged Edward Kynaston, who took many of the lead female roles in the early seasons of Rhodes' company and was remembered as 'a Compleat Female Stage Beauty, performing his Parts so well ... that it has since been Disputable among the Judicious, whether any Woman that succeeded him so Sensibly touch'd the Audience as he.'[10]

After a 1668 performance at court, *The Changeling* disappears from known performance records for some 250 years.[11] Two adaptations, however, from the late eighteenth and early twentieth centuries respectively, suggest the changes in taste that kept it off the stage. William Hayley's *Marcella*, published in 1784 and staged in 1789, whitewashed Beatrice-Joanna almost beyond recognition. Although Hayley never mentions *The Changeling*, it would seem the novelist Samuel Richardson had been reading it, and the suggestion for an adaptation had originated with him.[12] In Hayley's version, Marcella agrees to marry the lovingly importunate Lupercio despite her heart's misgivings, which prove prescient when she meets Mendoza. Too virtuous to confess her love to him (he overhears her soliloquy), and too honourable to bring reproach on her father by asking him to break the engagement (Mendoza is wealthier than Lupercio, so her father would risk appearing venal), Marcella is guilty of little more than the subterfuge of asking Hernandez, her father's elderly and deformed steward, to steal back a ring that will allow the honourable retraction of her promise. Horrified and filled with self-blame when Hernandez unexpectedly adds murder to the deed, she resists the threats by which he attempts to gain his reward, losing her virginity only when he feigns repentance, lures her to an isolated tower, and rapes her. She promptly confesses all to Mendoza and dies by self-administered poison in the arms of her stricken father. *Marcella* omits *The Changeling*'s subplot, injecting the theme of madness into the plot instead: Hernandez, we hear, was a model of 'Intelligence and duty' until 'depriv'd of sense' and driven to 'frenzy' by Marcella's ripening into beauteous womanhood, while Marcella herself ends as a 'lovely maniac', hallucinating Lupercio's ghost and begging Mendoza to kill her.[13]

Hayley's aims in rewriting Beatrice-Joanna are no doubt aptly represented by an 1815 comparison of the two plays, which praises his judgement in making 'considerable alterations in the principal incident', insofar as 'Marcella becomes in some degree an object of the reader's pity, whilst Beatrice can only be regarded with detestation and abhorrence'.[14] Despite its sanitization of the original – apparently taken even further in production, with Marcella's direct appeal to Hernandez omitted – the adaptation was a theatrical flop, its failure due only in part to a bit of theatrical skulduggery: Drury Lane, in an attempt to undermine its rival, Covent Garden, anticipated the latter's opening of *Marcella* with its own hastily scrambled together production on 7 November 1789, in which 'the performers were extremely imperfect in their parts'.[15] 'His *Work*, for a Play it cannot be called', sniffed the reviewer for *The World*, '... has scarcely a line, certainly *not one scene, fitted for the Stage!*' Rather more kindly, the *London Chronicle* called it 'an elegant trifle', but 'not sufficiently complex and intricate to create much suspense, or arrest much attention'. 'Modern theatrical taste', it concluded, 'will not very greatly admire a play, where the facts of the fable are wrought up with so little art'.[16]

After the failure of *Marcella*, no version of *The Changeling*, adapted or original, would be performed for over a century. Nineteenth-century critics James Russell Lowell and Algernon Charles Swinburne admired the main plot's poetry and skilful characterization, but it would take the changing social mores of the 1920s to make it conceivable that the play might return to the stage.[17] That decade's adaptation, *Beatriz Juana*, by drama critic William Archer, was less concerned with sanitizing Beatrice-Joanna's sins than with bringing the play into line with modern standards for psychological realism as established by Henrik Ibsen and George Bernard Shaw: that Beatrice-Joanna would choose the lustful, resentful De Flores as her assassin, and then react with helpless astonishment when he demanded his reward, struck Archer as ludicrous; the virginity test/bed-trick, moreover, was evidence that 'to the Elizabethan public, an ounce of sexual suggestion was worth a pound of psychological analysis or moral casuistry'.[18] His adaptation – published posthumously in 1927 – thus featured a protagonist who, 'consistent with her wily nature and survivor's instincts ... wades through the blood of fiancé, husband, and the stooge De Flores to engage yet another lover at play's end'.[19]

Archer, however, as he lectured at King's College on the superiority of the new British drama to the old, was avowedly doing battle with a resurgence of 'modish enthusiasm' for exactly the plays he deplored.[20] While his modernized version of *The Changeling* was never staged, discerning London audiences in the first half of the 1920s were flocking to the Phoenix Society's productions of early modern plays previously 'considered to be dull, unstageable and, in some cases, obscene'.[21] By 1925, a second company, the Renaissance Theatre, also catered to the appetite for such plays, and in the context of their celebration of John Fletcher – a three-play series drawing 'large and fashionable audience[s]' to sold-out shows – we discover what was *almost* the first modern revival of *The Changeling*.[22] Flush with its Fletcherian success, the Renaissance Theatre followed its announcement of *The Wild Goose Chase* with a list of sixteen planned future productions, including '*The Changeling*, by Thomas Middleton'.[23] Four of the plays on the list, among them *Arden of Faversham* and *The White Devil*, made it to the stage between 1925 and November 1926, but after that the Renaissance Theatre disappears from record. The Phoenix Society dissolved around the same time, 'owing to lack of resources': the literati, it seems, had turned their attention to the Film Society.[24]

Fashionable theatre enthusiasts of the same era in New York had somewhat better luck, becoming, on 19 February 1922, the first audience since the Restoration to watch De

Flores blackmail Beatrice-Joanna into his bed – but no more, as the prepared typescript of the full main plot was at some point whittled down to 3.3 to be presented as part of the MacDowell Club's 'Evening with Elizabethan and Jacobean Dramatists'. The scene from *The Changeling* was the finale to an evening that included excerpts from Lyly, Webster, Massinger and Heywood; programme acknowledgements for costume-making, and for loans of both 'Spanish' and 'Elizabethan' furniture suggest an effort to recreate the period. Blanche Yurka played Beatrice-Joanna to Ian Keith's De Flores: both were at the start of successful acting careers, and also happened to embark that same year on a short-lived marriage to each other.[25]

For its first full twentieth-century revival, *The Changeling* had to wait until 9 December 1938, when the Birkbeck College Literary Society staged the first of two performances. The actors, in accordance with the Society's tradition, were not named in the programme, but an annual report thanked Mr W. Summers for directing, and for playing De Flores, 'in a finished manner, which recalled ... such past performances of his as Captain Bobadill and Black Will'.[26] Photographs show a largely bare proscenium stage, with an interesting costuming choice distinguishing the castle from the madhouse: a picture of Lollio brandishing a whip while Alibius writes at a desk shows men in Puritan-style garb, while Vermandero – moustachioed like a melodrama villain – and his family wear Cavalier velvet and lace. The *Manchester Guardian* spent more time doubting the merits of the play – Archer was quoted with approval – than evaluating the production, but nonetheless expressed appreciation that Birkbeck, in its twenty-first year of reviving 'the dustier early masterpieces in drama', was keeping up 'the valuable work done by the ever-lamented Phoenix Society'. The female lead was praised for her performance in 'the best scene', where she was 'clearly aware of that passionate sweep in the writing which seems always about to catch up with poetry's self'; otherwise, the reviewer castigated the 'revolting' comic treatment of insanity, and summarized

*The Changeling* as 'a murder, a ghost, an example of wife-substitution, a case of arson, and a couple of violent deaths', all presented by 'a number of young men, very few of whom seemed to have any zealous idea of distinguishing themselves as actors'.[27] Nevertheless, the Society recorded that 'Financially, and artistically also, by general agreement of the spectators connected with Birkbeck and otherwise, this was the best production for a number of years.'

Other amateur and university performances followed through the next two decades. The Magdalen Players at Oxford took the tragedy to a chilly outdoor venue for three evenings in May 1949: photographs in *The Tatler and Bystander* showed a lank-haired De Flores on a bare, artificially-lit apron stage, and a boyishly pretty Alsemero clutching an elaborate plumed hat. *The Times* reported that 'De Flores is far and away the most interesting character, and Mr. David Symon makes him so', while 'Miss Pat Gray's unhappy lady is more frail than wicked, which is as it should be.' From the remark that De Flores' tragedy is to 'want [Beatrice-Joanna's] love and merely win her body', one can guess something of the sexual dynamic between them, while a sense of modern superiority toward the play's focus on virginity suggests itself in a comment on the production's 'nice appreciation of the preoccupation of the time with what we should now term, a little mockingly, the facts of life'.[28] Amusement, if not mockery, was the response to the Pegasus Society's efforts in 1954: 'in performance [*The Changeling*'s] macabre quality is in continuous danger of deteriorating into the ludicrous', observed one reviewer, adding that the 'friendly' audience stopped taking the tragedy seriously after 'the pharmacy scene'.[29] The Oxford Experimental Theatre Club had better luck two years later, with a Beatrice-Joanna who ably conveyed 'childish light-heartedness and ... tragic lack of comprehension', and an innovative approach to the subplot, which used *commedia dell' arte* masks and mime to provide 'malicious commentary on the main action'.[30]

By the time Tony Richardson mounted London's first professional *Changeling*, which ran for four weeks in 1961 at the Royal Court, Middleton and Rowley's play had seen at least six amateur productions in England, plus three in the United States and one in Canada.[31] Richardson himself had directed the Pegasus Society production in 1954, and looked back on it as 'quite disastrous'. Remembering the hilarity that had greeted the murder of Alonzo, the severing of the finger, and the death of Diaphanta, he described getting the right tone in these scenes as 'walk[ing] on an exceedingly difficult tightrope'. One of the things that drew him to *The Changeling*, however, was precisely its 'curious and ironic mixture of styles . . . of abrupt switches from farce to thriller, from thriller to tragedy', which struck him as oddly modern, 'a sort of super Hitchcock'; this, together with the existentialist theme of being 'solely and wholly responsible for your own actions', and the 'almost Strindbergian love-hatred relationship' between Beatrice-Joanna and De Flores, led Richardson to judge the play as 'tremendously in tune with the contemporary theatre audience'. Richardson's attraction to these 'contemporary' elements, and his desire for both audience and actors 'to relate the play to their own lives, not to regard it as a remote and holy classic' led to a certain amount of rewriting to modernize the syntax and minimize the number of asides.[32] *The Guardian*'s Philip Hope-Wallace objected to these cuts, further lamenting that 'no one cared much for the text, for the wound [*sic*, i.e. sound] of the words, the accent, the inner rhythm and tone', but T.C. Worsley in *The Financial Times* lauded the 'rapid and clear' exposition and the 'elegant but not elevated language'; *Punch* called the language 'lean and often magnificent', adding that 'the Royal Court is to be congratulated on exhuming such an exciting play in such a good production'. There was also high praise from Lawrence Durrell, who, in an interview a month or so afterward, recalled Richardson's revival as evidence that England was becoming less parochial, more European: 'The food's much better here now, and life seems more free and easy. I went to see a production of *The Changeling* that would have made Shakespeare jump with joy. You know how we tend to stuff our old plays with reverence – as if they're something at Madame Tussaud's. Well, this had tremendous power, even a mix of accents – North Country, Cockney, not anonymous or class-ridden stuff.'[33]

The deliberate mix of English accents on a stage where the costumes and sets were pure 'Goyaesque Spain' suggests a production concerned at least as much with *The Changeling*'s class dynamics as with its sexual ones. Harold Hobson began his review by observing that 'One is always being told that until lately the working classes have never been shown on the English stage except as comic or stupid' – a charge refuted, he added, by the 'true grandeur' of Robert Shaw's 'unshaven, tight-lipped, malevolent' De Flores: 'Among the dukes, lords, and fine ladies . . . he is as terrible as an eagle among sparrows', and 'as capable of lust, murder, sensibility, and courage as any aristocratic Shakespearean here.'[34] Shaw, born near Manchester, may have provided the North Country accent that impressed Durrell. In what was a fairly standard assessment of the lead actors, *The Times* reviewer was disappointed that Mary Ure, displaying all 'the prettiness and lifelessness of a doll', failed to give Beatrice-Joanna the requisite 'indomitable will . . . in keeping with her aristocratic upbringing', but praised Shaw as 'masterly'.[35] Whether due to Richardson seeing shades of Strindberg's *Miss Julie* in what transpires between De Flores and Beatrice-Joanna, or to the sexual chemistry of a real-life affair between Ure and Shaw – she would divorce her first husband for him in 1963 – the production also offered early glimmerings of what would become the standard interpretive subtext, criticized by Roberta Barker and David Nicol as anachronistically Freudian, textually unsupported, and anti-feminist: Beatrice-Joanna's subconscious attraction to the man she ostensibly loathes.[36] Describing Shaw's De Flores as 'still and strong, unswervable and dynamic', Kenneth Tynan remarked that 'one understands why Beatrice prefers his company to that of her pretty new husband: a villain who shares one's guilt is inevitably more attractive than a hero convinced of one's innocence'.[37]

Richardson recognized that the madhouse subplot, in its apparent detachment from the tragic plot, posed a 'special difficulty'. His Goya-inspired set and costumes, he felt, helped to lend a kind of unity by infusing both plots with 'a quality of insanity', but he added some further unifying touches of his own, by 'introducing certain of the minor characters into the main plot at points where they were not originally written'. Rather oddly, he sought to establish the subplot's modern relevance by treating Antonio's flowery wooing language as 'a sort of satire on the pop song of the time', and had Robin Ray rehearse the part 'in terms of pop singers ... so that he could relate it to his own experience': the 'original casting', he claimed, would have had the equivalent of a pop idol, 'the Tommy Steele or Adam Faith of the day' for 'the great popular part' of Antonio.[38] While evidence suggests the Jacobean Antonios were more like the John Cleese of their day, the Royal Court audience nevertheless followed their early modern counterparts in finding the madhouse hilarious: in a bit of unintentional irony, Hope-Wallace complained that the 'piteous lunatics' he believed were intended to 'shock and stun the audience of 1622', sent the theatregoers of 1961 into 'gales of hearty public school laughter'. Reviewers, on the whole, enjoyed the subplot less than audiences did: Worsley called the 'privately run looney-bin' 'irrelevant but entertaining' and Tynan appreciated Lollio's 'leering earthiness' up against Isabella's 'busty insolence', but Robert Muller considered it 'a monotony of ... gurgling, cackling, flagellation, cuckolding, and groaning, that sickens when it's not being unintentionally funny' – a view seconded by J.C. Trewin's indictment: 'I cannot believe that there is any good excuse for this stuff.'[39]

Richardson's 1961 *Changeling*, however, was not the first professional revival of the twentieth century, provided one does not take 'professional' to mean either 'paid' or 'London'.[40] In 1956, Joseph Papp, founder of the New York Shakespeare Festival, chose *The Changeling* for his Shakespearean Theater Workshop, then working out of the converted Emmanuel Presbyterian Church. Though composed of professional actors, including J.D. Cannon as a 'horribly birthmarked' De Flores, and Peggy Bennion (then married to Papp) as a 'spirited, insidious, altogether believable' Beatrice-Joanna, the troupe worked for free, and the pay-what-you-can admission adhered to Papp's ideal of 'reach[ing] people who do not ordinarily attend Shakespearean plays'.[41] The stage was bare, the props minimal, and the costumes black and white – five-dollar deadstock wedding dresses for the women, the men in their own black trousers and white shirts – but the result, in the words of Jerry Tallmer's almost giddily delighted review for *The Village Voice*, was 'the biggest bargain in town': 'How can anything not be a bargain if it's excitingly good and costs you, if you lack the wherewithal, exactly nothing?' Calling it 'a love-sex-hate play of utmost interest and immense vitality' performed by 'as splendid a permanent company of young actors as you will find anywhere, on or off Broadway', Tallmer recounted the plot up until the climax of 3.3, whereupon he breaks off with gleeful mock-prudery: 'And the rest of "The Changeling" I am not going to tell you about, because nice girls aren't supposed to act that way and this is after all a family newspaper.'[42] Accompanying the review is a photo of the dying Beatrice-Joanna, kneeling beside De Flores to touch his face with what seems to be affection. Tallmer's praise extended to the 'brilliantly comic-bawdy' actors in the 'parody counter-plot', praise echoed in a brief *New York Times* review focussed almost entirely on the subplot, which featured a skilfully danced duel between Antonio and Franciscus.[43]

In the press surrounding the next American revival – the ill-fated 1964 *Changeling* by the Lincoln Center's Repertory Theater – the only allusion to Papp's shoestring success would seem to be the reference to 'full-scale', in a note that the new production, directed by Elia Kazan, was *The Changeling*'s 'initial full-scale production in the United States since it was written in 1622'.[44] The photo accompanying the *New York Times* review showed Alsemero (John Philip Law) and Beatrice-Joanna (Barbara Loden) in sumptuous Elizabethan dress, and Glenn Loney described an elaborate set: 'When the lights went up on David Hays' tortured maze of walks, designed to suggest cramped castle corridors, expectation mounted. A twisted, brooding Christ hung from a large cross suspended above the stage.'[45] The intended visual effect, according to Kazan, was 'the spirit of the Renaissance' emerging from 'the body of the Middle Ages'.[46] What did emerge, though, was a disaster, to the point that the production's run was cut short, refunds were issued, and Kazan resigned as co-director of the theatre.[47] Reviews, scholarly post-mortems and Kazan's own reflections offer insight into what went wrong and why. The director's private life was in turmoil – his wife had died suddenly the previous year while he was having an affair with Loden, his Beatrice-Joanna; he later admitted, moreover, to having 'no feeling or genuine interest for any but contemporary plays on contemporary subjects'.[48] Like Richardson before him, Kazan perceived *The Changeling* as 'very modern in spirit' – 'an ironic, realistic, hard-headed view of the way humans behave ... wear[ing] masks in order to get by when their real impulses and their real feelings are something else' – but it proved stubbornly resistant to taking direction *as* a contemporary play.[49] 'Part of the fault lay in attempting to read the poetic language as though it were merely commonplaces of contemporary conversation';[50] another part, as Kazan realized in retrospect, lay in his actors being trained only in the techniques of Stanislavskian psychological realism, and thus 'never really succeed[ing] in wedding the necessary vocal force, clarity of speech, dexterity with words, and love of the language to the emotional techniques of the Stanislavski-Strasberg method'.[51] Loden, critically acclaimed just months earlier for her portrayal of the Marilyn Monroe-inspired Maggie in Arthur Miller's *After the Fall*, was universally excoriated for bringing the same vocal patterns and affect – her 'virtually uninflected little-girl talk' – to the 'self-indulgent, evil woman' that is Beatrice-Joanna.[52] Kazan defended Loden's 'little-girl manner' as an artistic choice, comparing Beatrice-Joanna to morally deficient modern teenagers who plead youth and emotional impulse for their failings: 'I wanted her to be wilful, spoiled, arrogant, insistent on what she wants at all cost, blind to consequences – a 15 year old of that time.'[53] Critics like Loney, though, were having none of it: 'If this is valid, why not set the play in Flatbush? Beatrice can be a sophomore at Midwood High ... Juliet was also a teenager. Does this mean the actress should behave like Patty Duke?'[54] The actors playing Alsemero and Tomazo were equally at sea with the language of Jacobean tragedy; Barry Primus as De Flores garnered some lukewarm approval as the best of a bad lot.[55]

The clash between Kazan's modern vision and *The Changeling* went beyond the acting. Robert Brustein launched a scathing attack on its 'mindlessness and vulgarity', objecting particularly to the onstage sex scenes: Kazan, he mocked, must have had a bed left over from *Cat on a Hot Tin Roof*, and was 'willing to sacrifice everything – plot, character, theme, language, the sense of the past – for the sake of a few prurient giggles from the gallery'.[56] The *Times*' New York drama critic raised the reasonable objection that casting a black actor as Alonzo vilified Beatrice-Joanna beyond warrant by adding racial prejudice to her already substantial list of sins.[57] Richard Shechner summed up the production's central failure as a philosophical one, Kazan's attempt to force the play into a moral stance foreign to the original:

> In much of his work before *The Changeling*, implicit in both his choice of plays and in his direction, is the sentimental belief that remorse is equivalent to forgiveness, that *feelings* can remedy actions. Such is the psychological fallacy, and it is not limited to Kazan. *The Changeling* does not submit to this interpretation, and some of the most amateurish moments in the LCR production came when Kazan tried to brute the material to his taste: at the final moment Vermandero sits interminably, his head bent in sorrow, his figure bathed in *soft* light; Alonzo's ghost panhandles pity up and down the stage in more scenes than one can bear; Beatrice poses in her room, immobilized by her follow-spot,

as others speak of her or enact what she has initiated; Tomazo returns again and again to the castle's front door pleading his murdered brother's cause until even many of the audience have gone home. All this staging is there to prompt us to pity. But why? *The Changeling* was not written for pity.[58]

Not all reviews were unrelievedly damning. Harold Taubman appreciated the spectacular murder of Alonzo, whose body plummeted from a height while Beatrice-Joanna prayed downstage, and the 'tautness' of Kazan's direction of the final scene, where 'the movement is so swift and controlled and the atmosphere so right in its blend of sombre justice and ultimate humility that even shortcomings in performance cannot stand between play and public'. And while faulting the production in general for 'emphasiz[ing] and linger[ing] on every scatological point', he conceded that 'Some of the comic scenes, where grossness is not ludicrously exaggerated, are handled with vitality.' Schechner, while criticizing Kazan's treatment of the main plot, admitted to enjoying 'the inferior madhouse scenes written by Rowley'. (Brustein, on the other hand, deplored an extra-textual decision that had Isabella, in direct violation of her role as foil to Beatrice-Joanna, 'bounc[ing] merrily into the sack as well'.) Given Kazan's reputation, and the critics' high hopes for the relatively new Lincoln Center troupe, a couple of reviews were optimistic that the performances would improve as the play's run continued.[59] Their optimism, as they soon found out, was misplaced.

The Lincoln Center fiasco, understandably enough, seems to have put American directors off *The Changeling* for quite a few years, though there was talk of Papp, championed by Brustein, revisiting it in 1966.[60] In Britain, however, the late 1960s and 1970s saw the flourishing of Middleton and Rowley's tragedy, with ten professional productions in the latter decade alone.[61] Before turning to the *Changelings* of the 1970s, a couple of productions from the late 1960s are worth a look for their unusual efforts at foregrounding the subplot. Frequently considered problematic and so pared down or simply omitted, Alibius' madhouse found itself suddenly fashionable after Peter Weiss's *Marat/Sade*, directed by Peter Brook for the RSC, became the theatrical sensation of 1964. *Marat/Sade*, in which a play-within-the-play is acted by the inmates of an early nineteenth-century insane asylum, appears to have inspired Frank Evans, directing the Oxford Stage Company in 1966, to situate the action of *The Changeling*'s main plot within the madhouse itself, with the inhabitants of the castle ducking in and out through flaps in the madmen's cage to play their scenes in the sand of the asylum's courtyard. B.A. Young, who judged the play 'grossly over-influenced by the modish concern with the "theatre of cruelty"', objected to this literalization of the subtle likenesses the plots draw between the mad and the sane: 'We are supposed to make this chilling discovery for ourselves, not to have it shouted at us in the first five minutes.'[62] *The Stage* appreciated the concept, but found that the 'overpowering atmosphere' of the madhouse submerged what were already weak performances by the actors cast as Beatrice-Joanna and De Flores; the latter, in a rather singular and perhaps asylum-inspired directorial choice, was played as a 'youthful, dim-witted servant'.[63] Later the same year, an Italian production by Luca Ronconi carried the *Marat/Sade* treatment even further: titled *I Lunatici*, it presented 'the much-maligned asylum subplot as if it were the main action', while the main plot became a play acted by the inmates.[64]

The asylum-centred treatments of the 1960s were among numerous *Changelings* that led up to the two major London productions of 1978: Peter Gill's at the Riverside Studios and Terry Hands' with the Royal Shakespeare Company at Aldwych. In 1970, Richard Eyre, later to direct the National Theatre Company in his racially-charged production of 1988, started out with a more conventional Goyaesque version at the Edinburgh Theatre Festival;[65] the following year, a young Sinead Cusack played Beatrice-Joanna for Gordon McDougall at the Gardner Arts Centre in Brighton, and further productions were staged in Birmingham (1973), London (1974) and

Glasgow (1976). The 1974 *Changeling*, at the South London Theatre Centre, appears to have been the first with a female director, Jill Clark: the single available review suggests a victimized Beatrice-Joanna, who fell into sin through a 'terribly, ghastly ... almost dreamlike' innocence and had her throat cut by an 'erect, defiant' De Flores, 'like an angel of destruction'.[66] Audiences in Glasgow, by contrast, were treated to 'an exquisite piece of kitsch' featuring a troupe of Spanish dancers who performed a bull-baiting on De Flores and 'tango[ed] sensuously' behind him as he deflowered his mistress; Michael Coveney, reviewing for the *Financial Times*, clearly found this cabaret-style show a great guilty pleasure and regretted only that director Philip Prowse had cut the subplot.[67]

Facing three new productions of *The Changeling* in late 1978 – the Riverside and the RSC among them – the reviewer for *Punch* was becoming peevish, remarking that the play's current popularity was 'for reasons still not entirely clear' and picturing his fellow critics 'desperately trying to grind out some sort of response' to it as 'a meaningful statement of the relationship between love and madness'.[68] *The Spectator*, on the other hand, embraced the onslaught: Peter Jenkins declared *The Changeling* 'a play for our times', not only in the usual parallels of Jacobean/modern 'moral instability, social fluidity, and political change' but in its 'compelling topicality' for audiences 'conversant with the committal of desperate deeds for appearances' sake and with the ensuing tragedy of cover-up' – a reference, it would seem, to the then-current scandal of Liberal leader Jeremy Thorpe allegedly hiring an assassin to silence his former (male) lover (a charge of which he would be acquitted at his trial in 1979). Jenkins' review of the Riverside production, the first of the three to open, highly approved of Gill's decision to avoid 'the conventions of revenge plays, all prancing and blood-spurting': his bare-stage production 'goes way to the other extreme: his players move with classical formality, mostly in straight lines like precision marchers, their footsteps echoing from the stone flags of the stage arena; when they have nothing to do they do nothing, no fidgeting or "acting," but stand motionless, frozen into stark Spanish tableaux, Velasquez-like'. The production's arresting visual effects, created on a bare stage with only the actors and lighting 'which seems almost to pierce the soul', drew praise from other critics for 'scenes as intricately composed as a dance', where characters 'freeze into erotic emblems', or are 'located to perfect visual satisfaction, as in a conversation-piece by Gainsborough'.[69] Brian Cox played a complex De Flores: sardonic, brutally intelligent and implacably efficient in his murders, but possessed of 'gentleness and a tender sense of guilt', an 'infatuated helplessness' around Beatrice-Joanna, and a 'soft, coaxing voice' with 'an outsider's North-country edge to his accent'.[70] Robert Cushman called him 'more likeabl[e] than even I would have expected'. Emma Piper's Beatrice-Joanna was a restrained portrait of an 'arrogant debutante', who dealt in 'delicate ambiguities and half-invitations to lovers and servants alike' and had the self-possession to regain her status around De Flores even after she submitted to his coercion.[71] Some reviewers found Piper *too* restrained, wanting in 'giddy capriciousness', 'spoilt-child pettishness', or a latent appetite for promiscuity and perversion, which Jenkins argued the character must have if she is accurately to reflect De Flores' 'insights'.[72] Michael Billington, by contrast, found she effectively conveyed 'the sado-masochistic fantasies of a reclusive virgin'; he was also not alone in taking Alsemero's 'there's scarce a thing that's both loved and loathed' out of context as elucidating 'the Freudian love-hate relationship in a nutshell' (see Nora Williams' discussion later in this volume), and praised Piper's 'fascinat[ion] from the start with De Flores' revolting pockiness'.[73]

When the RSC *Changeling* opened at Aldwych shortly afterward, the widely positive response to Gill's austere staging may have predisposed reviewers to criticize Hands' production as tastelessly overdone. Benedict Nightingale was in the minority when he preferred the 'erotic savageries' of the RSC to the 'Brookish severity' of the Riverside, though even he admitted that Hands' direction 'sometimes succumbs to overstatement'; J.C. Trewin more bluntly observed that 'Hands does so much with complicated atmospherics . . . that he perilously obscures the play', while Sheridan Morley complained of 'so much scenic effect that we are threatened with a circus'.[74] The set was a combination of sinisterly gleaming metal and 'leathery walls the colour of dried blood', conveying a 'feeling of poisonous ritual'.[75] Diana Quick, in a spectacularly low-cut velvet gown, was an overtly sexualized, 'voluptuous, spoilt-darling of a Beatrice-Joanna', who 'suggests from the start that [her] hysterical disgust conceals a cloying fascination'.[76] Jenkins, who had spent a good part of his review of the Riverside marshalling textual evidence for a kinkier, more depraved Beatrice-Joanna than Piper portrayed, praised Quick for making 'a qualified triumph of this difficult part'; he was willing to excuse – as several other critics were not – the illogic of a Beatrice-Joanna who flung off her shawl to 'thrust her luscious breasts toward [De Flores]' as she enticed him to murder, but was shocked when he claimed his obviously-promised reward.[77] Emrys James as De Flores, heavy-set and balding, 'manag[ed] to make menace tender and implacable sensuality gentle'; he played the climactic scene like a 'gentle, patient schoolmaster, quietly pointing out that she has not quite yet learnt her lesson and that honour and modesty are words she must forget'.[78] There was also a sense, however, that too much of the performance tipped over into black farce: as Morley put it, Hands offered 'a brisk, joky, mindless canter through a play which Gill asked us to stop and think about'. Irving Wardle, who liked the production despite finding it less 'emotionally powerful' than Gill's, noted loud guffaws from the audience during the virginity test; Jenkins objected to the audience's reaction to Alonzo's finger amputation – 'there is something wrong when an actor as good as Emrys James gets a laugh at what should be one of the most chilling moments of the play' – and even more strongly to the sequence that provoked further laughter at the start of 4.1: 'If Beatrice is to be had by De Flores on stage, and from behind what is more, bent over a chest, she cannot ... trip down stage and exclaim "This fellow has undone me endlessly."' The onstage deflowering occurred during the dumbshow, in which Alsemero married a manikin on wheels, masked and dressed to resemble his bride.[79]

Criticism of Hands' overblown staging – *Punch* compared the whole experience to witnessing 'an upper-crust orgy' – extended to his integration of the subplot. Pursuing the concept that the mad and the sane change places over the course of the narrative, Hands gradually changed the castle inhabitants' costumes to resemble those of the asylum inmates, and had the play begin with 'the sane voyeuristically watching the mad' but end with 'the mad sympathetically watching the contorted lusts and killing of the sane'; this sounded perfectly good on paper, remarked Billington, but 'theatrically it blows up in the inventor's face and leads to some rather frantic and noisy over-playing', to the extent that the audience ends the play 'bombarded into a state of virtual indifference'.[80] The same review recalled the quiet effectiveness of a scene in the Riverside production, where Gill suggested the subplot's relation to the plot by having Beatrice-Joanna and Isabella 'pass each other in opposite directions like two mirror images, each invisible to each other'.[81] Both productions, however, seem to have broken from the bawdy, comic Isabellas of earlier subplots: Gill's Isabella (Sharon Duce) conveyed an integrity that stood in explicit contrast to Beatrice-Joanna's vice, while Charlotte Cornwall in Hands' production played the 'disappointed wife' as 'both bitter and vicious'.[82]

The season of proliferating *Changelings* continued with four more professional productions through the end of 1978 and the first half of 1979, in Bristol, Manchester, Stoke-on-Trent and Birmingham: a certain weariness was evident when B.A. Young, reviewing his third in as many months, groused that the Bristol Beatrice-Joanna was likely to wind up dead no matter whom she married, murdered 'for her maddening way of making every movement at a run'.[83]

No longer an obscure Jacobean oddity, *The Changeling* returned to the North American professional stage in 1985, in a major production by the American Repertory Theatre in Cambridge, Massachusetts, directed by Robert Brustein. An assistant professor at Columbia when he had savaged Kazan in 1964, Brustein founded the ART in 1980 after leaving his position as Dean of the Yale School of Drama.[84] In a retrospective of the theatre's first five years, Richard Eder characterized it as enormously serious, dedicated to 'experiment and the unorthodox', and often, rather ponderous: 'The ART is magisterial; the trouble is that it can feel that way ... It is archepiscopal theater, whose audiences have the air of doing a worthy thing. There is little feeling of adventure, of danger, of busting out. There is more teaching than discovery.'[85] Some reviewers took exception to being taught, via Brustein's programme notes, that *The Changeling* was about 'the effect of a repressive society on an independent-minded woman', and that the subplot was an 'inferior contribution' not worth staging.[86] Carolyn Clay, who didn't mind that the omission of the madhouse produced 'something more like a Greek than a Jacobean Tragedy', could not summon the sympathy demanded by Brustein's claim that 'the repression of Beatrice-Joanna by a patriarchal society ... allots her none but radical recourse': 'there is nothing admirable in her cold-blooded means of defiance – or in her easier accommodation to mayhem than to sullied reputation'. The male characters, including John Bottoms as a jarringly comical De Flores – a Frankensteinian beanpole with a pustulent scalp, 'all snaky insinuation and Igor postures' – flaunted their sinister power in vaguely reptilian, codpieced leather jumpsuits; Jeremy Geidt's Vermandero was a 'tight, trim fascist' attended by a pair of teenaged concubines.[87] Diane D'Aquila, the mature, husky-voiced antithesis of Kazan's Beatrice-Joanna, played her as 'deeply and mysteriously troubled from her first entrance'.[88] The actors' treatment of the language was 'relentlessly contemporary', the steel-box set, backed with a sinister moon, evoked 'space-age weirdness', and Alonzo's body plummeted startlingly – as in Kazan's production – from a height.[89] The consensus: visually stunning but emotionally uninvolving, *The Changeling* as put through an 'intellectual juice squeezer' in which 'Brustein's formidable analytical powers ... filtered the raw material, neatened it, saved the audience the trouble and energy of messing with the unruly stuff of art'.[90]

Messing with the stuff of art, in a rather different sense, is what some reviewers felt that Richard Eyre was doing when he set his 1988 National Theatre production in a nineteenth-century Spanish slave colony and cast a black actor, George Harris, to play De Flores to Miranda Richardson's Beatrice-Joanna. The concept, according to the programme notes, was to 'make more visibly apparent the Jacobean interdependence of rank and money' and to show 'sex running riot across an oppressively stratified world'.[91] Comparisons to *Othello* abounded – Harris was 'a black Iago', or 'a hybrid of Iago and Othello', or 'a noble if disadvantaged black man, twice as proud as Othello'[92] – but the racial politics of a slave-owner's daughter discovering her desire (as the standard interpretation now had it) for a black major-domo transformed the meaning of the play: De Flores' 'external flaws [are] indicative of inner evil', objected the *TLS*, and 'to make him a member of a different race is to run counter to Middleton's [sic] point'. Some felt the dynamic elevated De Flores and made Beatrice-Joanna's eventual attraction to him all to her credit: Harris is 'tall, handsome, and immensely dignified. In a slave colony, a white woman's passion for such a man has very different connotations'; 'De Flores's pustules are tribal scars; her disgust for him is based on his negritude as much as his servile status. As a result, his passion becomes a noble thing, his simple sense of honour and debt far more worthy than Beatrice's girlish idea of social prerogative. Harris makes De Flores a hero.'[93] Others, disturbingly, thought that a black De Flores 'brilliantly exaggerates what is already there': Kate Kellaway, for instance, described Harris as 'unusually tall, ugly and black ... dominat[ing] in a glaring white suit that creeps up to his neck. His face is scarred, his tongue lolls in his mouth. He is all appetite and threat.'[94] Christopher Edwards for *The Spectator* found the whole thing simply a distraction: 'Visually, miscegenation is a permanent issue in the play, but the director is unable to make much of it as the text does not assist him.' The racially-charged visuals seemed to preoccupy reviewers at the expense of the acting: there were the inevitable gripes about neither lead fully meeting the challenges of Jacobean verse, and some scattered praise for Harris's 'remarkable containment' and 'cool, sometimes chilling nonchalance'.[95] Edwards defended Richardson's 'contained study of unknowing innocence waking up in a trap of sexual and moral consequences' as 'a more subtle performance that she has been credited with', but Alex Renton, labelling her 'suitably petulant and stupid-sexy', confessed himself irresistibly reminded of the 'delightfully dotty Queen Elizabeth I' that Richardson played in *Blackadder*.[96]

Critics were more united in their admiration of Eyre's set and its effectiveness in integrating the subplot. A sophisticated take on the *Marat/Sade*-inspired treatments of the 1960s, William Dudley's design transformed the stage into a burnished 'palace of cavernous halls, the walls thick with gilt but tarnished with greenish mold', with heavy back doors opening onto a brightly-lit tropical beach; this glowing interior, 'reek[ing] of sex and bleed[ing] old gold', was flanked by starkly-lit metal staircases that rose up through tiered cells to a gallery.[97] These represented the asylum, 'where lunatics and fools crouch in rags and straitjackets as other action takes place centre stage', 'as if the Marat-Sade were pressing in on a world of colonial opulence'.[98] The play opened with Beatrice-Joanna and Alsemero emerging, puppet-like, from a huddle of lunatics, to which they returned at the close, and a madhouse dance in which Isabella was suddenly revealed behind Beatrice-Joanna recalled, for Michael Billington, the 'great moment' in Gill's production when the two women crossed the stage as mirror images. Thematic parallels between De Flores and Lollio were reinforced by having the latter played by another black actor (Paul Barber), with both characters 'look[ing] ... down on this world of tormented white lust from a curved balcony high up in the roof'.[99] Alonzo was murdered on this balcony – though not thrown off it – and his blood dripped onto the stage with chilling effect.

By the 1990s, *The Changeling* was an established classic, inviting adaptation – Brad Fraser's *The Ugly Man* (1992) and Melanie Marnich's *Tallgrass Gothic* (1999) – and experimentation.[100] In January 1991, London had two productions playing simultaneously, both in modern dress and without the subplot.[101] Reviews of the fringe production at the White Bear, which billed itself as 'a comic horror story', testify to director Sophia Reed's decision to break from the now-canonical assumption that Beatrice-Joanna's loathing for De Flores springs from subconscious desire: *What's On* described this De Flores (Peter Cockett) as a man Beatrice-Joanna 'sincerely detests', while Malcolm Rutherford for *The Financial Times* objected to his being 'far too physically repellent – running sores all over his face – to make his later relationship with Beatrice as fascinating as it should be. It is blackmail, not mutual lust'. Elvis Presley's 'Love Me Tender', punctuating what *Time Out* referred to as 'Beatrice's unwilling submission to De Flores' lust', sounded an ironic challenge to the 'dark love story' convention, and the play closed, pointedly, with James Brown's 'It's a Man's World'.[102] The other 1991 production, directed by Mark Rylance for the British Chinese Theatre Company, set the action in the Golden Castle Chinese restaurant: Susan Leong played the owner's spoilt daughter, and Julian Lyon, 'a greasy untouchable with the face of a leprous Adonis', the obsessed cook who murders her bespectacled fiancé with a cleaver.[103] Most reviews expressed surprise at how well it worked: the dilemma faced by Beatrice-Joanna, 'a submissive daughter for whom there is no world outside the home', made sense in this 'world of courteous formality and arranged marriages', where the 'hermetic family setting' was ruled by 'a Chinese sense of hierarchy'.[104] Vengeful ghosts, as traditional in Chinese folklore as in Renaissance drama, included not only Alonzo, who manifested through a television set, but Diaphanta (Toshie Ogura), whose silent, accusing return at the end was admired even by critics who disliked the whole.[105]

Equally experimental, in New York toward the end of the decade, was Robert Woodruff's 1997 production with Theater for a New Audience. Woodruff had seen the ART *Changeling* in 1985, and disagreed with Brustein's excision of the subplot: 'Why anyone would want to give up the insane asylum is beyond me.'[106] His approach to the madhouse was to make it as dark as the castle, creating 'twin houses of horror, a bifurcated world of relentless darkness in which lunatic behavior overwhelms passion, faith and reason'. The sexual violence of the main plot was imported into the subplot by having Lollio perform painful gynaecological procedures – variously interpreted as clitoridectomies or abortions – on strapped-down female inmates while he bantered with Alibius; the violated women later appeared 'in copies of Beatrice's blood-stained wedding gown'.[107] Ten moveable glass booths changed from asylum cells to castle chambers to a blazing corridor down which De Flores led Alonzo to his death.[108] With an explicit mission to 'reclaim ... difficult classics for contemporary playgoers', Woodruff laid on a panoply of visual and auditory effects in what the *New York Times* called an 'acid-trip adaptation', complete with a flaming bed, a Blue Man Group-inspired ghost, Versace-esque costumes, frenzied flamenco dancing, a vomiting Beatrice-Joanna, a masturbating De Flores, and 'bloody crotches ... everywhere'.[109] Reviewers tended to agree with Francine Russo's conclusion in *The Village Voice*: a production in which 'the punctuation screams so loudly you can't hear the text'.

By contrast, the major London *Changeling* of the 1990s played it straight. Michael Attenborough directed the RSC, with Cheryl Campbell and Malcolm Storry as the leads, in a production that opened at The Swan in Stratford in late 1992, to be revived at the Barbican Pit the following spring. Whether reviewers appreciated seeing the play 'done plainly and not over-pictorialized as was the RNT's Goya-esque version', or found this 'traditional rendering' to be 'predictable, careful, and unmoving', the result was a renewed focus on the characters and the acting.[110] Stephen Wall for the *TLS* observed how Campbell's 'remarkable transparency enables her to convey what Una Ellis-Fermor called the 'snipe-like darts of [Beatrice-Joanna's] mind' with 'striking fidelity';[111] Campbell's 'whole body', wrote Kellaway, 'reveal[s] her state of mind, at once trapped and longing to flee . . . poised, breathless, on the edge of hysteria, exclamatory and greedy for love'.[112] While this Beatrice-Joanna began as 'an unimaginative brat for whom murder is in the fly-swatting category', she offered not a 'sadistic spectacle of purity defiled', but a woman of fully-developed appetites, undergoing 'not so much a process of corruption as a gradual and hair-raising admission of her desire for the detested De Flores'.[113] The 'warped love story' interpretation was very much brought to the fore, helped along, according to Malcolm Rutherford, by making De Flores 'much less ugly than he usually is': though his face was disfigured on one side with scars and burns, Storry's massive physical presence, combined with 'charm, wit, and intelligence' made it 'no surprise that . . . Beatrice begins to fall for him'.[114] This De Flores was also characterized by his 'frighteningly quiet control'.[115] John Peter, one of very few to dislike the production, called him 'a solemn, lumbering Malvolio' but most reviewers were with Kellaway: 'At first, he seems to lack electricity, seems disengaged from himself; speaks about his sexual appetites as if making a public broadcast to the audience. But gradually, terrifyingly, this calm man begins to show the cold will of a lunatic. His orderly manner is freakish; his disengagement is a form of amorality. The result is magnetic, chilling, absolutely right.'[116] The lunatic dimension of De Flores was further underlined, and cleverly integrated with the subplot, by the use of a grating-covered below-stage pit, akin to the traditional 'hell' of the early modern stage, to represent both the madhouse – its inhabitants emerged from below to act their scenes – and the closet out of which De Flores carries the wounded Beatrice-Joanna. The climax of 3.3 took place on the grating itself, lit from below to throw bars of shadow across Beatrice-Joanna and De Flores as she succumbed to his inexorable will.[117]

Both traditional and experimental stagings of *The Changeling* have continued unabated through the first decade and a half of this century. Karin Brown's list of British and American professional productions of early modern non-Shakespearean plays counts seven *Changelings* between 2000 and 2009, a number surpassed only by perennial favourites *Volpone* (eight productions), *The Duchess of Malfi* (eleven) and *Doctor Faustus* (thirteen); at least another seven have appeared between 2009 and the writing of this chapter, including a version translated into Slovenian and performed in Ljubljana under the direction of Australian Lindy Davies.[118] Since Sarah Dustagheer's essay in this volume explores four recent major London productions in detail, I will use the space remaining to offer a condensed overview of how twenty-first century directors have grappled with the challenges that have come to be associated with *The Changeling*: the limits of updating a play that hinges on seventeenth-century attitudes to virginity; the effective integration of the madhouse subplot; and the longstanding demand, as documented by Barker and Nicol, for explosive sexual chemistry between Beatrice-Joanna and De Flores, based on the problematic assumption that her loathing masks subconscious desire.

Modern-dress productions seem to have worked best when combined with a non-specific setting and an overtly theatrical aesthetic: with the 'brilliantly bonkers, goo-spattered' Young Vic production, where sex and death involved handfuls of red jelly, and De Flores took Beatrice-Joanna on her wedding-reception table while the guests danced the conga to Psy's 'Gangnam Style', a few reviewers objected to modern 'gimmickry', but none questioned the plausibility of the virginity dilemma.[119] Director Joe Hill-Gibbins was 'determined to avoid diluting the Jacobean play's power with twentieth-century realism' and relied instead on the inherent theatricality of the original: 'We don't disguise the fact that we're in the theatre; we use the mechanism of theatre explicitly to tell the story, that's something I like to do – but it also comes from Middleton [sic].'[120] With similar principles, Cheek by Jowl's widely-praised modern-dress version took place in the cavernous, stripped-down backstage area of the Barbican main stage, a space that 'looked more suited to a rehearsal than a performance', with a few items of functional furniture and a set of plastic chairs that served as prayer stands or asylum seating as needed.[121] Reviewers commented on the humanizing depth the company brought to Middleton and Rowley's characters, without questioning whether their motivations clashed with their (generically modern) clothes.[122] With greater specificity, however, came greater risk: Dawn Walton's 2002 *Changeling* at Southwark Playhouse evoked contemporary club culture, 'a multicultural 21st century world where slippery dealers and street-boys rule the day', and Beatrice-Joanna's 'glittering shoes and revealing clothes ... do little to assert her virginity'. 'Walton's task', wrote Rachel Haliburton, 'is to make the issues of Beatrice's purity and fidelity merit the life-or-death scenario that forms the crux of the play – a tall order in a modern world where both qualities are significantly devalued'. Most critics were simply puzzled by the incongruousness of it all.[123] Michael Oakley's production at the same venue in 2011 ingeniously updated the social divide between the main characters – Beatrice-Joanna was a rich businessman's daughter, De Flores a security guard stalking her through CCTV cameras in his grubby office – but did not escape the criticism that 'aggressively 21st century costumes do not sit easily with 17th century attitudes'; even less appreciated was Oakley's decision to modernize the play's many asides into pre-recorded voiceovers (as Sarah Dustagheer discusses in her contribution to this volume).[124] Even when transposed to an era in which similar attitudes to female sexuality might easily apply, the play needs to be staged so as to make the stakes perfectly clear: for the 2017 season of the Stratford Festival, Jackie Maxwell chose the Spanish Civil War as her setting, explaining in the programme notes that 'it was a time when the moral compass was spinning wildly, and danger and potential death were constants'. As the *Globe and Mail* review observed, however: 'The fascistic patriarchy of this Spain [was] not set up enough at the start to explain Beatrice-Joanna's drastic decision as anything other than cold and capricious.'[125]

While many directors continue to experiment with updating, few now choose to stage the play without its subplot. Oakley (2011) was roundly denounced by veteran reviewer Michael Coveney for doing so, although his younger colleagues seemed largely unperturbed.[126] A 2012 production by the Florida-based Resurgens company also cut the subplot: an odd choice for a group devoted to 'original practices productions of rarely-performed verse dramas', compounded with the even odder choice of staging Alonzo as a comic fop, complete with an effeminate wig that De Flores eventually used as a (literal) gag.[127] All other productions since 2000 have kept at least some version of the madhouse: the earliest, by Third Party in 2001 (dir. John Wright), revived a version of the *Marat/Sade* approach to create a 'Dickensian freak show' in which 'under the demonic tutelage of Dr. Alibius, the inhabitants of his Victorian madhouse act out plays for our entertainment'; the show involved heavy cuts to the text, an enormous terracotta wardrobe, and 'comedy by the vaudevillian bucket-load', but the reviews, though few, were positive.[128] Maxwell (2017) sought clarity by eliminating Franciscus from the madhouse, and included 'renegades' from the Civil War among its inmates – mentioned, and visible, but playing no other role.[129] For his 2004 production with Bristol's Tobacco Factory, Andrew Hilton had Dominic Power rewrite parts of the subplot, inserting offstage mad shouts that anticipated lines from the main plot, such as 'I am in pain and must be eased' and 'I am in a labyrinth'; they also included a scene in which Antonio set the inmates at large, allowing Alibius to proclaim the obvious connection: 'The madness that was fettered in this house is now abroad!'[130] Many reviews praised the clarity of this production, though one groused that the 'tidying' made the subplot no more satisfying, 'just less authentic'.[131]

Directors who adhered more closely to the original found inventive ways to tie the two plots together. Jesse Berger's 2015 Red Bull production brought the cast of both plots, excluding Alsemero, together for a dance of madmen, white-clad and unrecognizable in stylized full-head masks of the 'beasts and birds' that Isabella mentions in 3.2; the dance then morphed into the start of the bed-trick, as Beatrice-Joanna and Diaphanta unmasked and Alsemero led his veiled counterfeit bride into the windowed downstage asylum, while the dancers restrained her frantic mistress.[132] A full-cast 'wild wedding dance ... link[ing] love and madness' was also deployed by Cheek by Jowl (2006), but Declan Donnellan's main innovation was to 'literalize ... the play's figurative analogy' by having the main plot's actors remain onstage to become patients in the asylum scenes: 'As the action entered the madhouse, the seated characters of the main plot affected crazy repetitive habits – counting fingers over and over, chanting meaningless snatches, rocking to and fro – so that they became so many inmates.'[133] The Young Vic (2012) put its audience, quite literally, in the madhouse, 'blur[ring] the distinction between the witless and the sane and turn[ing] the theme into an overriding atmosphere': some audience members were seated onstage in wheelchairs, while others became the Bedlam gawkers, seated behind netting 'as if there to observe wildlife'. The asylum itself was filled with 'disconcertingly rattling boxes, cupboards and trunks that seem[ed] to be crammed with desperate, protesting inmates' but opened to release 'the sex-crazed principal players' instead.[134]

In a play so explicitly about the madness of sexual desire, Freud still makes an occasional appearance: on stage, for instance, in the 'egghead, beard, and little round glasses' of Donnellan's Alibius.[135] But in the thirteen years since Barker and Nicol objected to a tradition of performances based on Beatrice-Joanna's supposed subconscious attraction to the man she loathes, both companies and critics have become increasingly open to other ways of playing the central relationship. A brief survey of the four most recent major London full-text *Changelings* is illustrative. In 2004, Hilton's production surprised audiences by 'chang[ing] the dynamics of the principal intrigue': Lyn Gardner described how this Beatrice-Joanna, played by Saskia Portway as 'a spoiled little bitch', was in fact the corrupting influence on Matthew Thomas's De Flores, who 'suggests a good man, at least until he seizes the opportunity to become involved in Beatrice-Joanna's murderous intent'.[136] 'Almost until the end Matthew Thomas remains the servant', wrote John Thaxter, 'while Saskia Portway plays Beatrice as a prim Jane Austen heroine, more concerned with pregnancy testing and her lost maidenhead than below-stairs rough trade'.[137] While reviews were mainly positive, there were several calls for more 'creepy erotic fascination', with John Peter, the strongest proponent of an 'unconsciously . . . attracted' Beatrice-Joanna, demanding, 'So, then, what's the whole thing about? Why does she keep picking on him and insulting him, if not out of resentment that he attracts her?'[138] Two years later, Olivia Williams and Will Keen, under Donnellan's direction, changed the dynamic once again. Beatrice-Joanna from the start was 'trapped, stifled, clawing for any escape route', more psychologically damaged than unconsciously desirous: Kim Solga saw 'a longtime victim, and survivor, of sexual abuse at her father's hands. Williams told this back-story subtly but with unmistakable force early in the performance, allowing it to saturate Beatrice Joanna's future interactions with De Flores and every other male character on the stage'.[139] This Beatrice-Joanna's revulsion toward her servant was 'steady and certain', though after her deflowering – graphically staged on a desk where minutes earlier she had written him a cheque – it 'flipped into ardent attraction'.[140] Keen's De Flores took the route of 'eerily clipped, psychopathic self-control'; John Peter admiringly commented that 'The fierce sexual desire of a nervous, needy man is really shocking: both pitiable and ugly', and did not demand unconscious attraction from Williams' 'imperious, fastidious virgin'.[141] While the *Guardian*'s veteran reviewer

Michael Billington still clung to this requirement, and read it onto Williams' traumatized survivor – 'the heroine is a frenzied neurotic insanely attracted to the loathed De Flores' – few others now shared his expectations.[142]

By the time Hill-Gibbins (2012) and Dominic Dromgoole (2015) brought the murderous pair to the stage, Billington was virtually alone in requiring a Beatrice-Joanna whose 'constant criticisms of the "foul chops" of ... De Flores are edged with sexual neurosis', or who 'suggests there is something weirdly compulsive about her obsession with [him]'.[143] While he found what he was looking for in both Jessica Raine and Hattie Morahan (who inspired the two above comments, respectively), other reviewers perceived – and appreciated – a wider variety of dynamics. There was high praise for Daniel Cerqueira's 'disturbing and unusually convincing' De Flores at the Young Vic, who exchanged the role's usual sexual charisma for 'greasy hair, lumbering gait, slightly disfigured face, and old-fashioned dress' together with 'a weariness of voice as if poor self-esteem were slowing his pace': 'it is to this unsavoury depressive that Joanna is fatally bound', wrote Kellaway, in a very favourable review.[144] And when Morahan's 'posh, frivolous [and] ... frighteningly superficial' Beatrice-Joanna resigned herself to De Flores (Trystan Gravelle) 'with a sort of amusingly British stoicism', only one reviewer recorded a vague wish that 'more could be made of the sexiness of the story'.[145] Interviewed by Holly Williams for the *Independent*, Morahan acknowledged the feminist issues raised by a character who eventually 'expresses some kind of love' for the man who rapes her: 'You get into very murky political waters ... Beatrice refuses to play the victim ... One can choose to draw modern readings from it – is it some kind of Stockholm syndrome? [But] the play was written when it was and it's got enough integrity in terms of the psychological plotting to stand on its own two feet.'[146] And that might be as good a last word as any – until the next production – on the play now recognized as 'one of the greatest (and grisliest) Jacobean tragedies'.[147]

# 3

# State of the Art

## *Patricia A. Cahill*

## Authorship and collaboration

To peruse recent scholarship on authorship and *The Changeling* is to be reminded that while the play is one of the period's best-known collaborative works, the twenty-first century has seen little consensus about the nature of the joint playwriting enterprise. Thus, scholars debate not only how to interpret the play's internal textual evidence to identify authorial 'hands', but also, and more fundamentally, whether the concept of solo dramatic authorship is anachronistic in the early modern period.[1] One of the opening salvos in this century's lively discussion is a 2002 essay by Richard L. Nochimson examining the assumptions underlying attribution scholarship in general as well as the conventional attributions of *The Changeling*'s authorship in particular – namely, that Rowley penned the three hospital (or 'madhouse') scenes as well as part of the opening and closing scenes, while Middleton wrote the 'castle' scenes usually understood as constituting the play's tragic narrative.[2] Nochimson concludes that no good reason exists to support the notion that early modern collaboration necessarily entailed two professional dramatists taking on (or being assigned) discrete acts upon which each worked independently. More specifically, he urges a sceptical stance toward the claims, mostly originating in the late nineteenth century, about who wrote which part of *The Changeling*. Instead, Nochimson describes collaboration as a kind of 'intertwin[ing]' and 'interweaving' of the two plots.[3] Drawing on Michel E. Mooney's account of collaboration as involving the craft of 'framing', he further speculates that the play, which is famous for its coherence and unity, must have been a cooperative act, the product of two playwrights working especially closely together.[4]

In a chapter of *Joint Enterprises: Collaborative Drama and the Institutionalization of the English Renaissance Theater* (2004), Heather Anne Hirschfeld also turns to *The Changeling* as a case study in early modern collaboration, although rather than focus on what was shared between playwrights, she investigates difference.[5] Specifically, her study begins with the assumption that early modern culture recognized the practice of individual writers with distinctive styles at work on the same play. Evoking Pierre Bourdieu's sociology, she argues that many varieties of approaches to collaboration must have been possible in the early modern period. Significantly, Hirschfeld's objective is not to establish bibliographical facts but rather to consider how literary analysis helps to illuminate the psychodynamics of these collaborative writing relationships. In her discussion of *The Changeling*, she emphasizes that the professional alliance of the two playwrights seems intentional rather than haphazard, for it ran against their usual theatre company attachment. Moreover, in her analysis of the play as a 'critique of court decadence', she also highlights the play's repeated staging of a kind of linguistic violence whereby characters, especially De Flores and Beatrice-Joanna, confuse and misuse each other's words, often through punning.[6] By depicting characters who routinely steal each other's language for nefarious purposes, she proposes, the playwrights in effect imagine the inverse of their own collaboration, a writing relationship, she speculates, that was grounded in fellowship and likely aspired to what contemporary friendship treatises described as an ideal of mutual verbal sharing and apprehension.

In their commentary on *The Changeling* in *Middleton and His Collaborators* (2008), Mark Hutchings and A.A. Bromham also explore the joint enterprise of playwriting while veering away from traditional attribution studies.[7] Rather than focus on the intimacies of a writing relationship, they consider how collaboration plays out in performance. Specifically, they highlight parallels and resonances between *The Changeling*'s two plots, emphasizing that close connections are established on the stage between hospital and castle scenes. For example, the hospital servant Lollio (probably played by Rowley) serves as a kind of double of the castle servant De Flores just as Alibius, who runs the hospital, is a counterpart of Vermandero, who presides over the castle. For Hutchings and Bromham, the very structure of the play – its interweaving of the two plots – requires a continual reassessment of one's interpretation of the action. They thus propose a reading of the play's form as an allegory for the playwrights' collaboration: rather than conceptualize the joint work of playwriting as a matter of orderly deliberation, they suggest it be understood as a complex and recursive process entailing additions, deletions, negotiations and a great deal of unpredictability.

In a 2010 essay, Gordon McMullan also focuses on the play's two overlapping plots, although, for him, the remarkably interwoven structure is emblematic of the play's multifaceted concern with ugliness.[8] More precisely, drawing on psychoanalytic theorizations of ugliness as an all-consuming 'stain' or mark that inexorably blurs the boundaries between self and other, McMullan explores the play's embrace of this negative aesthetic, which he locates in the encounters between an outwardly repulsive De Flores and an inwardly degenerate Beatrice-Joanna. But somewhat counter-intuitively, McMullan also finds ugliness at stake in the play's 'tonal tensions'.[9] For example, he draws attention to the unease that attends the revelation in Act 4 that Alsemero, previously a conventional suitor, owns a virginity detection apparatus and, more generally, he emphasizes the perplexing presence of the hospital plot, which, as he notes, has often been ignored by scholars and viewed as problematic by theatre practitioners. By attending to the discomfiting aspects of the play, he suggests, one can see how Middleton and Rowley challenge prevailing ideas about both genre and authorship. Thus, for McMullan, the play muddies the conventions of revenge tragedy by turning to the low and 'grotesque' matter of the hospital plot; rather than follow a clear narrative path, they swerve from tragic form toward the hybrid genre of tragicomedy, something suggested by the fact that at the play's end Antonio remains alive and Isabella's marriage to Alibius has not been dissolved. Similarly, McMullan teases out the implications of the playwrights' embrace of ugliness in the play's last scene, the authorship of which remains for attribution scholars a matter of contention. According to McMullan, just as Beatrice-Joanna's last words home in on the idea of an elimination of all distinctions, so, too, do the playwrights pointedly repudiate the aesthetics of authorial unity.

One might be inclined to conclude that the scholarly debates about authorship and collaboration have come full circle, for in his account of the play's authorship in Gary Taylor and John Lavagnino's 2007 Oxford Middleton edition, Douglas Bruster indicates that the traditional authorial attributions mostly have been confirmed by later bibliographical work.[10] However, as is clear from David Nicol's extended commentary in *Middleton and Rowley: Forms of Collaboration in the Jacobean Playhouse* (2012), discussion of these matters remains somewhat contentious.[11] In his richly historicized account of the Jacobean theatrical world, Nicol revisits many recent challenges to traditional concepts of early modern authorship – for example, he dismisses Nochimson's scepticism toward internal evidence and attribution studies; he resists the idea of the two playwrights as, in effect, one author function, embodying a unified purpose; and he champions the jointly authored play as a product of two *distinctive* hands, while acknowledging that at times the playwrights may be intent on hiding their differences. One of the highlights of Nicol's approach to the authorial questions that swirl around *The Changeling* is that Rowley comes out of the shadows, emerging as a significant author in his own right – in fact, as the leading playwright for Prince Charles's Men. For Nicol, who remains sceptical about the extent to which the playwriting enterprise was rooted in mutual affection, the economic basis of this collaboration is significant, not least because Rowley, unlike Middleton, was a 'sharer' with considerable responsibilities, financial and otherwise, in his company. But Nicol also focuses on the play's stylistic differences and what he describes, without approbation, as the play's 'inconsistencies' and 'disunities'.[12] Significantly, for Nicol, these dissonant moments have everything to do with the play's neglected religious contexts. Thus he argues that the play must be recognized as a mash-up of Rowley's traditional and Middleton's Calvinist perspectives. Ultimately his author-focused reading offers a deep sense of the play's complexity as bound up with its engagement with contemporary theological debates and the two playwrights' rival understandings of such matters as moral choice, reprobation and damnation.

## Space and place

Twenty-first-century scholarship has witnessed many different approaches to the matter of the play's staging of space and place, though it is fair to say that critical conversations remain dominated by interest in the play's evocation of geographic spaces, especially Spain and England. In her 2007 introduction to the play in the Oxford Middleton, Annabel Patterson takes up the matter of Spain, including the division between King and Parliament over his pro-Spanish policies.[13] As Patterson elaborates on the significance of Spain in the play, she acknowledges that, as others have noted, the plot is clearly concerned with James's desired solution to the political turmoil – namely, his controversial plan to marry his heir, Prince Charles, to the Infanta Maria of Spain. However, Patterson forcefully dismisses the notion of the play as representing a thinly veiled anti-Spanish/anti-Catholic agenda, designed to thwart the period's censorship laws, an argument set forth by A.A. Bromham and Zara Bruzzi in 1990.[14] Endorsing the significance of Bromham and Bruzzi's insight that the play's source, John Reynolds's *The Triumphs of God's Revenge against the Crying and Execrable Sin of Murder*, was penned by a censored anti-Spanish writer, Patterson nevertheless argues that the play is far less 'schematic' than the two scholars claim. Opposing the notion that the play's evocation of Europe is tied to a precisely delineated politics, she suggests that its power inheres precisely in its 'ethical undecidability'.[15]

In two articles published in 2011 and 2012, Mark Hutchings also examines the play's attention to Spain. Following on the connection Bromham and Bruzzi drew between the play and the Spanish Match, Hutchings, in his 2012 article, explores the play's January 1624 revival at court in the presence of Prince Charles, who was newly returned from his secret mission to Spain.[16] Attending to the nuances of this politically tense moment – above all, the fact that Charles, upon his return, became an active opponent of the Match – Hutchings suggests that Alsemero would have emerged as the play's most significant character, for, in his quest for Beatrice, he would have been legible as both a double of the prince and as a choric figure who speaks the play's moral at the end. In line with this interpretation, Hutchings suggests that the play's courtly audience would have seen that even as the play welcomed the prince back from Spain, it offered a warning about the calamities that might have transpired had he been successful. In the 2011 article, Hutchings turns to the playwrights' use of theatrical space to understand the way it registers the anti-Spanish sentiment of English Protestant culture.[17] As he calls attention to a remarkable stage direction requiring De Flores 'in the act time' to hide his weapon shortly before murdering Piracquo, Hutchings considers what it means that the play asks De Flores to act so treacherously precisely at the moment designated for the play's intermission or interval, a time when tiremen would trim the wicks of the candles used to illuminate the stage. Underscoring the fact that this stage direction violates the norms of early modern indoor theatre, Hutchings assesses the theatrical impact of the moment. In his reading, De Flores is shown literally to embody a shadowy Spanish duplicity, for in that in-between moment, he enacts what was most dreaded: the 'trespassing' or invasion of Spain into England.[18]

In what might be thought of as a supplement to Hutchings's account of the theatrical dynamics of Spanish treachery, Barbara Fuchs also sets stage history alongside Anglo-Spanish politics in *The Poetics of Piracy: Emulating Spain in English Literature* (2013).[19] Characterizing *The Changeling* as a 'plotting play', Fuchs offers a literary genealogy in which she aligns this play with three Spanish dramas by Middleton. Taken together, these dramas, so she suggests, attest to the cultural demonization of the Spanish as Machiavellian and Jesuitical plotters. Put otherwise, she suggests, *The Changeling* endorses the anti-Spanish feeling famously writ large in Middleton's later drama *A Game at Chess* (a satire of the so-called Spanish Match) and which can also be seen in two earlier Middleton plays, *The Lady's Tragedy* (1611), and the collaboration with Ford, Dekker, and Rowley *The Spanish Gypsy* (1623). Acknowledging that *The Changeling* conjures Spain explicitly only in the vaguest of terms, she nevertheless argues that its sexual plot – especially its paradoxical depiction of Beatrice-Joanna as both a helpless victim and an immoral beauty – would have been immediately legible to the English as a warning about their own susceptibility to the changeable, indeed perfidious, Spanish. (See Berta Cano-Echevarría's essay in this volume.) Calling attention to the myriad ways in which Spaniards appeared as devious schemers in the English cultural imaginary, she thus brings *The Changeling* into clearer focus as a tale about the dangers of the potential dynastic union.

But what of the play's evocation of the Dutch? That question motivates a 2014 article by Mark Hutchings, which considers the significance of the moment early in the play when Vermandero asks Alsemero to confirm that the young man's father, and Vermandero's erstwhile friend, had indeed died in Gibraltar in a naval battle against 'those rebellious Hollanders' (1.1.176).[20] As Hutchings explains, scholars traditionally interpret this allusion to the Dutch victory against the Spanish in 1607 as part of the play's Hispanophobia, for by summoning up their co-religionist's conflict with the Spanish, it would remind the play's first audiences that James, rather than endorsing the Protestant cause, was seeking to align himself with Catholics. But Hutchings warns against reading *The Changeling* in terms of simple anti-Spanish sentiment and offers a wider political and cultural context: one that recognizes that, at the time of the play's performance, English tensions with the Dutch were on the rise as the Dutch empire was becoming increasingly powerful. Moreover, he notes, the play's allusion would have had renewed force after 1624 when pamphlets began circulating news of the 1623 torture and execution of ten English merchants accused of treason by the Dutch forces in what is now Indonesia. Throughout the seventeenth century, as Hutchings notes, this incident, which became known as the Amboyna massacre, was, for many in England, a byword for anti-Dutch sentiment.

*The Changeling*'s conjuring of *English* space has received scholarly attention from Kenneth Jackson and Carol Thomas Neely, both of whom emphasize that the play's hospital space, despite the play's Spanish geography, is referred to as Bedlam (3.2.21) and thus associated with a notorious London hospital that housed those deemed mad. For Jackson, who in his *Separate Theatres: Bethlem ('Bedlam') Hospital and the Shakespearean Stage* (2005), describes *The Changeling* as 'perhaps the best and most famous English madhouse play', Bedlam's significance on stage is deeply tied to its status in the early seventeenth-century period as a quintessentially Protestant institution.[21] Reading the play as an intervention into contemporary debates about the nature of charity, Jackson finds its staging of Bedlam to be strictly anti-Catholic. Indeed, his explication of the hospital plot – in which Isabella is pursued by counterfeit madmen – turns on his claim that the playwrights are directly responding to John Fletcher's endorsement of Catholic charity in his nearly contemporaneous romance *The Pilgrim,* which is also set in Spain and features a woman who pretends to be mad so as to avoid marriage to the man her father intends for her. In Jackson's reading, *The Changeling*'s main narrative transforms Fletcher's madwoman into Beatrice-Joanna, while its hospital narrative, in which the characters who visit Bedlam are motivated by corrupt sexual desire, offers a satiric takedown of Fletcher's depiction of good deeds. More broadly, as Jackson puts the play's hospital scenes into conversation with the spaces of Jacobean London, he explicates the politics of institutional benevolence in the period, suggesting, too, that the play provides a veiled critique of the monarch as well as of Bedlam's actual keeper, Helkiah Crook, who, despite allegations of financial corruption by city officials, received James's support.

In her commentary on *The Changeling*'s London hospital in *Distracted Subjects* (2004) as well as in a 2010 essay, Neely emphasizes, not the era's political and religious conflicts, but rather the institution's status as a performance space.[22] Overturning the widely held view of the historical Bedlam as a site where Londoners would go to view the mad, she points out that what did not happen in reality was conjured up by playwrights on the early modern stage. In a wide-ranging overview of early modern plays about madness, Neely thus observes that *The Changeling* is one of five Jacobean plays in which Bedlamites act, meta-theatrically, as performers. Yet she also notes that Middleton and Rowley seem far less interested in the Bedlamites than they are in the characters who spend time with them: Alibius, Isabella, Lollio, Antonio and Francisco. Underscoring the hospital's status as a performance site, Neely thus points out that the hospital is not only where the 'madhouse' dancers rehearse in preparation for Beatrice-Joanna's wedding; it is also where Isabella dresses as a madwoman to teach her would-be lover Antonio, who is also disguised as a Bedlamite, to recognize his foolishness. In Neely's view, the hospital plot thereby links madness with theatricality, revisiting ideas raised by the castle plot in a new setting and with middling sort characters. Equally important, so Neely argues, *The Changeling*'s hospital plot foregrounds the curative potential of theatre: in summoning up the English hospital as a performance space, she suggests, the playwrights effectively counter early modern anti-theatrical polemic.

In a 2004 book chapter, Neely further explicates how the national spaces evoked in *The Changeling* map onto its parallel narratives about two women and their suitors.[23] Focusing on the play's depiction of the malady of lovesickness and its indebtedness to geohumoralist notions of the Mediterranean as a locale for passionately overheated bodies, Neely argues that the play's corporeal language underscores the playwrights' opposition to the Spanish Match. In the castle plot, she suggests, the Spanishness of the lovesick Beatrice-Joanna and her three suitors (Piracquo, Alsemero and De Flores) is depicted in terms of their excesses of heat and lasciviousness, which (in the cases of two of them) ultimately lead to their deaths. By contrast, she argues, in the hospital space, Isabella emerges as a version of the witty English wife familiar from Jacobean city comedy: represented as well able to master not only her suitors but also her jealous husband, the chaste wife thus reveals the superior value of English womanhood.

Intellectual rather than cultural history comes into play in two recent studies that theorize space and the spatial thinking that subtends the play. In the first, a co-authored chapter on *The Changeling* in Bryan Reynolds's *Transversal Enterprises in the Drama of Shakespeare and his Contemporaries* (2006), Reynolds and Donald Hedrick offer a poststructuralist analysis of the play's depiction of the mobility of 'place' – a word, they note, which occurs some thirty-five times in the play.[24] Through close readings of De Flores's geometrical understanding of space and Beatrice-Joanna's repudiation of linear movements in favour of itinerancy, they show the play to be deeply concerned with conditions of placelessness. Indeed, they argue that the play embodies an important change in spatial thinking they identify with this historical moment: a turn, fraught with anxiety, away from traditional, localized notions of place – that is place, as defined by certain coordinates – and toward an idea of infinite and undifferentiated space.

A second theorization of space in *The Changeling* occurs in a 2014 essay in which Kim Solga considers several additional spatial matters, including the claim that Inigo Jones built the Phoenix Theatre and the nature of classical architectural theory.[25] Like Hedrick and Reynolds, Solga characterizes the representation of space in *The Changeling* as bound up with profound conceptual shifts in the culture. Like them, too, she contends the play participates in a 'key metaphysical shift' that she aligns with changing conceptions of space such that space becomes available as something replete with imaginative possibility, and place becomes understood as 'socially, culturally and sexually determined'.[26] As she returns to these philosophical discussions of spatiality, however, Solga also turns to gender and performance theory, especially Una Chaudhuri's suggestion that space is something to be performed and that modern theatre is founded on the idea of place as a problem.[27] For Solga, early modern place making is thus inextricably bound up with acting. She notes, for example, that the newly emergent way of thinking about space as 'place' in the early modern period may explain the anxious depiction of Beatrice-Joanna as herself a maker of space. More broadly, in her reading of Beatrice-Joanna as a subversive, obsessive and imaginative actor-architect, Solga invites attention to the performed spaces of *The Changeling* – from Vermandero's castle to Alsemero's closet – as fraught with gendered meanings.

# Sexual coercion and consent

In their 2004 survey of *The Changeling* on the London stage discussed elsewhere in this volume, Roberta Barker and David Nicol foreground the issues of sexual coercion and consent as they critique the tendency of modern reviewers of theatrical productions to read Beatrice-Joanna in darkly romantic or crudely Freudian terms: as a figure who unconsciously desires the man she claims to loathe.[28] Certainly, in this time of the #MeToo movement, *The Changeling*'s relevance as a narrative about female vulnerability to sexual coercion and consent has become ever more obvious. Any overview of twenty-first century scholarship on this theme properly begins with the much-cited feminist criticism of the last century, including Deborah's G. Burks's 1995 account of the play's politics of rape, which was republished in her *Horrid Spectacle: Violation in the Theater of Early Modern England* (2003).[29] Responding to the tendency of scholarship to focus on the extravagance of Beatrice-Joanna's desire rather than to the way she is strong-armed into sex, Burks calls attention to English legal writings on the crime known as ravishment, noting that the playwrights' attention to Beatrice-Joanna's morally weak will echoes early modern legal discourse about the possibility of female consent to the desires of their assailant. In early modern England, as Burks reminds us, ravishment was conceptualized as a property crime – that is, a crime in which men were understood to have been rendered bereft of their goods. Not surprisingly, then, so Burks argues, the play depicts male characters as the true victims of Beatrice-Joanna's sexuality and, in depicting Beatrice-Joanna's guilt, endorses the law's efforts to proscribe women.

Judith Haber's 2003 essay, '"I(t) Could Not Choose but Follow": Erotic Logic in *The Changeling*', also focuses on the way the play engages a cultural obsession with female chastity, which blurs distinctions between virgin and whore, between sexual desire and fear, and between marriage and rape.[30] In contrast to Burks, however, Haber sets the play in a wider literary context that embraces texts by Jonson and Spenser and underscores the play's aesthetic concerns, particularly its formal interest in linearity. Connecting this discussion of literary form with a sophisticated engagement with psychoanalytic theory, Haber suggests that the play both covers up and bespeaks the gendered fears and fantasies of early modern England. She points in particular to the play's paradoxical staging of dramatic sequence, connecting its linear structure – which she notes is depicted as both a formal problem and a solution – to its sexual logic.

Turning to performance theory as well as to Lacanian insights, Kim Solga's chapter on *The Changeling* in *Violence against Women in Early Modern Performance: Invisible Acts* (2009) also considers theatrical aesthetics and theatrical cover-ups, specifically the way the play frames Beatrice-Joanna's availability for sexual violation.[31] In the first part of her argument, Solga thinks about the play's complex way of locating female characters in space, noting that the play's representational strategies pointedly rely on occlusion – so that, for example, the playwrights do not indicate what sexual scenario Alsemero and Jasperino perceive when they together spy on De Flores and Beatrice-Joanna in the garden and determine that she is a whore. The second part of Solga's argument concerns the gendering of reception – that is, how the play positions audiences to see female characters on stage. Ultimately, she turns to the possibility and politics of audience witnessing and urges an ethical response to the depiction of violence and sexual violation. How, she asks, might *The Changeling* be staged today, so that audiences can see the sexual assault that the play puts under erasure and how might audiences be enjoined to be disturbed by what they perceive?

In an avowedly feminist essay published in 2011, Frances Dolan returns to the legal matters to which Burks drew attention, only to dislodge assumptions underlying many feminist analyses.[32] Pointing out that what happens to Beatrice-Joanna in the play does not, in fact, conform to what the playwrights' contemporaries would understand as rape, she invites us to think anew about seventeenth-century English understanding of sexual consent. For Dolan, the fact that the play mostly does not fit the mould of a rape play is a testament to its sophisticated investigation not only of male coercion but, more interestingly, of a woman's intention to survive her deeply circumscribed fate. Drawing on legal scholar Janet Halley (who critiques the way female rape victims are envisioned solely as passive victims of a crime) as well as on historical work documenting female testimony in cases of enforced sex, Dolan suggests we put aside the impoverished discourse of female guilt or innocence and instead explore how the play offers a more nuanced language for understanding female sexual agency. In Dolan's reading, Beatrice-Joanna's interactions with Diaphanta are nearly as important as those in which she schemes with De Flores and Alsemero, for in each situation the play considers the options available to women who may have very few options: that Beatrice-Joanna is forced to negotiate sex and that she may rely on her social status to make 'good' bargains is part of the story told by the play, which, in Dolan's view, invites us to question how Beatrice-Joanna might take control of her sexuality. Significantly, in this reading, Beatrice-Joanna's famous assertion that 'this fellow has undone me endlessly' (4.1.1) comes into view not as an acknowledgement of her utter ruin but rather of her need to participate continually in negotiations about the terms under which she will consent.

In a 2013 book chapter, Christine Varnado might be said to queer the critical discussion on sexual coercion and the matter of what can be seen in *The Changeling*.[33] Positing a kind of reader-response criticism in which audiences rely on their own desires to fill in what dramatic fictions leave unstaged, she contends that heteronormative critical practice has ensured that critics typically overlook a signal sex scene: the encounter between De Flores and Piracquo in 3.1 that leads to the latter's murder. More specifically, she considers that readers and playgoers are being solicited to respond imaginatively and erotically to the play's unconventional evocation of De Flores's sexual desire. In a *tour de force* reading of the scene, she notes its carefully choreographed sodomitical structure in its depiction of such actions as De Flores's squirrelling away of his 'naked rapier' (SD after 2.2.165), his proffered offer of service to Piracquo, his carefully choreographed movements in the castle's secret spaces, and his apparent coming upon Piracquo from behind. For Varnado, this scene moves perversely from homoerotic seduction to rape and murder, such that De Flores's notorious act of removing his victim's finger and ring evokes an unseen, sodomitical act of anal defloration. Moreover, Varnado also suggests that this early scene of violent seduction-cum-murder prefigures Act 5's rape and stabbing of Beatrice-Joanna in Alsemero's closet. In offering this more capacious view of the play's staging of sex, Varnado not only imagines De Flores as polymorphous in his desires, but she also aims to revise traditional understandings of Beatrice-Joanna. Unlike De Flores, who takes sexual pleasure in murder, Beatrice-Joanna, she implies, is fundamentally unlike the sexually-depraved figure to be found in past criticism of the play, for she is shown to be motivated simply by self-interest rather than the irrationalities of lust.

# Body narratives

As is clear from a number of the above studies, scholarly interpretations of *The Changeling* frequently depend upon readings of the play's narratives of embodiment. From the start of the twenty-first century, in fact, numerous critics have placed questions of embodiment, especially female corporeality, at the centre of their study. In a chapter of *The Female Hero in English Renaissance Tragedy* (2002), Lisa Hopkins examines the representation of Beatrice-Joanna's body alongside that of Bianca in Middleton's *Women Beware Women*.[34] Characterizing these protagonists as tragic agents who act defiantly to achieve their desires, she argues that they are made to pay for their resistance with death. Setting her close reading of the play's bodies in the context of anatomy books, she emphasizes their insistence on a supposed female ability to change shape and hide secrets. She also stresses that early modern discussions of female nature became increasingly invested in claims that the capacity for reproduction ensured that women were radically different from men. Highlighting these discursive contexts as she reads *The Changeling*, Hopkins contends that Beatrice-Joanna's most significant threat to patriarchal structures inheres in her embodiment.

Taking up the question of female bodies from a sociocultural perspective, Mara Amster's 2003 essay analyses the play in the light of seventeenth-century responses to the scandals around Frances Howard, which other scholars, including Hopkins, Margot Heinemann and others had previously addressed in lesser detail.[35] Amster highlights the play's oblique evocation of such episodes as Howard's divorce from Robert Devereux, third earl of Essex; her subsequent marriage to Robert Carr, earl of Somerset; and her trial with Somerset for the murder of Sir Thomas Overbury, who had strongly opposed their union. Refuting prior claims that the play's two virginity-testing scenes (i.e. Beatrice-Joanna's testing of Diaphanta and Alsemero's testing of Beatrice-Joanna) are inconsequential, Amster calls attention to an early modern obsession with the identification of chaste bodies. She thus discusses the court-ordered testing of Howard's virginity and rumours that the findings had been falsified, as well as other cultural texts, including contemporary responses to the scandal and books detailing methods for testing virginity, which rely on uroscopy and the like. Extending Marjorie Garber's earlier characterization of Beatrice-Joanna as an actor who 'proves' virginity through performance, Amster shows that the play's anxieties about female simulation and the impossibility of 'reading' female bodes with certainty are also visible in other cultural texts, such as archival documents connected with the Howard case (which fret about the verifiability of virginity), contemporary conduct books (which muse about how to appear chaste) and anatomy treatises (which disagree about the nature and meaning of hymeneal membranes).[36] Rather than underwrite the legibility of female bodies, what the play ultimately reveals, so Amster argues, is that it engages a cultural understanding of virginity as a performance that any woman might easily and convincingly counterfeit.

Sara Luttfring's discussion of *The Changeling* in a 2011 essay and in her subsequent book *Bodies, Speech, and Reproductive Knowledge in Early Modern England* (2016) considers some of the same questions that Amstar raises, while focusing on how the play shows female bodily performances to be complicated by linguistic ones.[37] Like Amster, Luttfring emphasizes the play's trafficking in the idea that a virginal body might, in fact, be indistinguishable from a sexually experienced one. But significantly, she maintains, female virginity is more than a bodily performance: it is also a narrative, a story that gets told. Supplementing Amster's account of how men grappled with female bodily illegibility, Luttfring thus explores how the play shows women strategically claiming 'epistemological control' over reproduction by creating and enacting 'bodily narratives' to resist male authorities. Returning to the Howard/Essex scandal, Luttfring observes that the court records show authorities trying to establish truth by moving between female words (especially Howard's account of her own body) and female bodies as key interpretative sites. In similar fashion, she contends, Beatrice-Joanna may be seen as shaping the discourse around her body. As she explores the anxieties underlying the play's depiction of Beatrice-Joanna as possessed of a deceitful exterior and a secret, inward corruption, she emphasizes that the play in fact acknowledges how profoundly patriarchal structures are dependent on women. Indeed, her reading of the play's conclusion underscores the melancholy of the male survivors who realize that, with Beatrice-Joanna's death, they have lost their own reproductive future.

Questions about female sexual agency are also prominent in Jennifer Panek's 2014 essay on the affective capacities of *The Changeling*'s depiction of female embodiment.[38] Drawing on Silvan Tomkins' theories of shame and focusing on the way the play identifies both shame and sexuality as being bound up with involuntary responses, Panek thinks about Beatrice-Joanna's reference to blushing at two key moments: just prior to her first offstage sexual encounter with De Flores and just before her death, in which Alsemero tells her publicly to re-enact sex with De Flores and she names her shame. In addition, Panek considers the voyeuristic pleasures of the play's first audiences as they encountered what she describes as a doubleness in the period's understanding of female sexual shame: the way, for example, that a blush was imagined both as attesting to sexual innocence and as inciting sexual arousal. In Panek's reading, the earlier of the two scenes she evokes is meant to arouse audiences with its staging of female sexual shame, while the later scene of Beatrice-Joanna's exposure should be read as offering audiences an unsettling return to the first one. Having solicited the audience's erotic desires, the play concludes, she suggests, by showcasing Alsemero's guilt, thus offering audiences a critique of the very dynamic upon which it relied for its narrative.

Jay Zysk's 2015 exploration of how the play grapples with the interpretation of bodily fragments starts with the proposition that previous studies of embodiment have overlooked the key place of relics or bodily remains in early modern religious debates and devotional practice.[39] Zysk stresses that in early modern English culture, relics would be recognized as inherently unreliable body parts not simply because they could easily be falsified but also because they necessarily are only partial: even if authentic, they offer persistent reminders that the whole body is absent. As Zysk considers several moments in the play in which body parts comes to the fore – Beatrice-Joanna's glove dropping, De Flores's presentation of Piracquo's dismembered finger, the virginity tests and Beatrice-Joanna's image of her body as polluted matter – he explicates how these moments are inflected by the paradoxes of a relic logic. Having considered the part/whole narratives that surround these moments, Zysk emphasizes that the play can be understood as staging a conflict between the theological and semiotic dimensions of the corporeal fragments to which it so persistently calls attention.

# Service and exchange economies

Given that De Flores's status as Vermandero's servant is central to the plot, it is hardly surprising to find a flourishing of scholarly interest in master–servant relations and in allied questions concerning the play's relationship to social and economic history, especially the transition from feudalism to capitalism.

Among the first to explore the play's representation of service in this wider social context was Michael Neill, editor of the New Mermaids edition (2006), who took up the topic in two essays dating from 2005. In the first essay, he explores the pervasiveness in early modern English culture of an idealized vision of the hierarchies of rank and the sacralized bonds of service.[40] As he traces the language of service in *The Changeling* as well as in the tragic narratives of *King Lear*, *Othello* and *The Duchess of Malfi*, Neill further explores how these texts interrogate the tensions between the ideal vision and the lived realities of service, an institution which, as he points out, was, historically, in the midst of crisis. For Neill, De Flores is a transitional figure who is compelling and even sympathetic partly because of his ambiguous social status: once a gentleman, he has been forced to become a servant in Vermandero's household. In his second 'service' essay from 2005, Neill again focuses on De Flores as he thinks about the ways in which gender and desire operate across hierarchies of rank.[41] Noting salient resonances between *The Changeling, Twelfth Night* and *All Well that End's Well*, Neill emphasizes that Middleton and Rowley, unlike Shakespeare, demonize the servant's erotic ambition as they emphasize the subversive way in which De Flores seeks to level the playing field. In Neill's reading, the tragic narrative turns partly on Beatrice-Joanna's offer of money for the murder of Piracquo, an indication that De Flores will be unable to claim or usurp the socially elite identity as a courtly lover that he craves. It is because Beatrice-Joanna fails to recognize that he might move out of his servant position that he takes aim at the chastity that undergirds her rank. In short, in Neill's reading, the sexual crime is also unquestionably an assault on the traditional social order.

Mark Thornton Burnett's 2006 essay also reads *The Changeling* against a historical backdrop in which the institution of service is on the verge of collapse.[42] Like Neill, Burnett stresses the topicality of the servant plot, for he points to historical data about the huge percentage of English labourers who had spent part of their life in servitude (as apprentices, unpaid household servants or wage labourers for their social superiors). However, drawing on Bakhtin, Burnett also suggests that, in staging the submission of Beatrice-Joanna to the will of her father's servant, the play offers not so much a tale of a singular social-climber but rather a carnivalesque vision of a world in which servants rule their masters. Radical in its critique of the social structures of the Jacobean world from which it emerges, the play's vision, Burnett suggests, is of a system in which social categories can easily blur and the all-too-fallible aristocratic masters can gradually be worn down by a tenacious servant.

In contrast to these De Flores-focused accounts, Michelle Dowd's 2010 essay on *The Changeling* looks at the question of service from the point of view of Beatrice's waiting-woman, Diaphanta, and in the context of early modern conditions of female servitude, which rendered women vulnerable to sexual coercion and abuse.[43] As part of her wide-ranging discussion of how women's domestic service was ideologically deployed in dramatic narratives, Dowd scrutinizes the constraints under which Diaphanta labours. As Dowd points out, Diaphanta, depicted paradoxically as both sexually voracious and overly eager to marry, shares with similar figures in *The Witch of Edmonton* (penned by Thomas Dekker, John Ford and Rowley [1621]), an association with threats of domestic disorder as well as a keen vulnerability to sexual assault. Calling attention to both cultural fantasies about female domestic labour and the material circumstances under which early modern women actually laboured, Dowd emphasizes the fault lines in the play's depiction of Diaphanta. For Dowd, Diaphanta is keen to do her mistress's bidding in the play's bed-trick, but ultimately serves as a scapegoat for the play's concerns about the disruptive potential of female servants in the household. Indeed, so Dowd argues, the play allows her horrifying murder to be depicted as necessary and deserving, for Beatrice-Joanna, as Dowd underscores, induces Vermandero to understand the murdered servant, in the wake of the fire, as a 'sleepy slut' (5.1.104). Moreover, so Dowd concludes, the play shows how the female servant's biography can willy-nilly be authored by her social betters, displacing the facts of the actual abuse of servants with fictions about the servant's untoward desire.

In a 2015 essay, John Higgins reconsiders these analyses of service in *The Changeling* and turns his attention to the textual records of the Overbury trial, particularly as they record the voices of Richard Weston and Anne Turner, the servant and lady-in-waiting of the Somersets who were later executed for their parts in Overbury's murder.[44] Arguing that 'early modern conceptions of service took shape, not as a stable and fixed ideology, but instead as an ongoing and collective struggle shaped by numerous voices', Higgins contends that during the trial the Somersets' servants repeatedly called upon a rhetoric of ignorance and vulnerability so as to cast blame upon their masters, gain public sympathy, and evade punishment for the poisoning of Overbury.[45] As Higgins considers *The Changeling* against this historical archive, he underscores the narrative similarities between the drama and the historical events: 'a young, aristocratic woman enlists the aid of a servant and a lady-in-waiting to help her commit a murder that will allow her to choose her own husband'.[46] In addition, he argues that the play, in its representation of the two servants, represents the contending views of service that the archive makes visible. That is, on the one hand, Diaphanta emerges as an unthreatening instrument of her mistress's will; she is an innocent and malleable woman, a version of the good servant that the Somerset servants sought to portray. By contrast, De Flores is shown to embody a grave threat to the hierarchies of the social order. Significantly, so Higgins claims, the threat that De Flores instantiates is not – as Neill and Burnett variously suggest – that the servant might rise above his station or topple the whole system. Rather, it is that he shows how easy it is for servants to feign subservience publicly. In Higgins's account, it is precisely when De Flores is most effective in acting the part of a servant that he manages to undermine the social order of the castle. Much like those who spoke at the Overbury trial, what De Flores seeks, so Higgins suggests, is to perform the role of the servant in such a way that it serves his own interests.

Approaching the play's economics from a strikingly different angle, Bradley Ryner in *Performing Economic Thought: English Drama and Mercantile Writing 1600–1642* (2010) considers the play's language of 'venturing' as signalling its interest in the intertwining of sex with economic calculation and the discourse of mercantilism.[47] Locating the play's origin in a period of tremendous economic instability, Ryner suggests that the conceptual problems faced by Middleton and Rowley's characters are much like those that historically arose from international currency exchange: how to assess the value and commensurability of objects and how to make sense of increases and decreases in price. He thus emphasizes that the play continually traffics in anxieties arising from the notion that men are vulnerable to disturbing assessments and might be viewed by women as fungible commodities. Such tensions, Ryner suggests, give resonance to the play's title and animate its narrative of sexual commerce.

# Science and nature

In recent years, critical fascination with the privy closet of Alsemero's physician has prompted studies of the play's engagement with early modern science and the allied field of natural history, which simultaneously have opened up new questions about the play's staging of race, affect and gender. In a chapter in *Barbarous Play: Race on the English Renaissance Stage* (2008), Lara Bovilsky discerns in the play signs of what she describes as seventeenth-century culture's growing desire for scientific certainty and objective data. She connects this Jacobean desire not only with Alsemero's virginity test but also with the play's investment in humoralist epistemologies, which identify sexual immorality with notions of contagion, deformity and polluted blood.[48] Indeed, as she draws on Gail Kern Paster's account of early modern humours and passions, she suggests that the play's materialist 'blood' metaphors, which conflate differences in social status, lineage and humoral identity, are part of the play's racialized discourse and bound up with its setting in a much-fortified Mediterranean castle whose inhabitants, she suggests, may be imagined as fearful of the inhabitants of neighbouring North Africa. In Bovilsky's account, the play's 'science' of humoralist physiology is used to explain specific characters' unwilled aversion to one other (such as Beatrice-Joanna's seemingly instinctual revulsion toward the disfigured face of De Flores), thereby obscuring the tragedy's actual origins in social conflict. As such, she suggests, the play's narrative is also indicative of an early moment in the 'affective history of racism', whereby biology is mobilized in the service of race, the truth of which is understood to be plainly written on the body.[49]

Scientific practice and unwilled bodily responses are also central themes in Patricia Cahill's 2012 essay, which, like Varnado's, contends that the play's erotic narratives disrupt the heterosexual frame in which it is usually viewed.[50] Identifying three scenes in which Beatrice-Joanna is imagined as engaged in intimate physical contact with others – her glove-dropping episode, her hands-on inspection of De Flores's disfigured face, and her testing of Diaphanta's chastity – Cahill reads the play as offering a kind of scientific investigation into the nature of touch and the literal matter of skin as a sensory organ. In her account, the play's attention to the sensitivity of cutaneous surfaces not only discloses its interest in vernacular science but also suggests its sexualizing of female scientific practice. Moreover, she concludes, the play's science narrative also reveals a fundamental challenge to the notion of individual agency, for the skins upon which the play lavishes such attention, she contends, have a way of going awry on their own.

As she considers the question of agency in her 2012 account of *The Changeling*, Gail Kern Paster returns to her pioneering work on the science of humoralism and the significance of emotions and passions.[51] Drawing attention to a reference in Act 1 to a conversation between Jasperino and Alsemero about a turning weathervane, Paster notes that this image, which likens Alsemero's desire for Beatrice-Joanna to shifting winds, not only stresses human susceptibility to sudden and volatile changes of feeling but also points toward a humoralist understanding of the embodied materiality of feelings. Focusing mostly on Beatrice-Joanna, Paster suggests that *The Changeling* is a narrative of 'emotional privilege' lost.[52] Thus Beatrice-Joanna initially rightly understands the world as constituted by bonds of sympathy and antipathy but wrongly assumes that she can control what she finds desirable or repugnant. Emphasizing the play's indebtedness to the idea that passions are not only embodied by individuals but also embedded within the world, Paster suggests that to understand Beatrice's internal transformation it is necessary to recognize that the playwrights represent Beatrice-Joanna not so much as a passionate individual but rather as a body in flux, engaged in 'transactions with a social and physical environment' that constitute an 'ecology'.[53] Offering a kind of natural history of attraction, the play, so Paster suggests, depicts Beatrice-Joanna as completely transformed by what she encounters: by Act 5, the beautiful noblewoman comes to recognize herself as a contaminated and contaminating body and comes to recognize De Flores not as her hideous opposite but rather as her twin.

In *Occult Knowledge, Science, and Gender on the Shakespearean Stage* (2013), Mary Floyd-Wilson contextualizes the play's representation of agency somewhat differently than Paster and focuses on female efforts to master the secrets of scientific knowledge.[54] Like Bovilsky, Cahill and Paster, Floyd-Wilson attends to the play's interest in seemingly unwilled affective responses, noting how the play evokes a sense of uncanny attractions and repulsions in Beatrice-Joanna, Alsemero and De Flores. Aligning the play's staging of such strangely compelled action and feelings with the early modern belief in human susceptibility to occult forces, Floyd-Wilson explores the play's staging of the quasi-scientific idea of natural sympathies and antipathies, which she also locates in Alsemero's Book of Secrets. In addition, in explaining Beatrice-Joanna's usage of De Flores, she underscores the play's attention to female facility with the homeopathic practice of curing one poison with another. Focusing on the play's conflation of scientific knowledge of nature with women's secrets, Floyd-Wilson ultimately suggests that the play, in staging Beatrice-Joanna's inability to succeed with her secret plot, thereby establishes scientific knowledge as the proper province of men.

# Looking ahead

As this survey indicates, the past two decades have seen a range of exciting scholarship on the play, with new areas brought into consideration and older themes revisited. Inevitably, given the sheer amount of criticism *The Changeling* continues to generate, this account is incomplete and this essay should be read alongside the discussions of theatre history and contemporary performance practice elsewhere in this volume, topics which have been deliberately omitted here. Undoubtedly, we can look forward to continuing reflection on the complexities of the play's performance and publication history as well as to scholarship that offers new perspectives on many of the topics of longstanding interest addressed in this review, such as the play's engagement with seventeenth-century geopolitics and its representation of space, embodiment and race. We can also expect to see scholars both focusing with renewed energy on the play's subplot, especially as it opens up questions of consent and confinement, and venturing into new fields, such as critical race studies, disability studies (see Nora Williams' essay in this collection) and ecocriticism.

# 4

# New Directions: Embodied Theatre in *The Changeling*

## *Peter Womack*

### Within

In 2015 *The Changeling* was revived at the Sam Wanamaker Theatre, the imitation Jacobean indoor playhouse attached to the Globe on Bankside.[1] For the first time since the 1660s, the play could be seen in a space quite like the one it was written for.[2] The production therefore had in part the character of a historical experiment, a performance on original instruments. What did it reveal?

The action happens on a platform in front of a wooden screen, the decorative upstage barrier classically known as the *frons scenae*. The platform is small and plain, whereas the screen is ornate and imposing, its columns and galleries rising almost to the high ceiling. Spatially, then, the *frons scenae* dominates the stage. Moreover, it includes three entrance doors side by side: this is the same arrangement as in the tiring house of an open-air amphitheatre, but here, because the stage is so much narrower, the doorways take up almost the whole of its width. The actors occupy the space immediately in front of a bank of entrances: it is rather like doing a show on the steps of a cathedral.

This configuration tends to tie the visible action to whatever is supposed to be behind the screen. We are constantly aware of a set of closed doors which may open at any time; and this compromises the autonomy of what we actually see. Rather than forming a complete object of attention in itself, the stage is like a forecourt or a vestibule, a place that is meaningful because of its relation to somewhere else.[3] One thing the space elicits from *The Changeling*, then, is the play's recurrent investment in places that are just out of sight. Scene after scene is structured by its proximity to a significant offstage location:

1. At the start of the play, first Alsemero and then Beatrice-Joanna enter as from the church where they first saw one another. (1.1)

2. In the madhouse scenes, the wards where Alibius's patients are confined are understood to be just off stage, intimated by cries and by the repeated exits and re-entrances of the keeper Lollio. (1.2, 3.2, 4.3)

3. Beatrice-Joanna investigates Alsemero's closet, and brings from it the potion to test Diaphanta; in the following scene, Jasperino brings out the same potion for Alsemero to administer to Beatrice-Joanna. (4.1, 4.2)

4. Beatrice-Joanna waits outside the chamber where Alsemero is in bed with Diaphanta. (5.1)

5. Later in the same scene, De Flores twice exits to, and re-enters from, the chamber where he starts a fire and murders Diaphanta. (5.1)

6. Just before the dénouement, Alsemero confines Beatrice-Joanna in what is presumably the same closet as in 4.1. De Flores joins her there, and they emerge from it together at the end. (5.3)

In all these instances, the scene itself is located quite vaguely: in conformity with the logic of a bare stage, the writing takes little interest in the question of where the action is supposed to be taking place. But the *offstage* location – the church, the confined lunatics, the closet, the marriage bed – is specific and charged with meaning. The stage stands for a place which matters not because of where it is but because of where it is *near*. Moreover, these symbolically fraught unseen places are all interiors: as in accordance with the normal language of early modern stage directions, offstage space is 'within'. In short, *The Changeling* is typically set somewhere just outside a closed and significant room.

This recurring pattern is the more suggestive in the Wanamaker because of the lighting. Although the *frons scenae* is disproportionately large in relation to the stage, it does not overpower the action because it is in semi-darkness. The little platform, and the performers upon it, are bathed in the glow from the candelabras and sconces, while the architecture behind them recedes into shadow. This theatrical chiaroscuro works exquisitely to enable the actors to command the visual field without strain, but at the same time it has a second and more unsettling effect: it sets the warmly lit people against a hinterland of darkness. When the screen doors open, or are left open, the audience peers into recesses which the candlelight hardly penetrates, occasionally picking out an impression of movement or a glint of metal. These inexplicit openings draw the eye: the clearly seen external action is haunted by a scarcely glimpsed interior. Is there somebody in there?

The question applies most literally to the scenes set in the madhouse. With the exception of a single dance, Alibius's genuine patients do not appear on the stage: the visible scene is populated by sane characters pretending to be mad. The real madmen are 'within', heard as offstage noises, or seen, masked, in a brief passage across the gallery. The stage is the place where madness is discussed, displayed, imitated, joked about and used as a metaphor, but the thing itself, the object of all these playful references, is just out of view behind the doors.

What is out on the stage is witty, artificial, conscious of itself: it is a version of pastoral.[4] What is inside is inarticulate and unrepresentable.

The force of this binary structure is felt above all at the climax of the main plot. When Alsemero discovers that his bride is an adulteress and a murderess, he locks her in his closet – that is, in theatrical terms, behind the same door that confined the lunatics in the earlier scenes. Then he allows De Flores to join her there, so that both of them are concealed 'within' when the rest of the cast enter to report the discovery of Antonio and Franciscus. There follows a kind of cross-talk:

VERMANDERO
    O Alsemero, I have a wonder for you.
ALSEMERO
    No sir, 'tis I – I have a wonder for you.
VERMANDERO
    I have suspicion near as proof itself
    For Piracquo's murder.
ALSEMERO              Sir, I have proof
    Beyond suspicion, for Piracquo's murder.

(5.3.122–6)

Wonders, suspicions, proofs: the snappy repetitions place the exchange ironically, almost parodically, in the realm of word play. This is all just talk. Then it is cut short by inarticulate sounds from the darkness:

BEATRICE
    (*Within*) Oh, oh, oh!

(5.3.140)

Alsemero opens the door and the pair erupt on to the stage, soiled, obscene, covered in blood, filling the onstage interlocutors with dismay. This is the *coup de théâtre* to which the spatial organization of the whole show has been tending: the darkness breaks out on to the illuminated platform, discharging the violent energy that has been pent up behind the door, and so bringing the performance to an end. The shock is visual, but more essentially it is cognitive. It is not only that the onstage characters' theory about the murder of Piracquo is instantly disproved. It is also that they seem in that moment to have been wrong about the world in general. Their discourse was made up of law, rhetoric, probability, honour, agreed proprieties governing the relations between parents and children, and so on. Now that language is silenced: *this* is what things are really like, these ungovernable appetites, these dying bodies. Just as the caged madmen interrupted the pretences of the intriguers in the subplot, so here the confined criminals break up the linguistic constructions that keep families and societies going. It is unworldly theatre, quasi-theophanic except that what it reveals is not a god but an interior: the closet, the lightless bedroom, the secret passion, the vagina, the blood.

# The unconscious

That brutal and asymmetrical opposition – on stage, mere talk; off stage, the real thing – is announced at the outset:

> *Enter* ALSEMERO.
> 'Twas in the temple where I first beheld her,
> And now again the same – what omen yet
> Follows of that? None but imaginary.
> Why should my hopes of fate be timorous?
> The place is holy, so is my intent;
> I love her beauties to the holy purpose,
> And that, methinks, admits comparison
> With man's first creation – the place blest,
> And is his right home back, if he achieve it.
> The church hath first begun our interview,

And that's the place must join us into one,
So there's beginning and perfection too.

(1.1.1–12)

The young man has fallen in love somewhere else, and now comes here to talk about it. And not only to talk, but to *argue* about it. The speech is not simple narrative exposition; it is an exercise in deliberative rhetoric, designed to refute the proposition that the church is an ominous place for the lovers to have met. It sets out the reasons for believing that, on the contrary, the location is auspicious: Alsemero's purpose is holy, so the church is an appropriate context for it; his aim is marriage, which is a sort of restored paradise; the wedding will be in a church, so the courtship will have been initiated and completed in the same place. As a piece of formal argumentation it works reasonably well, but as a dramatic gesture it turns against itself because it enforces the very suspicion it is intended to allay. There must be reason to think that the omens are bad, otherwise Alsemero would not have to work so hard to prove that they are good. Thus the very first words spoken in the play are undermined by their unspoken opposite.

That is how it appears to Alsemero himself when he looks back at this moment from the end of the play. When Beatrice-Joanna confesses to the murder, he exclaims:

Oh, the place itself e'er since
Has crying been for vengeance, the temple
Where blood and beauty first unlawfully
Fired their devotion, and quenched the right one –
'Twas in my fears at first; 'twill have it now.

(5.3.73–7)

Now, in the dénouement, the temple's cry for vengeance is heard on the stage; but back then, at first, it lived only 'in my fears'. Alsemero knew that his devotion to Beatrice-Joanna was unlawful, but also refused to know. His opening speech, then, was the onstage trace of two different kinds of offstage reality: the unstaged events in the church, but also the unacknowledged truth in his mind.

The same gesture of retrospective interpretation appears again, a few moments later, in Beatrice-Joanna's parting speech. Pointing at De Flores, she says:

> upon yon meteor
> Ever hung my fate, 'mongst things corruptible,
> I ne'er could pluck it from him; my loathing
> Was prophet to the rest, but ne'er believed.
>
> (5.3.154–7)

Like Alsemero, she looks back at her initial feeling, realizing, too late, what she knew all along. In the play's early scenes her loathing of De Flores is several times highlighted not only as intense, but also as incomprehensible to herself: at one particularly telling moment, she is distracted by it from the problem of her impending marriage to Piracquo and exclaims, 'Oh, I was / Lost in this small disturbance' (2.1.93–4). She was 'lost' in it, yet holds on to the reassuring idea that it was 'small'. As with Alsemero, the audience can see something that is invisible to her because she is denying it; only when her trajectory is complete, and there is no further point in denial, does it come to consciousness for her.

Thus the dark places behind the action, where the candlelight barely penetrates, come to stand not only for the interior locations required by the story, but also for closed rooms of the mind. At the very end of the play Alsemero declares, with startling explicitness, that it is better to keep them closed. Vermandero is contemplating the infamy that has overtaken his name, and Alsemero advises him:

> Let it be blotted out, let your heart lose it,
> And it can never look you in the face,

Nor tell a tale behind the back of life
To your dishonour.

(5.3.182–5)

Blot out the thing you're ashamed of, arrange for your heart to lose it, so that it can neither look you in the face nor tell tales about you: the speech evocatively recommends what we might call repression. What is done cannot be undone, but it can be consigned to the realm of the unconscious.

In an obvious sense, to describe the play in these terms is to dehistoricize it. 'Unconscious', as an English noun, was unknown until the nineteenth century, and not common until the 1920s, when it formed part of the new language of psychoanalysis.[5] It invokes in that sense a distinctively modern concept, and applying it to *The Changeling* is a trace of the play's career as a modern classic. Influentially praised by T.S. Eliot in 1927,[6] it was established in the literary and dramatic canon around 1960, with its appearance in student editions (Revels 1958, New Mermaids 1964, Penguin 1965) and its first professional revival in England in 1961. The director of that production, Tony Richardson, promoted the play as 'contemporary', and seized on the 'love-hate' sexuality of Beatrice-Joanna and De Flores, which he compared to Strindberg (see Jennifer Panek's essay in this volume).[7] The play was being rediscovered for the self-consciously post-Freudian theatre of Pinter and Osborne. In the half-century since then, regular performances and appearances on reading lists have sustained its reputation as Middleton and Rowley's masterpiece.

Reading it as a drama of the unconscious, then, if not exactly anachronistic, is a response to its second, twentieth-century life. When Beatrice-Joanna says that her loathing of De Flores was 'prophet to the rest, but ne'er believ'd', modern actresses and audiences usually understand her to mean that her phobic reaction spoke her repressed attraction to him.[8] It is unlikely, though, that this was the main import of the line in the seventeenth century. As is well known, Middleton and Rowley found their story in John Reynolds's collection of 'tragical histories', *The Triumphs of Gods Revenge, against the crying, and execrable sinne of Murther* (as Berta Cano-Echevarría discusses in the essay following).[9] This source suggests a frame of reference whose determining category is not so much the psyche of the heroine as the justice of Heaven. It invites us to take Beatrice-Joanna's words 'prophet' and 'believ'd' in their obvious religious senses, and to understand her loathing as a divinely prompted recognition that De Flores is destined to be the instrument of her damnation. God was warning her, but sin stopped her ears.[10]

But although these two readings of the line, and consequently of the story, are radically different, they are not wholly unconnected. Middleton and Rowley (and Reynolds, if it comes to that) lived and worked within the Protestant culture of their time, and as many historians have argued, it was intensely conducive to self-analysis.[11] This was a logical outcome of Calvinist soteriology. Christ died for our sins, and we seek assurance of salvation in the contemplation of his sacrifice, but the doctrine of election makes the assurance precarious. Forgiveness through Christ is not extended to everyone. Did he die for *my* sins? The universal formulations of Scripture cannot answer that, because really it is a question not about Christ but about me. As Charles Lloyd Cohen explains it: 'Election is revealed not in Christ but in thoughts and affections, the moods and motives that plot the Spirit's passage . . . [S]uch a perspective deflects attention from Christ crucified to the self anatomized.'[12]

Self-examination was also repeatedly enjoined. Interrogating one's own thoughts and affections was an integral part of godly living:

> He that makes Conscience of his Ways, and to please God his only Way, is to take him to a Daily Direction, and some set rules, thereby looking constantly to his heart all the Day

> ... if a man tie not himself thus to Rules, his heart will break from him, and be disguised one way or another.[13]

So there the story about the justice of Heaven is not unequivocally different, after all, from the story about Beatrice-Joanna's psyche. If a man's salvation entails 'looking constantly to his heart all the Day', then the psyche is exactly where the justice of Heaven is to be sought.

The point here is not that *The Changeling* is really a play about damnation, or that Middleton was really a Puritan – though both these views have been eloquently advanced.[14] Rather, it is that the injunction to self-examination is psychologically divisive. I must interrogate my heart constantly, I am told, because if I fail in regularity or rigour, it 'will break from [me], and be disguised'. My heart, then, is like an alien creature; it is possible for me to lose contact with it, or to fail to recognize it. The regime of watching and reflecting is designed to guard against this self-alienation, but at the same time it produces it by setting the conscientious self which is to carry out the surveillance against the wayward, untrustworthy self which is its object. 'I' split into watcher and watched. And the relation between the two is unstable because the watcher can never see everything; something always escapes; that is why the inspection has always to be repeated. The interminable examination of one's spiritual state produces as its inevitable consequence an unexamined residue: an unconscious.

The play's initial situation is made up of selves that are divided in just this way. Alsemero, on the point of leaving the town by ship, declares that the wind has turned against him:

> JASPERINO                  Against you?
>    Then you know not where you are.
> ALSEMERO                        Not well indeed.
> JASPERINO
>    Are you not well, sir?
> ALSEMERO               Yes, Jasperino –

> Unless there be some hidden malady
> Within me, that I understand not.
>
> (1.1.21–5)

Beatrice-Joanna, engaged to Piracquo but falling in love with Alsemero, confesses aside:

> I shall change my saint, I fear me, I find
> A giddy turning in me.
>
> (1.1.148–9)

And De Flores, constantly putting himself in Beatrice-Joanna's way, knowing that she will insult and humiliate him, wonders at his own behaviour:

> am not I an ass to devise ways
> Thus to be railed at? I must see her still;
> I shall have a mad qualm within this hour again –
> I know't, and like a common Garden-bull,
> I do but take breath to be lugged again.
>
> (2.1.77–81)

All these people are as it were spectators of their own hearts: for each of them there is a psychic activity – Alsemero's 'hidden malady', Beatrice-Joanna's 'giddy turning', De Flores' 'mad qualm' – which they 'find' in themselves, but cannot understand or control.

Beatrice-Joanna's arbitrary loathing of De Flores forms part of this network of dumb inner forces. She observes it in herself, but experiences it as if it came from outside:

> This ominous, ill-faced fellow more disturbs me
> Than all my other passions.
>
> (2.1.53–4)

And a few moments later:

> I never see this fellow, but I think
> Of some harm towards me, danger's in my mind still,
> I scarce leave trembling of an hour after.
>
> (2.1.89–91)

She speaks the language of introspection: she can report on her disturbance, her passions and what is in her mind. But she does not know *why* De Flores has this unsettling effect on her: once again, her state of mind has the character of a 'hidden malady' whose nature is obscure although its symptoms are felt. Her crisply phrased asides articulate the watching self, while the self that it watches is vague but dominant, expressing itself not in words but in involuntary movements of desire or anger or fear. As in the narratives of psychoanalysis, it is the thing inside you that you rationalize in vain.

# Flesh

One of the central texts of Calvinist self-division was the seventh chapter of Paul's Epistle to the Romans:

> 18 For I know that in me (that is, in my flesh,) dwelleth no good thing: for to will is present with me; but how to perform that which is good I find not.
> 19 For the good that I would I do not: but the evil which I would not, that I do.
> 20 Now if I do that I would not, it is no more I that do it, but sin that dwelleth in me . . .
> 22 For I delight in the law of God after the inward man:
> 23 But I see another law in my members, warring against the law of my mind, and bringing me into captivity to the law of sin which is in my members.
> 24 O wretched man that I am! who shall deliver me from the body of this death?
> 25 . . . So then with the mind I myself serve the law of God: but with the flesh the law of sin.[15]

On the face of it, this sets out a straightforward opposition of mind and body. The mind, the 'inward man', wills the good and delights in the law of God, but the flesh, the outward 'members', are subject to the law of sin, and constantly thwart the mind's intentions. Mental and physical modes of being pull endlessly against one another: so far, it is a simple statement of a very familiar idea. However, there are two complications, one inherent in the Biblical text, and the other imported by Calvinist interpretation.

The inherent complication is seen in the contortions of the first-person pronouns. In verse 18, Paul can say 'in me (that is, in my flesh)', as if 'me' and 'my flesh' are synonymous. But by verse 20, he is saying that the flesh makes him do things he wants not to do, and, to that extent, 'it is no more I that do it, but sin that dwelleth in me'. Now it seems that 'I' means 'my mind', and that the flesh is an alien force that opposes and enslaves 'me'. So is my flesh me or not-me? The question refuses to settle. It is me, but it is also my adversary.

The imported complication comes about because 'mind', from a Calvinist point of view, cannot, in this context, simply mean human thought or reason. The total fallenness of mankind implies that mind in that sense is no less corrupt than flesh, unless it is sanctified by divine Grace. Calvin himself explains:

> Therefore the inner man [i.e. the 'inward man' in verse 22] is not simply taken for the soule, but for that spirituall parte of the soule whiche is regenerate of God: the worde members signifieth that other part that remayneth. For as the soule is the more excellente parte of man, and the bodie the inferiour: so is the spirite more excellent than the fleshe. By this reason therefore, because the spirite occupieth the place of soule in man: and the fleshe (that is the corrupt, and contaminated soule) the place of bodie: spirite hath the name of inner man, and fleshe the name of members.[16]

By this logic, 'flesh' becomes the name of a part of the soul. It is therefore not merely a physiological entity, but also a psychological one, not the inert matter of a mechanical dualism, but a dynamic participant in the interminable conflict that constitutes human identity. Consequently the substance itself – that of an actual body on the stage of a theatre, say – is not merely a neutral vehicle for a person whose essence is moral and psychological. It is a dramatic agent in its own right, suspect, formidable and somewhat mysterious.

Here, then, is an older name for the divisive presence which the characters of *The Changeling* find within them, the opaque yet undeniable self of which they are intermittently aware. Rather than assimilating it to twentieth-century psychology as 'the unconscious', what might we discover by trying to imagine it as 'flesh'?

Around the end of the twentieth century there was a surge of critical interest in the 'embodied' early modern self.[17] The dominant pre-Enlightenment conception of what a person is, it was argued, was grounded in Galenic medicine, which made no hard and fast distinction between psychology and physiology. According to this model, impulses and emotions which today we attribute to the psyche were 'material events, bodily in origin, humoral in nature'.[18] Humours, in particular, were definingly psychosomatic, being fluids within the body whose names – choler, melancholy, phlegm – nevertheless denoted moods and character types, as they still do. Occasionally that can make the system sound like a physiological determinism, as if a person's emotions were simply dictated by the natural chemicals in their bloodstream. But that was, and is, a selective and polemical way of putting it. The more usable view, both for medical practice and for natural philosophy, was that the relation between blood and subjectivity was reciprocal: 'As Burton wrote, fear and sorrow are simultaneously symptoms and causes of melancholy, "they beget one another and tread in a ring"'.[19]

At the centre of this interactive dance are the passions: fear, desire, hope, anger and so on. In them, soul and body meet. As Joseph Roach sums it up,

Because they derive from the humours and in turn influence [them] . . ., they are of the body. Because they are called into existence and directed by sensory, mnemonic or imaginative functions of the mind and spirits, they are of the soul.[20]

Accordingly, passions are, as it were, double-coded. Katharine Park explains that they can be given 'parallel psychological and biological accounts'; thus the sixteenth-century encyclopaedist Gregor Reisch 'interpreted wrath as both the impulse to resist evil and a dilation of the heart, which drives the blood and vapours in veins and arteries towards the extremities'.[21] This harmonious superimposition of psychology and biology is not surprising given the underlying assumption, derived from Thomas Aquinas, that the passions are behaviours of the organism, either 'concupiscible' (seeking what is good for it) or 'irascible' (attacking what is harmful to it). They may be thought of as events in the soul, but in that case the soul itself is being thought of as the body's representative and guide; irascible and concupiscible passions are mechanisms to ensure *its* survival and reproduction. In this respect, human beings are not essentially different from other animals.

This model of the person could almost have been designed for the theatre. The player, considered (as he often was) as an exponent of passion,[22] produces the 'double coding' in schematic form: insofar as wrath is an impulse to resist evil, it is part of the fictional situation given by the words he has memorized; insofar as it is a dilation of the heart, it is an event in his body, occurring not in the virtual time of the story, but in the immediate present. Acting consists precisely of bringing these two heterogeneous elements, the verbal and the visceral, into a functioning unity; it is the psychosomatic art form *par excellence*. Not only that, but the opposition of concupiscible and irascible passions suggests a syntax for the interaction of bodies on the stage, resolving emotion into motion 'towards' and 'away from'. The opening situation of *The Changeling* is a textbook example. Alsemero was intending to leave the town, so his servants are pulling him away, but a new impulse moves him towards Beatrice-Joanna; she is gravitating towards him, which takes her away from her father, but the father's hospitality draws Alsemero towards him. All that is on top of Beatrice-Joanna's violent movement away from De Flores, and his obsessive approaches towards her. The action as a whole seems to call less for a narrator than for a choreographer: it is a dynamic pattern of proximities. The plot is embodied in a way that makes naturalistic drama look bloodless by comparison.

But this integration of body and soul works smoothly only if we forget our Biblical starting point. Wrath, after all, is not only an impulse to resist evil and a dilation of the heart, it is also, thirdly, one of the deadly sins. If, rather than imagining the soul as a bundle of cognitive and motive faculties, we think of it, with St Paul, as the spirit of God within us, the flesh appears less as its complement than as its prison. One of the texts that modern scholars use as a source of early modern psychological ideas is *The Passions of the Minde in Generall* by the Catholic theologian Thomas Wright, published in 1604. At the end of a long survey, Wright lists over a hundred questions about our souls and bodies to which we do not know the answers. One of them is:

> How are the Soule and body, Spirit and Flesh coupled together, what chaines, what fetters, imprison a spiritual Substance, an immortal Spirit in so base, stinking and corruptible a carkasse?[23]

The same imagery shapes his explanation of our inability to answer this and other questions about our own nature:

> [O]ur capacities [are] too feeble, the meanes to attayne vnto such knowledge, too difficult: our Soule dwelleth in the tabernacle of flesh & blood, it is drowned in humors and fatnes, it is blinded with vapours & mists, it sees thorow carnall windowes, and cloudy spectacles.[24]

The incongruous yoking together of spirit and flesh makes us what we are, and at the same time defeats our attempts to know what we are. Our bodies are obscure to us because their very grossness impairs our capacity to perceive them. Carnal existence is a patchwork of insights and blind spots, conscious and unconscious states of being in intricate conflict with each other.

This is the psychological world of *The Changeling*. It is enacted for example through the play's malicious interest in involuntary reflexes. We saw that encountering De Flores makes Beatrice-Joanna tremble for 'an hour after'. Later, at the end of the scene in which he claims her sexually, he comments on her response to his touch:

> Silence is one of pleasure's best receipts:
> Thy peace is wrought for ever in this yielding.
> 'Las, how the turtle pants!
>
> (3.4.168–70)

There seems to have been a belief that a turtle-dove pants when it is stroked: Middleton used the same fragment of natural history in two other plays as well.[25] In all three instances, the turtle-dove represents a virgin who has been caught by a sexual predator, and the panting – which the actor performs – may be heard as panic, or as sexual arousal, or as a queasily pornographic mixture of the two. Whichever way it plays, the woman is deprived of words and shown in the grip of her automatic response. For the moment, she *is* her body. In all three instances, too, her reaction is framed by the comments of the predator. This makes the dramatization of the body brutally reductive. Suddenly the girl is exposed, *as* flesh, to a knowing male regard. Whatever she may have been saying about chastity and honour is literally silenced by the contraction of her heart and the crisis in her breathing. As before, language is trumped by the authority of an unspeaking objectivity. She is 'yielding'; she can't help herself.

The same logic governs the scene of the virginity test. If a woman who swallows Alsemero's potion is a virgin, it will cause her to yawn, sneeze and laugh, in that order. Beatrice-Joanna reads out the instructions and then administers the medicine to Diaphanta, who innocently displays the predicted symptoms. This puts the audience in a position like that of the knowing rapist. The yawning, sneezing and laughing, like the trembling and panting, are reactions in which flesh expresses itself independent of conscious intention, but which we observe in full consciousness of their meaning. Diaphanta's body is telling us the truth about itself without her knowledge.

These gestures of forcible embodiment are also reductive in the sense that they efface personality. The observed subject is an instance of a species, like a bird or an animal: she is doing what they always do. This anonymisation prepares the next move, which is the substitution of Diaphanta for Beatrice-Joanna on the wedding night. The 'bed trick' assumes that the husband will not notice that he is making love to the wrong person – it therefore works as a cartoon-like representation of the idea that one sexually available woman is much the same as another. The flattening of individuality is doubly satiric. It demystifies the distinctions of rank: mistress and maid are indistinguishable in the dark. And it mocks the language of love which originally set the plot in motion. Alsemero and Beatrice-Joanna both spoke as if each were for the other the only possible partner: 'this was the man was meant me' (1.1.85). In the upshot, though, both of them make do with somebody else, so the rhetoric of uniqueness ends up sounding pretentious. As in the *double-entendres* that pervade the dialogue, high-sounding words are made to disclose their low meaning. In that sense, despite the tragic momentum of the plot, the insistence on flesh has the character of comic debasement.[26]

The spokesman of this generically dubious reduction to the corporeal is De Flores. Positioned outside the play's respectable society by his ugliness and his menial status, he begins as a kind of clown, lowering the tone of the show with dirty-minded asides. Take for example his reaction to Beatrice-Joanna's friendliness:

> Oh my blood!
> Methinks I feel her in mine arms already,
> Her wanton fingers combing out this beard,
> And being pleased, praising this bad face.
> Hunger and pleasure, they'll commend sometimes
> Slovenly dishes, and feed heartily on 'em,
> Nay, which is stranger, refuse daintier for 'em.
> Some women are odd feeders.
>
> (2.2.145–53)

Blood, arms, fingers, beard, face – the connection is made out of detailed physical sensations. And the conceit that follows is aggressively materializing, not merely making eating a metaphor for sex, but imagining it as 'feeding' – coarse, needy, animal-like. Moreover, the reflection on 'odd' preferences takes the thought back to the idea of the involuntary. Sometimes (as proverbially in pregnancy) women just want to eat weird things; rational choice is overridden by an obscure impulse from within; again, literally, the body appears as the seat of the unconscious.[27]

The daydream of 'her wanton fingers combing out this beard' is one of a conspicuous series of references to fingers. Early on, De Flores picks up a glove that Beatrice-Joanna has dropped; she angrily throws down the other one, leaving him with the pair:

> She had rather wear my pelt tann'd in a pair
> Of dancing pumps, than I should thrust my fingers
> Into her sockets here.
>
> (1.1.232–4)

When, for her own purposes, she fakes an interest in his health, his reaction is again focused on her hands:

> DE FLORES  Her fingers touch'd me –
> She smells all amber!

BEATRICE   I'll make a water for you shall cleanse this
  Within a fortnight.
DE FLORES           With your own hands, lady?

(2.2.81–4)

The recurrence is not merely verbal; it is embodied on the stage at every point: '*this* beard', 'her sockets *here*', 'a water ... shall cleanse *this*'. Finally, when the murder is done, he brings her one of the victim's fingers. This last move is often read as a moral statement, but it is also, again, a materializing one: flesh – the visible, tangible stuff – is the thing you deny in vain.

Here we are close to the source of what actors always find in the relationship between Beatrice-Joanna and De Flores: its perverse eroticism. It is not necessarily that she unconsciously desires him; it is, much more simply, that the connection between the two actors on the stage is scripted for their bodies. Neither De Flores' lust nor Beatrice-Joanna's loathing has anything to do with personality. Both impulses are bound up with the other's literal proximity: with breath, smell, touch, presence. When Beatrice-Joanna touches De Flores' diseased face, we know because of what she has said earlier that she is forcing herself to do it, fighting down her revulsion. However we interpret that, it electrifies the instant when skin makes contact with skin. The touch that disgusts her excites him: both of them are in a state of violent responsiveness. Nothing that passes between Beatrice-Joanna and Alsemero has anything like the same intensity.

In her pretended solicitude, Beatrice-Joanna attributes De Flores' skin condition to 'the heat of the liver' (2.2.80). In other words, his face carries the marks of his physical constitution; it is impossible to forget that he is a body containing blood, appetites, internal organs. The most intense apprehension of this is voiced not by Beatrice-Joanna, but by Tomazo de Piracquo:

              he's so foul
One scarce would touch him with a sword he loved
And made account of; so most deadly venomous,

He would go near to poison any weapon
That should draw blood on him – one must resolve
Never to use that sword again in fight,
In way of honest manhood. . . . – What again?
He walks a-purpose by, sure to choke me up,
To infect my blood.

(5.2.15–25)

For Tomazo, as for Beatrice-Joanna, De Flores' sheer bodily presence is toxic: he threatens your health by walking near you; if you wounded him, you would have to throw away the sword you had used so as not to poison a subsequent opponent. Of course, one reason for Tomazo's paranoid vehemence is that De Flores is the murderer of his brother. He does not yet know this: it is another case of unconscious recognition. If a murderer approaches his victim's body the wounds will bleed afresh, and what is happening in this scene is an extension of the same principle.[28] Tomazo is 'of the same blood' as Alonzo, and it is this shared blood that is reacting to the presence of the man who shed it. Blood is the medium of occult influences, communicated wordlessly from one physical interior to another. Once again, the play's determining relationships, half seen in the shadows of incomprehension or denial, are those between the bodies on the stage.

And in the end, it is as a body that De Flores takes control of the dramatic situation. It is a question of theatrical rhythm. At the beginning of the role, he is a hanger-on, trailing after Beatrice-Joanna and getting in her way, hovering ineptly on the fringes of her decisiveness. In the wedding night scene (5.1), on the contrary, she is wretchedly hesitant, and he has three purposeful exits and re-entrances in fifty lines. The action is punctuated by exclamations at his efficiency: 'How rare is that man's speed!', 'That fellow's good on all occasions.', 'Ha, there he goes. – 'Tis done.' (69, 91, 94). His potency, as the bride's covert lover, is indecently dramatized by his brisk entrance carrying a gun which, he says, he proposes to fire up the chimney to dislodge the soot. Everything in the scene's construction invites the actor's movement to be energetic and relaxed where those around him are agitated and vague. Thus his progression from marginality to authority, which structures the play, is not primarily a moral or thematic development, but a phased takeover of the time and space of the show. His eventual supremacy is indisputable because it is not an idea but a physical accomplishment.

# Allegory

*The Changeling*, then, is a script from a radically embodied theatre. The staged person is not only a nexus of social relationships and ethical choices, but also an organism which breathes, touches, trembles. It is easy to see how this dramatic language appeared in the early 1960s as excitingly 'modern'. The revival at the Royal Court was part of a cultural moment that included the new accessibility of Freud in English, the ascendancy of D.H. Lawrence, the English discovery of Artaud, the earliest work of Edward Bond and the crumbling of theatrical censorship.[29] It fitted readily into the ambient narrative of physical and sexual affirmation. But of course, the play's assimilation is not as straightforward as all that. As far as we can tell, the last professional performance in England before 1961 was in the 1660s: its dramaturgy is on the far side of a wide historical gap.

To retrieve something of that earlier theatrical language, we can take advantage of a chance echo from one that is earlier still. In *The Life and Repentaunce of Marie Magdalene*, a moral play probably written in the reign of Edward VI (1547–53), there is a sequence in which Mary, who has been laughing and flirting with a quartet of attractive Vices led by Infidelitie, encounters an admonitory figure called Knowledge of Sin.[30] Knowledge of Sin is hideous, and Mary and Infidelitie try to get rid of him, but he explains that now she has met him he will always be before her sight. There is no evidence that the passage could count as a 'source' for *The Changeling*. But it does suggest a different way to read the relationship of Beatrice-Joanna and De Flores. This stage routine – the sociable, light-hearted girl and the disturbingly ugly man who attaches himself to her and cannot be shaken off – has been done before: it means something.

What carries the meaning is allegory. Considered as a theatrical resource, this is above all a drastic motivation of the actors' physical characters and relations. This particular scene, for example, enacts Romans 3.20: 'for by the law is the knowledge of sin': an actor playing 'The Law' brings another actor, playing 'Knowledge of Sin', onto the stage. A little later, Mary has a crisis of faith and the script reads, '*Here entreth Christ Iesus*' (1230): the sentence is at once a practical stage direction and a doctrinal statement. In the most literal sense, the play presents religious truths by *embodying* them.

Viewed in this frame, De Flores 'bad face' would not be an incidental disfigurement but the visible form of his significance. This, you could say, is what Beatrice-Joanna's sin looks like.[31] By the same token, his sexual occupation of her would be understood, not as something that happens as a result of her fall, but as the fall itself. At the start of the vices' campaign against Mary Magdalen, Pride of Life says to Infidelitie,

> If thou once be rooted within the heart,
> Then maist thou make an entrance by thy craft and art
> So that we may come into hir at pleasure,
> Fillyng hir with wickednesse beyond all measure.
>
> (287–90)

The vices 'come into' Mary in the sense that they join her on stage, but the spatial imagery also implies a kind of rape: the vices enter her body. The vocabulary of allegorical theatre effaces the distinction between physical and psychological events.

We tend to think of allegory as a convention of medieval drama, and certainly Wager's play, a deliberate adaptation of fifteenth-century forms for post-Reformation purposes, had long been obsolete by the time *The Changeling* was written.[32] All the same, it was by no means an archaic or unfamiliar mode for Middleton. Throughout his career as a playwright he also wrote triumphs and pageants whose idiom was primarily allegorical, as was his famous satire of 1624, *A Game At Chess*. And consider this sententious speech in *The Spanish Gypsy*, which played at the Phoenix the year after *The Changeling*:

> O, what vile prisons
> Make we our bodies to our immortal souls!
> Brave tenants to bad houses; 'tis a dear rent
> They pay for naughty lodging: the soul, the mistress;
> The body, the caroch that carries her;
> Sins the swift wheels that hurry her away;
> Our will, the coachman rashly driving on,
> Till coach and carriage both are quite o'erthrown.[33]

The elements of this image are neatly moralized: mistress, coach, wheels and coachman signify, almost pedantically, soul, body, sins and will respectively. But then on top of that, the rapidly sketched action – the lady abducted in a speeding coach – is the kind of thing that might easily happen in a Middleton play: the ambush of Bianca in *Women Beware Women*, and the rape of Clara in *The Spanish Gypsy* itself, are incidents of just this kind. So the entrapped woman is no less present in the little narrative than the imprisoned soul she stands for. Almost imperceptibly, the soul turns into a character, and the body that brings it/her to ruin clicks into focus as a man. There are two registers – the high-life anecdote and the psychomachia – and each has access to the other. That suggests how *The Changeling* itself, while it is obviously not an allegorical play, is nevertheless open at the side, as it were, to an allegorical dimension. Allegory is present as a sub-text, or a haunting.

This metaphor of the coach represents, among other things, a subversion of hierarchy. If the soul is 'the mistress', then the coach ought properly to be under her control. The coachman (will) is a servant, and the mistress (the soul) will leave her vehicle (the body) once she has reached her destination (death in Christ). So for the will and the body to drive off somewhere else is a kind of insurrection: the servants are hijacking their mistress. The same narrative of mutiny appears in one of the earliest texts to synthesize Galenic and Christian models of the person, Nemesius' *On the Nature of Man*, which circulated widely in Latin and was translated into English by George Wither in the 1630s:

> The body being an instrument which the soule useth, if it bee well fitted for the same, is a helper unto the soule; and she the better useth it to her own contentment. But, if it be not every way framed and tempered for the soule's use, it becommeth her hinderance, and much adoe hath she to strive against the unfitnesse of her instrument. Yea, so much, that if shee be not very wary and diligent in rectifying the same, she her selfe is perverted aswell as the instrument; even as a musitian misseth of true musick, when his harp is out of tune.[34]

Again, this spills the denaturalizing light of allegory on to the central events of *The Changeling*. As Wither's sentences extend themselves, the repeated pronouns – 'she', 'her' – make it harder to keep in mind that what is being talked about is the soul: instead, the words conjure up a woman in a story, and the story is Beatrice-Joanna's. The mistress adopts the servant as her 'instrument', hoping to use him to her own contentment, but ends up first striving against his unfitness, and then being herself perverted by it. De Flores' rebarbative physicality makes a new kind of sense in this context: he performs the body's rebelliousness as such. It refuses to be the equable means to the soul's ends; it had its own agenda, all along.

Finally, then, pursuit of the play's allegorical dimension brings us back to St Paul's conflicted co-existence of soul and body, the 'other law in my members, warring against the law of my mind'. Those verses from Romans were much interpreted by Calvinist preachers; one example, a pair of sermons by Willem Teellinck, was printed in London in 1621, the year before *The Changeling* was written. Its text is 7.24: 'O miserable man that I am, who shall deliver mee from this body of death?' Teellinck understands the 'body of death' to signify natural corruption, from which not even the apostle was free, and which is aptly imagined as a body 'because it lyeth, and hangeth vpon vs, euen as our owne bodie, or flesh ... For whither we goe or stand, we carry it with vs as we doe our owne body, and flesh.'[35] You cannot escape it because, as De Flores points out to Beatrice-Joanna, you are one with it (3.3.140). But it is also hideous, 'a most vgly, deformed body of death, a fearefull, and deadly monster'. The monstrosity measures, once again, the perversion of inner hierarchy:

> And if it so be, that it bee a monstrous thing when in a bodie, the members are all mishapen, and misplaced, and moreouer, in themselues exceedingly depraued; so must this naturall corruption needs be held to be a monstrous thing, wherin the vnderstanding, which should be gouernour and leader of the will, and fleshly lustes, and affections, not onely lieth subdued vnder them both, but also is in it selfe vtterly obscured, & darkned: and the will, and affections in themselues altogether peruerted, and disordered.[36]

Of course, the play is not a dramatization of this or of any sermon. But it is striking how intensely it comes from the same discursive world. Beatrice-Joanna's eventual situation is, precisely, that there is no-one to deliver her from this body of death, which is fearful and ugly but also intimately joined to her. It has subdued and darkened what should have been its governor and leader, and left her altogether perverted and disordered. At this half-buried level, the play stages, as in some demonic baroque allegory, the triumph of the flesh.

So it really does exemplify the disturbing and immediate dramaturgy of flesh and blood that recommended it to the actors and directors of the 1960s and 1970s as they struggled to free themselves from what felt like centuries of genteel euphemism. But what that rediscovery understandably overlooked was the ferocious negativity of the play's embodiedness. Its vivid notation of corporeal life resists being recuperated as any kind of affirmation. Rather, the vividness is the effect of an anathema: flesh is palpable on this stage *because* it is imagined as the enemy of all that is good. What ultimately underlies the physical excitement of *The Changeling* is the play's residual contact with a religious stage and its conception of the flesh as incurably depraved.

# 5

# New Directions: Doubles and Falsehoods: *The Changeling*'s Spanish Undertexts

## *Berta Cano-Echevarría*

When, in 1727, Lewis Theobald entitled his revised version of Shakespeare and Fletcher's lost play *Cardenio* (*c*.1613) *Double Falsehood* he was giving prominence to the duplicity and cheating that his Spanish characters perform throughout the play, as they do in Cervantes' original story.[1] Famously, this is the only instance that we know of where Shakespeare drew material directly from Cervantes, and it is regrettable that the only extant version, or rather trace, of this significant textual encounter is the watered-down play-text Theobald produced a century later. Shakespeare was not alone in borrowing from Cervantes and other contemporary Spanish writers, and their presence can be better appreciated in a number of other, extant English plays. *The Changeling* is prominent among them. Although its Spanish elements tend to be glossed over in general (and generic) terms as simply providing a (safe) foreign setting, so allowing oblique comment on topics closer to home, there is, in this case, a tapestry of references and borrowed episodes that resonate throughout, inviting us to understand it as a play that establishes a dialogue with texts, occasions and locations far beyond English frontiers. As Jennifer Panek's essay in this volume observes, modern productions of the play have sometimes evoked the paintings of Goya (or, less anachronistically, Velazquez) in seeking to express its Spanish flavour. There is a deeper truth underlying these artistic decisions. While editors since N.W. Bawcutt in 1958 have identified the two main sources on which Middleton and Rowley drew (John Reynolds' and Gonzalo de Céspedes' prose narratives), the second of these has received conspicuously little attention.[2] Both offer a rich connection between *The Changeling* and contemporary Spanish culture and literature, a link which, it will be proposed, articulates a 'deep structure' of influence in this most Spanish of early modern English plays. This essay argues that what might be termed *The Changeling*'s 'undertexts' insinuated a trope of doubleness and falsehood, especially concerning the honour of women, which had a particular resonance for English audiences following years of tense and uneasy peace between the two countries.

From the outset, deceit is the play's leitmotif. In greeting Alsemero, Beatrice-Joanna laments, 'This was the man was meant me' (1.1.81), and upon the arrival of her father, Vermandero, with his unwelcome, peremptory injunction – 'Thou must be a bride within this sevennight' (1.1.183) – she immediately seeks to put off the wedding day with the now-unwanted Piracquo, hoping to manipulate her father by claiming it is too soon to part with her virginity (which he dismisses as a 'toy' [1.1.190]). Later, in 4.1, following her wedding to Alsemero, Beatrice-Joanna instructs a kind of doppelganger to replace her on her wedding night because her own body is no longer untouched. With the introduction of her servant Diaphanta into her bed, Beatrice-Joanna becomes in effect two, and experiences a 'second de-flowering' through a surrogate. De Flores' presentation is more complex, initially at least, since it is unclear whether we should pity him for the abuse he receives from Beatrice-Joanna or appreciate his apparent humility and loyalty; but by the end of the first scene we learn that nothing will stop him from getting his 'will' (1.1.230), his docile behaviour being no more than a mask. Indeed, Alsemero is also an ambiguous figure, an acceptable match for Beatrice-Joanna but compromised by his possession of a grotesque virginity test kit. Other doubles, of course, are presented by way of the parallel plots and the mirrored characters – De Flores/Lollio, Beatrice-Joanna/Isabella – sometimes, as in the case of Antonio and Franciscus, being almost interchangeable.[3] But since duplicity and hypocrisy were two of the most recognizable traits of the Spanish stereotype that circulated in England at the time, the doubleness of the play is particularly apposite, as the integration of the source material illustrates.

# Reynolds' Spanish doubles

John Reynolds' *The Triumphs of Gods Revenge* (1621) is acknowledged as the primary source for *The Changeling*. It has been speculated that Reynolds produced this collection of tales on the violent consequences of unhappy marriages as an acceptable way of promoting support for the Protestant cause in England, since his pamphlet *Vox Coeli* (published in 1624 but in circulation earlier) had proved too provocative.[4] Indeed, as it happened, Reynolds would be extradited from France and imprisoned. *Vox Coeli* is one of the numerous printed documents that focused on the figure of Don Diego Sarmiento de Acuña, Count of Gondomar. His arrival as an ambassador for Spain at the court of James I (1613), after having been the Corregidor (Mayor) of Valladolid at the time of the English embassy to the city to ratify the peace between Spain and England (1605),[5] proved controversial from the beginning. He refused to strike the banners of his ships as he entered Portsmouth harbour, despite the threat of being sunk if he did not oblige, which gave him a reputation for arrogance. But beyond that, the threat he posed for English Protestants concerned the negotiations he conducted to procure a marriage alliance between the English heir to the throne (first Henry and subsequently Charles) with a Spanish Infanta (first Ana María and later María Ana). The image of the Spanish ambassador as a Machiavel capable of manoeuvring England towards subjection under Catholic Spain proved a fruitful topic for pamphleteers. Barbara Fuchs argues that the potent stereotype of the Spanish people as plotters owes much to the recurrent characterization of Gondomar in the literature of the time.[6] In his pamphlet Reynolds represents Gondomar as receiving a letter from the ghost of Mary Tudor, praising him for having 'tyed to king James his Eare and his Maiestie to your Girdle', and then instructing him on how to act in order to secure the final triumph of Spain over England.[7] This image of Gondomar as a direct threat to English sovereignty is revisited in the stereotype of the false and duplicitous Spaniard that is ubiquitous in *The Changeling*, and not only in the characterization of De Flores.

Valladolid, the seat of the Spanish court when the Anglo-Spanish peace was signed, features in both main sources for *The Changeling*.[8] The fourth tale in *The Triumphs of God's Revenge* has a very specific Spanish setting and was probably inspired by Reynolds' experiences during his time as a merchant and traveller. If we accept what he asserts in the preface, he did not take his stories from another written source, or invent them: 'I have illustrated and polished these Histories, yet not framed them according to the model of mine own fancies, but on their passions, who have represented and personated them.'[9] All of them show desire is the driving force of crimes, and all are set outside England, mostly in France, Italy and Spain, 'because it grieves me to report those that are too frequently committed in our Country'.[10] Allowing for a degree of sensationalism, Reynolds is intent on presenting a flavour of the cultures and territories he was familiar with, painting them (in *implied* contrast to England) as sites of deceit and debauchery. Significantly, contemporary records place him in the harbour of Valencia in 1604 and then again in 1605, just at the time of the signing and ratification of the peace treaty.[11]

The tale in the volume entitled 'A Spanish History' is set in Alicante, where the Castle of Santa Barbara, the church of Santa María and the country retreat of Briamata stand as the three locations of the story. Reynolds was especially thorough in giving a recognisable historical and geographical setting to his plot.[12] Don Pedro de Alsemero, the protagonist and *villain* here, travels to the court in Valladolid to seek from the Duke of Lerma an appointment as a captain to fight under the Arch-Duke Albertus in the wars in Flanders (which had continued, following the Anglo-Spanish peace), and thus avenge the death of his father, who had lost his life at the battle of Gibraltar (1607). However, a truce with the Dutch ensues, followed by a new peace treaty, and so the career of Alsemero as avenger is frustrated. This allows us to situate the story shortly after 1609, when a peace to end the war in the Flanders was signed in Antwerp.[13] Still intent on soldiering, however, Alsemero travels from Valladolid to Alicante, planning to sail to Malta and fight against the Turks; but once more he is prevented, first by contrary winds and subsequently by spotting a beauty in church whom he decides to court – the very point, of course, where *The Changeling* begins. Reynolds' moralizing narrator presents this as follows:

> It is both a grief and a scandal to any true Christians heart, that the Church, ordained for thanksgiving and prayer unto God should be made a stews or at least a place for men to meet and court Ladies; but in all parts of the Christian World, where the Roman religion reigneth, this sinful practice is frequently practised, especially in *Italy* and *Spain*.[14]

The Beatrice-Joanna in Reynolds is a woman whose descent into crime is gradual, starting with her slight misbehaviour in church by responding to Alsemero's gaze. Subsequently it is driven by a growing desire to outmanoeuvre her male protectors. For a long time she withstands her father's pressure to marry Alonso de Piracquo and only with reluctance does she accept Alsemero's courtship; but during her forced seclusion in Briamata she convinces herself that she is in love with Alsemero and entices one of her father's followers, De Flores, to kill her first suitor, Piracquo, to get him out of the way. Her marriage to Alsemero seems to be happy enough until he becomes unreasonably jealous and, as her father did before, decides to seclude her. Her reaction – rebelling and embarking on an adulterous relation with De Flores – seems to be motivated principally by a desire to defy her husband. Predictably, Alsemero discovers the couple in flagrante, and in a passion kills them, only to be later executed himself – for having killed Piracquo's brother in a duel earlier. De Flores, in contrast to Alsemero, is a rather uninteresting secondary character, lacking the powerful ugliness of his successor on the stage: 'a Gallant young Gentleman of the Garrison of the Castle',[15] he murders Piracquo because he is besotted with Beatrice-Joanna, but he only obtains his reward months after the marriage, once the married couple's relationship has deteriorated. The story presents a society of deceit and repressed passions, where murder is merely a solution to eliminate an inconvenient suitor and female desire seems uncontrollable, subject to and yet opposing the patriarchy. Reynolds' version differs in many ways from *The Changeling*, but one of the most noticeable aspects is the handling of time. In *The Triumphs of God's Revenge* time is extended and this allows for the characters to develop and change. Alsemero spends a long time courting Beatrice-Joanna before she relents, following many conferences, meetings and exchanges of letters. Likewise, once married there is a lapse of three months until he becomes unreasonably jealous of Beatrice-Joanna, motivating her to stop loving her husband: 'he watcheth her everywhere and sets spies over her in every corner; yea, his jealousie is become so violent as he deems her unchast with many, yet knows not with whom'.[16] Compared to the Beatrice-Joanna of

*The Changeling*, she manages to handle the situation by herself, until almost the last moment when, discovered by her husband, she faces death together with her lover. More than duplicitous, Beatrice-Joanna is a true 'changeling' in this story, adapting to circumstances to escape male control.

Reynolds' story has been criticized for its awkward construction and the text's 'jerky and episodic technique',[17] but it establishes the main storyline for *The Changeling* and provides a set of characters as well as a geographical and historical setting. What has not been noted, however, is how the recurring trope of female seclusion to which Beatrice-Joanna is subjected and from which she rebels in the Reynolds version is echoed in the secondary plot of *The Changeling* – for which editors have not established a source – where Isabella is practically kept prisoner by her husband, who fears her supposed appetite for other men. Isabella and Beatrice-Joanna represent two distinctive responses to commitment and courtship, but they both derive from the same origin. It is tempting at this point to see the double plot structure of the play as originating in a split that divides Spain and England in much the same way as *A Game at Chess* represents the two 'houses' in black and white. In *The Changeling*, the castle and the madhouse are not in direct opposition, but they invite comparison by the striking contrasts between them (as some modern productions, as well as criticism, have demonstrated). The apparent solidity of the fortress hides unspeakable corruptions that will eventually destroy its inhabitants, whereas the chaos of the madhouse can be contained – and, paradoxically, reveal rather than conceal its secrets, in the denouement of 5.3. As has been pointed out (see Patricia Cahill's essay in this volume), since the subplot evokes London's Bedlam (Bethlehem Hospital), the play presents these three scenes as *English* in locale. Significantly, the names, Lollio and Alibius,[18] sound less recognizably Hispanic than Antonio and Franciscus, who are *infiltrados* from the castle determined to seduce Isabella (though Antonio's dual status activates the popular English term for fool, 'Tony'). The stupidity and greed of the madhouse keepers is venal, and overt – city comedy material, as commentators have noted – compared to the dark primal forces that motivate the inhabitants of the Alicante castle. Spanish duplicity can readily be traced in this reduplication of plot structure where the characters of Antonio and Franciscus repeat the same plan and are discovered by the same procedure. Isabella's purity is thus intensified as she has been able to detect the fake fool and the fake madman and remains loyal to her ('albus'/white) husband; it is tempting to think here of *A Game at Chess*, where the white pieces resist the sexually-voracious black house, and its 'checkmate by discovery' (5.3.160–1) at the denouement.[19]

# Representations of the Spanish 'honra'

Like several of the tales in *The Triumphs of God's Revenge*, contemporary Spanish drama was obsessed with the preservation of women's honour, and rape was at the centre of this anxiety.[20] Crucially, Middleton and Rowley, rather than relying entirely on an Englishman's text of uncertain provenance, also dramatize authentically *Spanish* material in their play. As we shall see, the Spanish fixation with the concept of honour, '*la honra*', penetrates *The Changeling* in ways that radically transform the original material in Reynolds. Two of the most famous plays of the period, *El Alcalde de Zalamea* (*The Mayor of Zalamea*) (c.1636) and *Fuenteovejuna* (c.1612–14), examine the consequences of rape and, in both, the rapist, a powerful lord who takes advantage of a peasant girl, is subsequently killed. These plays also share a clear political and legal theme as they consider the options of rebellion against an oppressor who exerts his power through sexual violence. In Lope de Vega's *Fuenteovejuna* the whole village assumes responsibility for killing the aggressor, a commander of the Order of Calatrava, while in Calderon de la Barca's play it is the father of the victim who, despite his social inferiority, exerts his power as mayor of the village and dictates the execution of the captain of a troop of soldiers. In both plays the Catholic Monarchs and Philip II respectively restore order by understanding that a wrong has been righted and that the rapists deserved their death.[21] But this need for the monarchs to step in as *dei ex machina* is testimony to the controversy over legal responses to rape in early modern Spain. Of course, silence for this type of crime was the most common response of most women and their families, to avoid the shame of dishonour; but in the reported cases of statutory rape (as happens in both these plays), where the victim is a virgin and therefore she and her family are deprived of the most valuable asset for her marriage, the case would be commonly settled by paying financial compensation to the father of the victim. This would provide the family with money for her dowry or with a means to sustain the daughter if she was to remain unmarried. Seldom would the perpetrator marry the victim: although the law stated this as a means to right the wrong, only rarely was it enforced by the court. Sentencing the culprit to death, even though enshrined in the canons of law, was rare indeed, so *Fuenteovejuna* and *El alcalde de Zalamea* ought not to be considered as representative of actual practice.[22]

Loss of '*la honra*' was an obsession, specifically of its aspiring middle classes and lower nobility. Loss of property, or even life, was as nothing compared to blemishing the name of a reputed family. As the avenging mayor in *El Alcalde de Zalamea* expresses it:

I'll give up life and property
At the King's word. But honour is
The offspring of the soul of man.
And the soul, God tells us, is his.[23]

Honour was defined by social class, reputation within that social class; *hombría* or virility for men, and virtue for women. But the woman's virtue spoke for the virility of the men in her family, her husband – if she was married – and her father and her brothers. Women could not lose their honour, because it did not belong to them: it was the responsibility of the male figures around to protect it. Gustavo Correa argues that loss of honour was the annihilation of the male individual, who was thus dispossessed of his value and his virility, as well as of his social standing, given that he would no longer be accepted by his community.[24] Loss of honour was expressed in Spanish Golden Age literature variously as an offence, a reason for mockery, or a punishment, but a recurring metaphor was a stain that needed to be cleansed and purified, as we see evoked in the closing sequence of *The Changeling*. In this process the stain would be sublimated into a symbolic ritual of purification, acquiring an almost religious significance, accompanied by violence and bloodshed. Such plays in the Spanish *Siglo de Oro* are full of murder and revenge, but also with the symbolic purging of fire, as in the case of Tirso de Molina's *El Celoso Prudente* (*The Jealous Prudent Husband*, c.1630), where the supposedly cuckolded husband plans to burn the house with his wife inside.

These extremes may seem to be at odds with the more pragmatic responses, such as paying or marrying the victim, but of course, in the cases where the rapist belonged to a lower social class, this kind of compensation became impracticable. That the woman was to be held responsible for her loss of honour when she was the victim of rape meant that it was she who was punished because she held the family's *honra*, since it could only be transmitted through her line. In an infamous case in 1577 in Lorca, not far from Alicante, it was reported that a priest of no social standing, taking advantage of the acquaintance he had with the powerful Bienvenguds family, committed statutory rape against the Bienvenguds' youngest daughter. According to the records the guilty priest was only sentenced to exile; one of the brothers, however, unable to endure the stain on the family's name, killed his own sister and her child when she was eight months pregnant.[25]

Given the centrality of rape in Spanish Golden Age drama it is not surprising that rape and loss of honour is a recurring theme in Middleton's 'Spanish trilogy'. Notoriously in *A Game at Chess* the plot is constructed around the sexual appetite of the Spaniards. Though it is mainly the Black Bishop's Pawn (a Jesuit) who is implicated in the attempted rape of the White Queen's Pawn (a virgin), the whole black house participates in this sin of venery, and so it is confessed by the character of the Black Knight (representing Gondomar) when he tries to seduce the White Knight (taken to represent the Duke of Buckingham, who had accompanied the Prince of Wales on his mission to Spain in 1623) into coming over to his side:

> The trifle of all vices, the mere innocent,
> The very novice of this house of clay. Venery?
> If I but hug thee hard I show the worst on't.
> It's all the fruit we have here after supper;
> Nay, at the ruins of a nunnery once
> Six thousand Infants' heads found in a fishpond.
>
> (5.3.125–30)

The English white house eventually escapes unscathed, but the threat of castration, rape and sodomy defines the Spanish side. Moreover, repeated attempts against the virtue of the White Queen's Pawn are all done under the disguise of religious habits, just as Franciscus and Antonio, subversives from the castle, conceal themselves beneath their Bedlam robes.

In *The Spanish Gipsy* (1623), based on two of the *Novelas Ejemplares* (*Exemplary Novels*, 1613) by Cervantes, Middleton and Rowley (with John Ford and Thomas Dekker) build a very complicated dramatic structure around the rape of a young virgin by Roderigo, the son of the Corregidor (Mayor) of Madrid. Kidnapped while walking home in the company of her parents and taken to the house of the Corregidor, Clara is attacked in a dark room. As she cannot see the face of her rapist the only proof of her ordeal is a crucifix she takes away with her. Her first option is to remain silent, but in order to conceal her lost virginity she must reject a suitor, Luis, who happens to be a friend of her rapist. As in other Spanish and English plays of the period, the woman who is abused by a social superior can only recover her honour through marriage to her attacker, and this was understood to represent a 'happy ending' since this new, higher status would compensate for the woman's past sufferings.[26] Clara is appropriately united with Roderigo at the end of the play, thanks to the intervention of the Corregidor to whom Clara pleads for justice, holding the crucifix as both a symbol of her ordeal and proof that she had been in his house:

> CLARA [*showing the crucifix to Roderigo*]
> CLARA
> By this crucifix
> You may remember me.
> RODERIGO             Ha! Art thou
> That lady wronged?
> CLARA                I was, but now am I
> Righted in noble satisfaction.
>
> (5.1.46–9)[27]

Clara could have married Luis, who proposes to her earlier in the play, after (unbeknown to him) she has been raped, but she seems to believe that she belongs to her aggressor and to no one else. In Cervantes' original novella, *La Fuerza de la Sangre* (*The Force of Blood*), the victim's suffering is intensified since she bears a child after the rape and has to hide her maternity for seven years, before the supposed 'resolution' of marriage.[28] No one proposes to her during this period. The poignancy of this solution is softened in *The Spanish Gipsy* as the denouement of Clara's story is mixed with other parallel (but comic) plots that come to similar marital conclusions.[29]

Rape in *The Changeling* (chronologically the first in this trilogy) is much more controversial. In the not-so-distant past some critics adhered to the view that Beatrice-Joanna was a corrupt, foolish girl who falls into her own trap, and correspondingly rape did not enter the equation.[30] A more psychologically complex interpretation, drawing on Freud, proposed by Joost Daalder, among others, presents her as sexually attracted to De Flores, her initial insults and comments about his physical repulsiveness in fact concealing her desire: 'Beatrice's conscious loathing is in some way a manifestation of unconscious love'.[31] This erotic component complicates our understanding of what happens between De Flores and Beatrice-Joanna in the audience's imagination during the interval between acts three and four. Some critics regard it as rape, while others discuss the complexity and ambiguity of the moment and present a range of possible interpretations. In 'Re-reading Rape in *The Changeling*', Frances Dolan opts controversially to 'un-rape her', arguing that in contemporary legal cases women who claimed to have been raped had to prove it through their damaged bodies, while women who were charged for their sexual behaviour could relate other forms of sexual relations which gave them some control over the situation:

> What would happen if we took a break from describing what happens in *The Changeling* as rape? Only then can we assess the complex distribution and abuses of power between De Flores and Beatrice-Joanna and in the play more generally.[32]

Similarly, Judith Haber studies the erotization of virginity and the thin line that separates images of rape from the recreations of the nuptial first night in some literary works of the period, pointing out how De Flores' lines at the end of 3.3 echo the epithalamium Ben Jonson wrote for the Howard-Essex marriage in 1606.[33] For Haber, in *The Changeling* rape is conflated with marriage.[34] Conversely, Deborah Burks argues that the play exploits contemporary male anxieties about the difficulties of ascertaining the facts of women's sexuality because in early modern law virginity, desire, consensual intercourse and rape depended on testimony. On these grounds she reads De Flores' actions as forceful and violent, rather than ambiguous:

> When he forced Beatrice-Joanna to sleep with him, DeFlores murdered her honor; now he finishes his crime with her actual murder. Her body, when DeFlores drags her out onto the stage, bears visible signs of his violation, signs which are a literalization of the violence their sexual union committed on her body and her honor and, by extension, on her family.[35]

Reading the episode in the light of the play's setting and sources offers an additional, complementary perspective that frames the rape and its consequences in 'Spanish' terms.

## The Céspedes undertext

In Reynolds, there is no rape scenario, explicit or otherwise. It is in the second source that we find the material that inspired the characterization of Beatrice-Joanna as the bride to be who finds herself deprived of her honour on her wedding night. *Poema Trágico del Español Gerardo*, by Gonzalo de Céspedes y Meneses, was published in Madrid in 1615 and in translation as *Gerardo the Unfortunate Spaniard* by Leonard Digges in London in 1622.[36] This source, first identified by Bertram Lloyd and included by Bawcutt as an appendix in his edition,[37] is little discussed. Joost Daalder grants that 'some detailed similarities exist ... [but] they are ultimately trivial'; Barbara Fuchs goes further, asserting that 'No Spanish sources have been identified for Middleton and Rowley's *The Changeling*.'[38] However, as we shall see, Céspedes provides more than a tangential inspiration for the playwrights, presenting Middleton and Rowley with key traces of characters and situations that are central to the play. If they were not familiar with the original in Spanish then they must have read the voluminous translation in haste to make use of an inserted story told by a pilgrim to Gerardo that serves as a diversion from the main story. One of the curiosities of this is that it is told twice: first by the pilgrim, a naïve husband who recounts his life and marriage, unaware of the falsehoods that were being committed behind his back; and then through a letter of confession written by his wife Isdaura on her deathbed. Roberto, the husband, is a penitent man on his way to Santiago de Compostela to purge his sins, not for having done much wrong, but (not unlike Alsemero in the play) for not having discerned the truth as it was taking place.

Most interestingly, this double story of Roberto and Isdaura adds two key characters not in Reynolds: the servant who rapes Isdaura before her wedding night, and the maid servant who takes the place of her lady in the nuptial encounter. The first of these characters is an antecedent of De Flores in ways that the original De Flores in Reynolds is not. Moreover, this character seems to come directly (or indirectly) from *Don Quixote de la Mancha*, in the Biscayan who fights with Don Quixote, just after the famous windmill episode. Don Quixote stops a carriage that is taking a lady from the Basque country to Seville where she is going to bid farewell to her husband, who is about to leave for the Indies.[39] Don Quixote believes this lady to be a kidnapped princess and halts the group in order to rescue her. The lady's squire, a Biscayan with an unintelligible speech and a strong will, confronts him, but the knight errant refuses to fight with a mere servant. Outraged, the latter exclaims: 'Biscayan on land, hidalgo [gentleman] at sea, hidalgo at the devil, and if thou sayest otherwise thou liest', at which point they begin to fight.[40]

Céspedes, inspired by Cervantes, is surely drawing on this character for his own Biscayan squire. In his story, however, the nobleman who goes to the Indies, leaving his wife and daughter behind, returns with a fortune. This Leonardo Argentino, upon arriving in Spain, decides to marry his daughter Isdaura to Roberto, the narrator of the story and son of his business partner in Peru. Roberto has never met his future wife, but obedient to both fathers' wishes travels to Toledo, where the wedding is unexpectedly postponed by the sudden death of 'their old servant, the trustie *Biscayner*, [...] laid under a blacke Herse strooke thorow with fiue cruell wounds'.[41] The following day the union takes place, but Roberto only partly enjoys the wedding night; shortly after he falls asleep he is awoken by Isdaura with 'sudden affrighten shriekes' announcing that the house is on fire. And in the midst of the 'wringing and wailing' another disaster happens when they find how a 'handsome discreet maid-servant [...] having been earnest to draw water to quench the fire (whether with some fright or sudden accident falling in) in an instant (there being no meanes to save her) was drowned' in the well.[42] Roberto confesses to his listeners on the way to Santiago that, despite all this having taken place long ago, grief is still with him: 'neither can I forget those propheticall boadings of my wretched marriage'.[43] Indeed, the marriage ends tragically years later, with Roberto killing his best friend and provoking the death of Isdaura because of a supposed infidelity between them.

It is from the letter that Isdaura writes before she dies that Roberto and the reader learn what actually happened in the two consecutive nights that doomed their marriage. The night before the wedding the 'trustie Biscayner' had entered Isdaura's room, prepared to take by force what her father had taken from him by marrying her to Roberto:

> Who would have thought of thy Father, that hee should so unthankefully have recompenced the paines, which in thy education, and honest substaining his family in his absence, I have undergone: only because I hoped to reape the benefit in thy amiable desired companie, which uniustly, my *Isdaura*, he deprives mee of.[44]

The Biscayner uses a dagger to coerce his victim; the very dagger that Isdaura uses to kill him once he has fallen asleep. From this point on, Isdaura enters into a frenzy of deceit and doubleness. She has to dispose of the corpse and feign grief in front of her parents and her newly arrived fiancé, but she also needs to solve the problem of the wedding night, having lost her virginity.

Mirroring her own deflowering by a servant, she arranges things so that her maid servant can be deflowered by her husband, which Middleton and Rowley incorporate in their reworking of Reynolds. In this case Julia does not undergo a virginity test, but, like Diaphanta, she comes to bed in darkness and stays there longer than she has been instructed, arousing distress and jealousy in her mistress:

> I knew not which in mee was most, my iealousie or feare, and my rage increased the more, when (hearing the Clocke strike three) I saw so little memory in her of my danger. This and the difficulty of waking her without being perceived by you made me undergoe a desperate course, as that of the *Biscayner*.[45]

The parallel in *The Changeling*, and notably the detail of the clock striking three times (5.1), is clear. Here, however, Isdaura has to act on her own: she sets the house on fire, urges her husband out of bed, creates confusion in the household and, in the midst of the chaos, pushes Julia into a well.

How much this inspired Middleton and Rowley has not been sufficiently considered. True it is that De Flores is a more sophisticated Machiavel than this garrulous Biscayan, but the common trait they share is that they resent their social status as servants, roles imposed upon them as a result of their declining fortunes. When the Biscayan in Cervantes' episode attacks Don Quixote, he is protecting (as he sees it) his mistress's right to continue with her journey, but also defending his honour as a 'hidalgo'. Basques in early modern Spain had the reputation of being violent and rough, but were also characterized as being proud of the ancient origins of their lineage.[46] The Biscayan Don Quixote encounters is a comic figure but the *Biscayner* in Céspedes shifts register from comic to tragic; after years of being the de facto master of the house he is displaced by an unwelcome suitor and he reclaims his position, obtaining by force the most valuable asset of his master, his daughter. De Flores holds a similar undefined position in his lord's household; esteemed and trusted, he has aspirations towards Beatrice-Joanna that are clearly above his station. To obtain his prey De Flores is much more subtle, his outward appearance perhaps a projection of the Biscayner's roughness and psychological domination; unlike the Biscayner, De Flores does not need to use a dagger. However, the dagger is meaningful in another moment in the play when De Flores hides the rapier with the purpose of later killing Piracquo. This weapon, charged with sexual significance, is subsequently used to cut off the finger with the ring that symbolically unites in murder his fate and Beatrice-Joanna's, which the dagger seals in 5.3. De Flores is thus a composite character, more distant from the patient squire in Reynolds and closer to the sexual predator servant in *Gerardo*. Like him, he uses coercion to obtain the sexual prize that he desires, and like the Black Knight in *A Game at Chess* he displays all the abilities of a Machiavel to manipulate circumstances to his advantage.

A particularly striking parallel – one, again, that does not appear in Reynolds – is between Isdaura's maid Julia and Beatrice-Joanna's Diaphanta. Their bodies are equally objectified, although Diaphanta shows her readiness to lose her virginity while Julia is reluctant to substitute for her mistress, agreeing only out of loyalty. Neither sees the risk of being recognized in the dark, their physical body distinctiveness seeming to disappear once their only tangible quality becomes their hymen. Such logic goes unquestioned by all the parties involved. Roberto does not ask himself how he could not have noticed the difference:

> having to my unspeakable joy [I] reaped from my Bride the sweet fruit, amorously passing the rest of it, at length (our bodies mutually in each others Armes interlaced) we fell asleep. But no longer were our weary limmes laid to soft

rest, when my Wife with her hands and sudden affrighting shriekes awoke mee.[47]

At this point the switch has taken place, the hands and cries that awake him are Isdaura's, while Julia is still in bed by his side, as we learn from Isdaura's version:

[hoping] you would take no notice of ought but my cries, embracing you closely and crying Fire, fire: you awoke and frightfully leapt out of your bed and the chamber, leaving me with *Iulia*.[48]

The pleasure both Julia and Diaphanta enjoy is shown by the abandonment with which they fall asleep and needlessly prolong the time in bed, while their ardent passions are symbolically quenched, one by water, the other by fire, thus erasing the trace of their doubled identities. Julia and Diaphanta suffer similar punishments for their impersonation: having saved their mistress's reputation they cannot be pardoned.

Reynolds' salacious tale provided Middleton and Rowley with the scaffold for their main plot, but it is to Céspedes that is owed the undertext that gives the play its Spanish Golden Age flavour (and which lies at the heart of the play's appeal today). *Gerardo the Unfortunate Spaniard* inspired the three key elements that enabled the playwrights to transform the narrative in Reynolds into an arresting drama: the character of the villain, the rape and the bed-trick. *The Triumphs of Gods Revenge* has rightly been criticised for its 'clumsy construction and unconvincing motivation', though as N.W. Bawcutt points out, Reynolds was a moralist, not a novelist.[49] For the literary element the playwrights drew on authentically Spanish material that takes us, obliquely, all the way to Cervantes, via the Biscayner whose social status Middleton and Rowley graft onto the Antonio de Flores taken from Reynolds. It is through its adaptation of Céspedes that *The Changeling* may be regarded as rather more than simply an English portrait of contemporary Spain playing to Protestant conceits. If the rape of a lady by a social inferior evokes a cultural anxiety surrounding *la honra* (rather than simply functioning as the casual demonizing of Catholic Spain as a society driven by lust), the bed-trick is similarly double-facing. The folkloric origins of the bed-trick are keyed to its providential function stemming from the Bible.[50] Early modern English drama tended to follow this tradition, the device being used to rectify a wrong and resolve a social crisis, such as we find in *All's Well That Ends Well* (c.1604) and *Measure for Measure* (1604; revised by Middleton in 1621). As Julia Briggs points out, the bed-trick in literature may be regarded as a cultural response to male desire, as a means of accommodating and policing male sexual fantasies:

> In its most basic form – a wife substituted for a mistress in her husband's bed – this plot does not merely enact but embodies sexual fantasy, providing an imaginary freedom and an actual safety, while leaving unresolved questions about the place of such desires within marriage.[51]

*The Changeling* both follows and departs from this tradition; in this it is not unique, but the debt to Céspedes is significant. Typically, the device is used to trick the male, at the instigation of a woman or sometimes (as in *Measure for Measure*, for example) a man (the Duke). Isdaura uses Julia to trick Roberto, and Beatrice similarly employs Diaphanta to fool Alsemero: in each case the wife/mistress substitution is inverted, the trick's providential function converted to conceal a rape that otherwise threatens the nuptial bliss of the bridegroom in order to save – hardly providentially – the bride's honour. Céspedes takes pains to explain the trick, Isdaura's letter, a deathbed confession, recited by Roberto to Gerardo, for the benefit of the reader; Middleton and Rowley adapt this to show Beatrice, onstage, providing a running commentary on the offstage, unseen activity in Alsemero's bed.

Perhaps understandably the play's editors have tended to give most credit to the playwrights. Michael Neill, for example, while acknowledging that the Digges translation associates the Biscayner with 'service' and 'will', terms whose doubleness Christopher Ricks has shown to be central to the text's performance of wordplay, nevertheless concludes that '[f]rom such small details, Middleton and Rowley worked up the story of sexual insurrection and domestic betrayal that transformed the crudely moralised sensationalism of Reynolds' narrative'.[52] As this essay has argued, *Gerardo the Unfortunate Spaniard* not only helped facilitate such a transformation of Reynolds, but also imported onto the English stage authentically Spanish material. While *The Changeling* activates anti-Spanish feeling that was intensifying towards the end of the first Stuart reign, ironically it did so, in part, through its appropriation of concerns that were central to Spanish Golden Age literature. And whether deliberately or not, the *Spanish* bed-trick deployed was deeply ironic in another way, since in calling up the Frances Howard scandal at points through the play – and most starkly in Diaphanta's aside, 'She will not search me? Will she? / Like the forewoman of a female jury?' (4.1.99–100) – the playwrights skewered the countess by linking her family's Catholicism with the kind of doubleness and falsehood associated with Romish Spain.

# 6

# New Directions: Performing *The Changeling*: 2006–2015

## *Sarah Dustagheer*

In 3.1 De Flores leads Alonzo on a tour of Vermandero's castle.[1] 'Yes, here are all the keys' (3.1.1) the seemingly benevolent servant tells Beatrice-Joanna's unsuspecting fiancé as they descend through the 'narrow' (3.1.6) passageways of the 'impregnable fort' (3.1.4). There is a growing tension for the audience, who know De Flores's murderous intentions; his lines promising Alonzo that he shall 'see anon / A place you little dream on' (3.1.11–12) take on a macabre dramatic irony. Moreover, the servant's aside about his own 'safety' (3.1.15), in contrast to Alonzo's vulnerability, ensure that the audience are in many senses as much cornered as the murder victim, finding themselves unable to escape De Flores's callous cruelty and his black-humoured running commentary. The scene ends with servant murdering master and a dismembering of the body: struggling to remove the ring Beatrice-Joanna had given to Alonzo, De Flores decides on a 'speedy course' (3.1.34) and cuts off finger and ring together. 3.1 exemplifies much of the dramaturgical power of *The Changeling* – the ways in which Middleton and Rowley weave the tragic events and corruption of characters into the materiality of the stage space and dialogue structure. The aside becomes an important tool for examining the growing discrepancy between public honour and private malignancy, especially for De Flores and Beatrice-Joanna. De Flores's keys, foreshadowing his menacing control of the castle, and Alonzo's engagement ring, that will not yield even in death, are two of a number of props with potent symbolic meanings. Like the other violent actions of the play, Alonzo's death is mapped onto Vermandero's castle. *The Changeling*'s settings – the castle and Alibius's madhouse of the subplot – become increasingly palpable sites of claustrophobia and depravity.

With this reliance on embodied performance, *The Changeling* has proved alluring to modern theatre-makers and is an established part of the non-Shakespearean repertory. In this chapter I want to explore four recent stagings in relation to key features of the play's dramaturgy: Declan Donnellan for Cheek by Jowl at the Barbican (2006); Michael Oakley at Southwark Playhouse (2011); Joe Hill-Gibbins at the Young Vic's Maria Studio (January to February 2012; revived with a different cast in the Main House, November 2012); and Dominic Dromgoole directing at the Sam Wanamaker Playhouse (2015).[2] All, except Dromgoole's, were set in contemporary times and used modern costumes; Dromgoole's *Changeling* had a seventeenth-century setting. How do modern productions portray Vermandero's castle and Alibius's madhouse, and bring together the two plots of the play? What role do the play's many asides have in different theatre spaces, and how does this early modern dramatic device affect contemporary audiences' engagement with the play? In what ways do designers and directors make use of the play's symbolically rich materiality? In addressing these questions this chapter seeks to examine the appeal and meaning *The Changeling* has for theatre practitioners, theatre reviewers and audiences in the first two decades of the twenty-first century.

# A 'perennial problem': Main plot and subplot

The relationship between the castle main plot and the madhouse subplot has intrigued scholars and performers across the play's history. Michael Neill notes that while *The Changeling* appears to offer the 'bald juxtaposition of two almost unrelated stories', the play's 'critical and performance histories have amply demonstrated [... their] thematic and poetic coherence'.[3] In twenty-first-century productions contending with the two plots has remained a focus for theatre-makers and reviews. Discussing Cheek by Jowl in 2006, Michael Billington praised the first major twenty-first-century production of *The Changeling* because it 'solve[d]' the 'perennial problem', bringing together the 'grim tragedy' of Beatrice-Joanna and De Flores with 'the comic subplot in which a madhouse keeper's wife is assailed by counterfeit lunatics'.[4]

Cheek by Jowl transformed the main house of the Barbican, London, by not using the *c.*1,100-seat auditorium for the audience. Instead, Donnellan and designer Nick Ormerod placed audience members on the Barbican stage, creating a much smaller and intimate playing space where actors and spectators were in close proximity. In what has become Cheek by Jowl's signature aesthetic, the set was minimal; beside the backstage Fire Exit (used for actors' entrances and exits in this production) was a fridge, a sink and a small CCTV monitor; the set was completed with a desk and a dozen orange plastic chairs. In part Donnellan unified the two plots of the play as this set provided the backdrop for both. In addition, though, during the madhouse scenes, the characters of the main plot sat on chairs and 'affected crazy repetitive habits – counting fingers over and over, chanting meaningless snatches, rocking to and fro, and so on'.[5] As characters of the main plot (notably Beatrice-Joanna and De Flores) became mad inmates, Donnellan's cast embodied the thematic links between the two plots. The castle inhabitants and madhouse inmates were one and the same, equally maddened and corrupted by love and lust. The production won universal praise for 'underlying the madness of love that drives the central characters to murderous extremes'; showing the links of 'love and madness'; and 'literaliz[ing] the play's figurative analogy between its two main plots [. . .] everyone in this play was maddened'.[6]

Six years later, Joe Hill-Gibbins at the Young Vic took a similar approach; reflecting on his interpretation of the castle and madhouse, he observed:

> Even though they're set in the same city and overlap, they feel like they're in separate universes. But the more I worked on the play, the more I began to feel that, actually – and I didn't anticipate this at all – they're the same story told in two completely different ways.[7]

Hill-Gibbins extended the doubling seen in Donnellan's production as main plot actors were not just inmates in the madhouse, but also took on specific roles. Main and subplot characters were doubled as follows: Jasperino/Lollio, Tomazo/Antonio, Diaphanta/Isabella and Alonzo/Alibius. Again, as at the Barbican, the two plots of the play were acted without changes of scenery. Within the small concreted breezeblock space of the Maria Studio, the audience were seated in the round: some on the same level as the set, on wooden benches, but the majority were seated on an upper level of red scaffold seating which was encased in a large net. Designer Ultz created a fairly minimal set complete with mattress, table and a small offstage plywood boxed room. Completing the set were a series of cupboards, closets and boxes on wheels that, alongside the actors' bodies doubling roles, became the site of the blurring between castle and madhouse. In Alibius's madhouse noises and banging were heard from these enclosed spaces and, by the end of the first scene, the main plot characters burst forth to continue the play's action. Like its 2006 predecessor, this production suggested that all the characters were inmates of the madhouse and won praise for demonstrating an 'air of lunacy' and 'all-embracing madness of the world'.[8] Billington stated he was 'won over by a production that, like Declan Donnellan's 2006 version, suggests madness is the play's real theme'.[9]

Yet madness is only one of the linking and mirroring interactions between the main and subplots – the objectification and containment of female sexuality (as examined in work by, for example, Deborah Burks, Sara Eaton and Judith Haber) might offer an equally compelling link between the plots.[10] It is reductive to limit the 'real theme' of *The Changeling* to one idea; and Billington's word choice alerts us to the way in which trends in performance, influenced by the current moment, become crystallized in critical thinking as the most authoritative interpretation of a play. Therefore, while madness is certainly significant, it is important to view these productions within their contemporary circumstances, specifically in terms of an increasing sophistication in thinking about mental health. Certainly Cheek by Jowl frame Rowley and the subplot in anachronistic terms, ascribing to the playwright somewhat modern insights: 'He is crystal clear about the difference between mental illness and mental handicap which many plays before (and since) are not.'[11] At the Young Vic a major strand of research and development for the production was 'looking at the nature of the madhouse and its inhabitants'.[12] The production's Schools' Resource Pack (prepared by the Young Vic 'Taking Part' education team) frames this research work in a modern context, listing the modern names for conditions that 'Fools' and 'Madmen' had (for example, schizophrenia, personality disorder, obsessive compulsive disorder) and noting 'we are considerably more enlightened and people with mental health problems are treated much more humanely'.[13] It is apparent that the Young Vic invited students to use Hill-Gibbins's production as the starting point for a discussion of contemporary treatment of the mentally ill. Part of *The Changeling*'s modern appeal is that it offers a way into thinking about current concerns with mental health. Having said that, in light of recent developments in Disability Studies, no recent production to date has exploited the potential of the subplot's portrayal of physical/mental disabilities and institutionalization; and it remains important to consider the wider politics of *acting* disability, as Nora Williams does in the final essay in this volume.

Michael Oakley's 2011 production at the Southwark Playhouse found a radically different way to reconcile Middleton and Rowley's two plots by simply cutting the madhouse scenes. Oakley explained that this decision was one for the most part dictated by practical and financial reasons in that he had 'six actors, two weeks of rehearsal and a limited budget' for his fringe production at the south London theatre.[14] Nonetheless he did find an artistic imperative in his cutting of the text, arguing that the themes of madness 'didn't interest him' as much as the central relationship between De Flores and Beatrice-Joanna and the play's portrayal of 'sexual obsession and fascination' and its 'dark sexuality'. For some critics, Oakley achieved this focus. Maddy Costa noted that in cutting the madhouse scenes '[w]hat's left is a taut, claustrophobic sex drama', and for Alisdair Hinton the 'play is more focused on the intricate sexual politics and manoeuvrings of the key players'.[15] Six years on, however, Oakley reflected on the effect of cutting the madhouse scenes:

> I think it all happens too quickly ... Rhythmically the madhouse scenes make the play work because they allow the Beatrice and De Flores plot to marinate; when you come back to [the main plot] you see the characters' development because in the offstage action of the play you can believe time has passed, things have happened.

The director points out a simple but often overlooked dramaturgical relationship between the main and subplots; the plots do have a 'thematic and poetic coherence', but also work together as a temporal performance experience for the audience.[16]

Other reviews of the Southwark Playhouse production were very critical of Oakley's decision to cut these scenes. In perhaps an example of the crystallization of a particular interpretation of the play as noted earlier, Natasha Tripney wrote:

> Snip, snip. Snip, snip. Michael Oakley's production of Middleton and Rowley's Jacobean tragedy has taken the secateurs to the text. Gone is the madhouse subplot [...] But this secondary narrative strand does more than provide a comic counterweight to the central story, it feeds into it, shadowing it, paralleling it. Insanity takes many shapes, many forms in this play.[17]

In a review of the Young Vic production (which followed just a few months after Oakley's), Michael Coveney praised Hill-Gibbins's editing of the text because it 'gloriously entwined' the two plots in relation to the 'feeble butchery' of the Southwark Playhouse staging.[18] The vitriol of Coveney's language and to a lesser extent Tripney's playfulness ('Snip, snip') confirms *The Changeling*'s canonical status in the non-Shakespearean repertoire. Middleton and Rowley's play is one with which mainstream theatre critics are familiar enough to register and rebuke cuts to the text, a practice more consistently seen in reviews of Shakespeare (as work by Stephen Purcell and W.B. Worthen attests).[19] Moreover it is possible to see an emerging consensus around one particular reading of *The Changeling* as a play with two plots linked predominantly – or even exclusively – by ideas of insanity and madness. Deviations from this reading are registered and sometimes heavily criticized by reviewers. In this way, as with Shakespeare's plays, a particular interpretation of *The Changeling* is enforced and consolidated; I will return to what this critical response says about the play's twenty-first-century status in the non-Shakespearean canon at the end of the chapter.

## 'I am in a labyrinth': Physical and psychological enclosure

In an echo of the streamlining created by cutting the madhouse scenes, Oakley's *Changeling* was set almost exclusively in one location: the underground office of security guard De Flores (the wedding scene of 4.1 was played under minimal lighting so that De Flores's office temporarily gave way to an imagined church space). Designer Fotini Dimou's set was a functionally furnished modern bunker. The brick back wall of the Southwark Playhouse was exposed and in front on stage stood a large desk covered with a bank of CCTV monitors, a phone, a fax and desk lamp; there were two filing cabinets, a few boxes of notes, a printer and a metal cupboard that functioned as Alsemero's closet. The use of CCTV is a modern spin on *The Changeling*'s voyeurism and surveillance. In one of the play's seminal speeches Beatrice-Joanna warns 'Our eyes are sentinels unto our judgements' (1.1.68), these opening lines foreshadowing a play of sexual gaze, objectification and spying. CCTV also made an appearance in Cheek by Jowl's staging of the play, where at one point (according to the rehearsal notes) it showed 'bad quality recording of sex scenes'.[20]

Oakley's play opened with several CCTV monitors showing a close-up shot of Beatrice-Joanna and De Flores staring intently at her, while a voice-over delivered a speech transposed from later in the opening scene:

> Fates do your worst, I'll please my self with sight
> Of her, at all opportunities,
> If but to spite her anger. I know she had
> Rather see me dead than living, and yet
> She knows no cause for't but a peevish will

(1.1.98–102)

The strange intensity of the central characters' relationship was, thus, the focus of the production from the beginning.

Beatrice-Joanna found herself increasingly present in De Flores's office, trapped and contained in his domain. In the production's graphic depiction, De Flores pushed Beatrice-Joanna up onto one to the filing cabinets in an act of violent sexual aggression.

The psychological and physical enclosure conveyed in modern productions is, of course, deeply embedded in the language and ideas of the play. As studies by Nicholas Brooke and Thomas L. Berger demonstrate, the play's narratives are mapped onto the increasingly claustrophobic spaces of castle and madhouse.[21] Inmates are physically contained in the madhouse, as is Isabella, all under the watchful eye of key holder Lollio. In the main plot, De Flores is Lollio's counterpart, a key holder who traps its inhabitants: Alonzo is permanently bound in the castle walls by death and Beatrice-Joanna is psychologically enclosed by her actions – 'I'm in a labyrinth' (3.3.71) she exclaims once she realizes what De Flores wants in reward for murder. Ultimately both Beatrice-Joanna and De Flores are physically contained in Alsemero's closet, making literal their pre-existing moral and psychological enclosure. In many respects this theme maps well onto the play's original performance space, the Phoenix. Penelope Woods has demonstrated that a 'complex condition of proximate voyeurism' existed in small, indoor, candlelit spaces, where audience members were seated in close proximity to the stage action.[22] If we remember that the Phoenix was an intimate, sensory-heightened and voyeuristic space it is apparent that *The Changeling* played into the spatial dynamics of indoor early modern theatre.

As an 'archetype' of an indoor Jacobean theatre, the Sam Wanamaker Playhouse (SWP) gives us some insight into the possible performance conditions under which *The Changeling* was first performed. In academic terms discussions of the insights that the SWP offers are tempered by the anxieties of theatre essentialism and the wider theoretical debate about the purpose and value of reconstruction.[23] However, understandably in short reviews, mainstream theatre critics tend not to engage in this more nuanced debate; and so the response to Dromgoole's production at the theatre emphatically linked space and play. For Susannah Clapp the production 'might have been crafted for the Sam Wanamaker Playhouse [. . .] This glowing coffer, with its beeswax candles, its gold leaf and its concealed corners, is a mirror of the labyrinthine, claustrophobic drama'.[24] Similarly Billington noted the suitability of the play in such a 'seductive chamber theatre'; Tripney observed that a 'play of murder and deception sits well in this intimate candle-lit room'.[25]

Certainly there was a synthesis between text and space in the production. For example, in 3.1, the awkward movement of De Flores and Alonzo removing their weapons in the narrow doorway of the stage door, the sound of their voices as they moved offstage and their swift re-appearance on the other side of the stage evoked the confines of the castle and of De Flores's increasingly powerful control of the space. Yet to focus solely on the seemingly perfect fit between text and space in this production is to elide the interpretative and creative work of Dromgoole and his designer Jonathan Fensom. The set was designed to underscore feelings of entrapment and claustrophobia. The stage doors were fitted with metal gates which were the backdrop for both castle and madhouse. De Flores and Lollio were linked aurally through the sound of the heavy set of keys they both carried with them at all times, the regular jangling creating a cumulative feeling of menace.

As part of the play's spatial logic, Beatrice-Joanna and Alsemero's courtship is located at a secret 'place' (2.2.1), which the potential husband is led to by Diaphanta; it is in this 'place' that Beatrice-Joanna goes on to ask De Flores to murder her fiancé Alonzo. It is perhaps also this private location where Beatrice-Joanna and De Flores have their illicit meetings, eventually observed by Jasperino who notes the mistress leaves her servant via the 'back door' (5.3.11). Fensom created this 'place' on the SWP stage with a small metal rectangular fence that was placed on stage for 2.2 and 3.3; Beatrice-Joanna's dialogue with Alsemero, and then with De Flores, was played within the confines of this fence, thereby reducing the already small playing space to something like a metre squared. The effect of this piece of scenery was to reduce the physical distance between Beatrice-Joanna and her intended fiancé, and then between her and De Flores in the moment of her requesting his help and the rape scene that follows. It is worth noting that even in a performance space which, for many critics, made the play's theme of enclosure immediately obvious, Dromgoole and Fensom identified this theme of the play as one that needed further embodiment and emphasis. Thus Middleton and Rowley's portrayal of spatial and mental entrapment continues to intrigue modern theatre-makers.

# 'Ha!': Staging asides

The claustrophobia of *The Changeling* is not confined to its characters. In many respects the play encourages audiences to experience a sense of enclosure as the play's asides – delivered primarily by Beatrice-Joanna and De Flores – ensure that the audience find themselves implicated in the unfolding tragedy. It is important to note, however, that the 1653 quarto does not indicate *any* asides and so it has been left to editors and directors to identify the asides of the play, as Nora Williams has explored.[26] Overall, though, the majority are implied clearly within the text and so the play has become well-known 'for its liberal use of asides'.[27] Sara Eaton points out that the 'corrupted private language' of asides is juxtaposed with the 'public language'; it is the audience who find themselves in the midst of this juxtaposition, enveloped in the corruption.[28] As several scholars have demonstrated, direct address was a major dramaturgical feature of a playing environment where actors and audience shared light and existed in close proximity.[29] Played out in a similar environment, the SWP production provided a glimpse into the possibilities of the aside in its original performance conditions. Hattie Morahan (Beatrice-Joanna) noted that her character has 'a very intimate and colluding relationship with the audience'; and that 'It's part of the dramaturgy, that characters share their inner thoughts, which immediately forces an audience to be complicit.'[30] For Tripney, 'the heightened relationship between audience and performers' made possible in the SWP worked 'in the play's favour'.[31] Indeed it was evident that Morahan's Beatrice-Joanna and Trystan Gravelle's De Flores drew on the close proximity and shared lighting not only to deliver their asides, but also to make regular eye contact with the audience, thereby creating a cumulative relationship of collusion.

Yet, while undoubtedly the space of the SWP might especially encourage an intimacy between actor and audience, the experience of audience complicity in watching *The Changeling* is not exclusive to a Jacobean theatre space. One of the effects of Cheek by Jowl's radical re-shaping of the Barbican playing space was to bring actors and spectators into close proximity. Paul Menzer argued that 'Donnellan's transformation of the Barbican space gave his players intimate access to the audience, which they took advantage of with sinister ease'.[32] The minimal aesthetic of the design foregrounded actor's voice and body and, thus, audience/actor interaction. David Benedict noted that 'Nick Ormerod's deliberately uncluttered production design accentuates a plot turning on whispered secrets that must not be overheard. Everything rests upon speaking and listening, which puts acute pressure on the actors'; for Claire Allfree, 'With no set, and the props extending only to red chairs, the emphasis is firmly on the actors'.[33] Despite the difference in production space and aesthetic, then, Cheek by Jowl company members talk in a similar way about the audience's role in this play as Hattie Morahan at the SWP. Indeed Olivia Williams (Beatrice-Joanna) describes engaging with the audience in an intimate way, noting that they are so close 'you can whisper to them ... it's confidential'.[34] Similarly Donnellan argues that 'We become intimate with these people' and in turn this feeling creates a complicity which, ultimately, leads the audience to question its own ethical position.[35]

Both these productions suggest that staging *The Changeling* in spaces where actors and audiences are close to one another brings a certain aspect of the play – its ability to create a complicit role for the audience which troubles their moral position – to the fore. In other productions, in different spaces, this aspect shifts and/or diminishes, affecting the perceived success of the interpretation. When the Young Vic production moved from the Maria Studio to the Main House audiences found themselves distanced behind a much larger net, no longer as closely surrounding the stage as before. Annegret Maerten felt that the 'the space and the stage in the main house are a bit too wide to allow the viewer proper submersion into the story' and that the netting 'detaches the viewer from the action on the stage'.[36] Maerten speculates that the detachment created by the netting is 'probably the point of the whole thing' and goes on to say (somewhat sarcastically) 'so well done to the design team [. . .] for actually reading Brecht and shoving an alienating device in my face'.

However, other reviewers did not detect a problem in the audience's relationship to the play in the Young Vic Main House. For Billington 'Where the intimacy of the studio made us feel guiltily complicit in the action, we now become more like detached spectators, watching a pageant of sex and death through wire netting'.[37] For Peter Kirwan, Hill-Gibbins's *Changeling* 'was deeply concerned with the question of who, exactly, was being watched', arguing that 'At the heart of this inventive and inverting production, then, stood the key question *Quis custodiet ipsos custodes*? – who watches the watchers, and who is sane enough to pass judgement on others'?[38] Voyeurism, as I have discussed, is an overriding concern of *The Changeling* and it seems that Hill-Gibbins's Main House production – in layout and set – encouraged audiences to became voyeurs, engaging with the play via this ethically-loaded role as uncomfortable witnesses to disturbing events.

Oakley's Southwark Playhouse production most altered the role of the audience with a radical production choice: all asides were delivered as pre-recorded voice-overs, a technique more familiar in cinema than theatre. The programme notes describe the decision as an 'experiment' ('We have decided to take that risk and see'), and Oakley outlined the thinking behind it as follows:

> There are so many asides in it. I remember reading it thinking, wouldn't it be fascinating to do a workshop where the asides are not spoken but just thought and see what it did? [. . .] I did a workshop on the asides a year before [the production] and there was a wonderful moment, when she has asked him to do it [kill Piracquo] and in aside she refers to him as 'dog face' [I shall rid / Myself of two inveterate loathings at one time: / Piracquo and his dog-face' (2.2.144–6)]. What was wonderful was what we could do was have her smiling and yet we heard her say 'his dog face' while smiling at him [. . .] It revealed the duplicity of the aside, and what it was good for was their eyes locking, they did not have to move their head to the audience. It created these moments where they were utterly locked and engaged with each other, so sometimes it paid off brilliantly.

In an interview with *Exeunt Magazine* Oakley reiterates his point, arguing that 'This is a play about duplicity, about people acting one way and being another. That was the reason.'[39] The lack of direct address from actor to audience changed the role of the latter. As Oakley suggests, 'It makes the audience observers, rather than participants, voyeurs, which is sort of what we are aiming for. You should be uncomfortable watching these people [De Flores and Beatrice-Joanna].'

Some reviewers were sympathetic to Oakley's experimentation. Maddy Costa echoed the director's ideas when she writes: 'When it works, in the harrowing central scene in which Beatrice-Joanna entices the disfigured servant De Flores to murder her hapless fiancé [. . .] it allows the actors a physical proximity that addressing the audience might preclude.'[40] Nonetheless, she goes on to point out that when the cinematic asides did not work, 'which unfortunately is most of the time, the tactic distances the characters from the audience, halts the action, diverts our focus'. Other reviewers similarly criticized Oakley on the basis that the aside, especially in *The Changeling*, is a device to create complicity. Alisdair Hinton argued that the asides 'bring the audience into the action, making them in some way complicit in the drama'.[41] Paul Taylor described asides as 'oblique confidences' and that voice-over asides used by Oakley demonstrated 'ill-advised pseudo-cinematic pretensions'.[42] Michael Coveney offered much harsher criticism, calling the voice-over asides 'a bad and silly idea'.[43]

The 'risk' that Oakley took clearly did not pay off. In part there were the technical and sound difficulties one might expect in a small fringe venue (as opposed to more heavily subsidized and professionalized theatres like, for instance, the National Theatre). The voice-overs were sometimes hard for audiences to hear and occasionally mistimed so that they played while actors were speaking, or at the wrong point in the scene. Aside from technical problems, Oakley felt that the technique did not work because pre-recorded asides often mismatched the emotional tempo of the live and changeable individual performances of the actors, which jarred. Leaving aside the practicalities of its execution, the voice-over asides did not work because they denied a fundamental quality of Middleton and Rowley's work. *The Changeling* prescribes, especially through its heavy use of asides, audience immersion, which creates a complex ethical role for the spectator; a role that is central to the rich experience of watching the play. Certainly, as well as confidants, the audience can be voyeurs, submerged in the world of the castle and madhouse as uncomfortable witnesses; a role foregrounded in Hill-Gibbins's Main House Young Vic interpretation. Some form of submersion and connection is, I suggest, key to the performance of *The Changeling*. At the Southwark Playhouse, the choice to cut the asides and thereby diminish direct engagement between actor and audience was a distancing effect too far. Yet I respect Oakley's creative courage in taking a 'risk' derived from an intelligent and by no means outlandish reading of the play: duplicity is at the heart of many of the asides; so why not experiment with a technique that encourages characters to remain 'locked and engaged' with one another during moments of high drama? I want to suggest therefore, when I return to the question at the end of this chapter, that some of the very harsh language used about Oakley's production choices ('bad and silly', Coveney; 'ill -advised . . . pretensions', Taylor) again exemplifies *The Changeling*'s status in the non-Shakespearean canon and a policing of that status.

## 'Loved and loathed': Staging sex and violence

Middleton and Rowley embody their exploration of sex, violence and madness in the objects and physical actions prescribed in dialogue and stage directions. De Flores's moral depravity is expressed in his disfigured face; Beatrice-Joanna's feelings for the servant are represented (arguably) in her dropping her gloves; De Flores produces a macabre love token for Beatrice-Joanna in the form of Alonzo's severed ring finger; Alsemero's implicit patriarchal misogyny is reflected in the virginity test. The play contains an onstage murder, an offstage rape, a burnt corpse brought onstage, and an onstage murder-suicide. How do modern theatre practitioners make sense of this carnival of blood, viciousness and sensuality?

All of these productions used make-up to create various levels of disfigurement on De Flores's face. At the Southwark Playhouse David Caves's De Flores had large red swollen carbuncles on his cheeks; in Cheek by Jowl's production Will Keen had weeping lesions all over his face. Theatre-makers involved in both performances drew attention to the importance of ugliness in the play, especially for a modern audience surrounded by body-beautiful images in contemporary culture. Michael Oakley noted that 'the sexual politics' of the play are fascinating 'with her being beautiful and him not ... that's something you never see, we are so image conscious now as a world'. Likewise Olivia Williams (Beatrice-Joanna, Cheek by Jowl) reflected that part of the appeal for modern spectators was the 'sexualisation of ugliness'.[44] She also goes on to state that De Flores does not rape Beatrice-Joanna; she discovers an unconscious desire for him and finds him 'massively attractive'.[45]

Williams articulates what Roberta Barker and David Nicol have identified as a well-established interpretation of the text, traceable through theatre reviews and some critical work across the twentieth century: 'critics have developed a reading of Beatrice-Joanna as a spoilt child whose amoral decision to murder her detested fiancé is only a precursor to her slow realization of her repressed, subtextual desire for De Flores'.[46] Their seminal article demonstrates, though, that this interpretation is both deeply anachronistic – it is based on the premise that Middleton offers us proto-Freudian ideas – and sexist, misreading the sexual violence and exploitation in Beatrice-Joanna and De Flores's relationship. Alongside Williams's reading of her character, we can see that this particular interpretation of the play has continued into the twenty-first century. For all four productions it is possible to find reviewers who articulate Beatrice's subconscious desire for her servant. 'The heroine is a frenzied neurotic insanely attracted to the loathed De Flores', Billington wrote in his Cheek by Jowl review.[47] 'The repulsive has its perverse, magnetic attractions. We can lust for what we loathe', Paul Taylor comments in his opening to a review of the Southwark Playhouse production.[48] Peter Brown noted that although the Young Vic's Beatrice-Joanna 'hates De Flores, she is also magnetically attracted to him'.[49] And Quentin Letts's response to the rape scene at the SWP is especially disconcerting in its attitude to sexual violence: 'Should there not be something more? Should there not be a feral awakening of her sexuality and selfishness?'[50]

Nevertheless this reading of Beatrice-Joanna is losing some of its purchase. Hill-Gibbins describes Beatrice-Joanna's narrative in a very different way, noting that *The Changeling* is 'centred on a woman battling to assert the way she wants to live romantically, to establish a relationship with a particular man'.[51] Rather than sexual desire, at the centre of Beatrice-Joanna's narrative, for Hill-Gibbins, is power and assertion. This reading is more in tune with the progressive one offered by Barker and Nichol in their challenge to traditional and sexist interpretations of the play. Some critics were able to pick up on this different narrative for Beatrice-Joanna, Kirwan noting the 'rigid distaste with which she endured [De Flores's] attentions' and the 'power dynamic [of Beatrice-Joanna and De Flores's relationship] that was repeatedly returned to'.[52] Critics also found a different reading of Beatrice-Joanna and De Flores in Dromgoole's 2015 production. Matt Trueman identified 'a fierce feminism at work in Dominic Dromgoole's production: a gritted outrage at men that push themselves – through force or duplicity, successfully or not – on women'.[53] Certainly interactions between Lollio and Isabella, and Beatrice-Joanna and De Flores, were marked by a noticeable physical aggression – these male characters pushed, grabbed, eyeballed and invaded personal space, literalizing the play's sense of patriarchal dominance. Furthermore, Holly Williams argued that at the SWP 'feminist anxieties surrounding Beatrice-Joanna and De Flores's relationship – that she expresses some kind of love, after being, in effect, raped by him – are left open, without any slanted, modern interpretation'.[54] The openness Williams detects, I think, was largely a product of Morahan's performance in which her response to De Flores remained one of shocked bewilderment, with little indication of growing affection.

One challenge all productions have to face is the nature of physical contact between its central protagonists. At the Southwark Playhouse De Flores and Beatrice-Joanna's exchanges in 3.3 were deeply aggressive and violent, De Flores using the furniture of his underground bunker office to trap and then violate her. Trying to escape his advances, Beatrice-Joanna threw an office chair at him; territorially he proceeded to grab her and restrain her in this chair before pushing her against the filing cabinets to rape her. The act of sexual violence here was perhaps more shocking because of the prosaic and mundane objects (chair, filing cabinet) used as weapons. Cheek by Jowl's production similarly did not shy away from the violence of the play. Peter J. Smith gives an account of the final scene:

> As the company looked on, we saw Joanna's naked buttocks slamming against the glass door as De Flores brutally penetrated her. The door opened and she, in diaphanous white night gown, staggered downstage, a huge red blood stain across her belly. As she lay dying, De Flores brandished his knife and thrust it down his open trousers. With a gut-churning cry, he severed his penis and crumpled over to die next to Joanna.[55]

In spite of Williams's traditional interpretation of Beatrice-Joanna's feelings for De Flores, the sexual violence of the Cheek by Jowl ending suggested dominance, power and patriarchal aggression, not subconscious desire and affection, as a way of reading the central narrative. Beatrice-Joanna and De Flores's final interaction was one of sexual violence and the servant's self-castration a metaphor for the dominance of what Barker and Nicol have termed the 'patriarchal ideology' in Middleton and Rowley's text.[56]

Six years after this visceral and naturalistic representation, Hill-Gibbins's made a very different artistic choice. In an interview with *Exeunt Magazine,* Natasha Tripney outlines the director's reflections on the play's sex and violence:

> The question [. . .] is how you present a play which is so 'full of sexuality rolling out of control'. He wanted to find a way of 'expressing this mess'. But because the play is also full of innuendo [. . .] 'there was something about making the sex completely explicit that didn't sit right either'. He digresses: 'sex on stage, just like violence on stage, is very hard to do. The accepted conventions often take you out of the moment

and in trying to be realistic it can become really phoney'. He wanted instead to find a theatrical way of conveying the play's sex-soaked quality without 'being crassly illustrative, without making a piece of "shit theatre"'.[57]

Moving away from realistic conventions, the director literalized the play's imagery of food, sensuality and lust: a rich wedding feast of punch, custard and trifle was deployed for acts of sex and violence and gradually splattered all over the white flooring of the Maria Studio. De Flores murdered Alonso by drowning him in punch; Diaphanta and Alsemero's 'wedding night' saw both actors cover themselves in symbolic blood-red jelly; and the play culminated in characters throwing jam and jelly at De Flores and Beatrice-Joanna. As Laura Estill pointed out, 'the onstage food and drink [...] were material manifestations of the unclean and immoral acts in the play'.[58] Moreover the anarchic mess foregrounded the chaos and subversion within the play: as Tripney noted, Hill-Gibbins's production was 'messy and excessive in a way that is only fitting'.[59] Yet it is also apparent that this very representational form of conveying the play's sexual violence can obscure and diminish its frightening power. One reviewer suggested the production 'sometimes borders on pantomime and farce'; another summed it up as 'brilliantly bonkers, goo-spattered'.[60] Of course there is much humour in *The Changeling*, and Hill-Gibbins's use of food is rooted in the linguistic and imaginative language of the text. Nonetheless there is a danger that 'bonkers' and 'pantomime' portrayals of misogynistic violence, rather than anarchic, are conservative in that they gloss over disturbing and unsettling content with levity and humour.

## Canon-formation: Conclusion

In their collection of essays on the non-Shakespearean canon, Pascale Aebischer and Kathryn Prince note the 'cultural function' of this canon as a 'counterpoint' to an 'implicitly conservative, institutionalised Shakespearean canon'; but, they wonder, 'Are some of these plays gradually being absorbed by the conservative canon to which they were once the alternative'?[61] The productions I have examined in this chapter provide a somewhat ambiguous response to this question. I have highlighted occasions where the growing status of this non-Shakespearean play has resulted in a sense of critics seeking to punish creative risk-taking and possibilities, and to police its 'real' themes, dramaturgy and characterization. Yet despite this potential creeping conservatism, *The Changeling* has been a site for exciting and at times risk-taking work: cinematic asides, thinking about mental health, foregrounding psychological enclosure, dynamic interactions between actor and audience, and feminist readings of sexual violence. It seems more than likely that the richness and complexity of Middleton and Rowley's play will continue to maintain its place in twenty-first-century theatre-making.

# 7

# New Directions: Loving and Loathing: Horror in *The Changeling* from Text to Screen

## *Nathalie Vienne-Guerrin*

'There's horror in my service, blood and danger' (2.2.119), says Beatrice-Joanna, when she asks De Flores to rid her of Alonzo de Piracquo so that she can escape a forced marriage. Once he has agreed to kill Piracquo, De Flores – previously called 'the basilisk' (1.1.110), 'this serpent' (1.1.218), 'Thou standing toad-pool' (2.1.58), 'thou thing most loathed' (2.1.72) – becomes agreeable to Beatrice-Joanna, who exclaims: 'How lovely now / Dost thou appear to me!' (2.2.135–6). Beatrice-Joanna's change of perspective in this scene is emblematic of the mixture of fascination and repulsion that characterizes *The Changeling*, a mixture that Alsemero theorizes in the play when he comments on Beatrice-Joanna's horror of De Flores with the aphoristic phrase: 'There's scarce a thing but is both loved and loathed' (1.1.120).[1] Her double name expresses this very reversibility – what she calls 'a giddy turning in [her]' (1.1.149) – and inscribes it in the character and at the heart of the play. The numerous occurrences of the word 'fear' and the omnipresence of loathing suggest that *The Changeling* feeds disgust both within the play and in the viewers and conjures up what Julia Kristeva has termed 'abjection'. De Flores can be seen as an abject object who contaminates the world around him, especially Beatrice-Joanna, who, in her turn, may contaminate the world around her, as is suggested at the end of the play when she warns her father: 'O come not near me, sir, I shall defile you' (5.3.149).

The purpose of this chapter is to study the anatomy of horror that the play delineates and to see how the horrid abjection that can be found in the text is translated on screen in the 1998 film, directed by Marcus Thompson, a version that Courtney Lehmann describes as a 'horror film'[2] and that has inspired both attraction and distaste among critics.[3] I explore the combination of fascination and repulsion that is created by the play and analyse how it is conveyed by Thompson's film. This chapter examines the way horror is created in this film and what it may tell us about the play itself. Taking into account other scholars' work on the play on screen – especially Pascale Aebischer's work on Jacobean plays on screen and Lehmann's study of *The Changeling* on film – this essay focuses on the uncomfortable viewing that the film entails, which is in keeping with the way the play cultivates a sophisticated balance of showing and not showing, leaving to directors the choice to show or not to show the horrors in the plot.

## *The Changeling* or the anatomy of abjection

There looms, within abjection, one of those violent, dark revolts of being, directed against a threat that seems to emanate from an exorbitant outside or inside, ejected beyond the scope of the possible, the tolerable, the thinkable. It lies there, quite close, but it cannot be assimilated.

It beseeches, worries, and fascinates desire, which, nevertheless, does not let itself be seduced. [. . .] Unflaggingly, like an inescapable boomerang, a vortex of summons and repulsion places the one haunted by it literally beside himself.[4]

This is how Julia Kristeva approaches abjection in the opening lines of her *Powers of Horror. An Essay on Abjection*. In her book on abjection and representation, Rina Arya reformulates Kristeva's thesis by pointing out that 'we are both repelled by the abject (because of fear) and yet attracted to it (through our desire)' and that 'the ambivalent nature of abjection means that we find it difficult to tear ourselves away from the experience'.[5]

One can find an anatomy of abjection in *The Changeling*, in many respects. Etymologically related to the act of rejecting or dejecting (*ab-jacere*, to throw off, away from), the term may first describe the horror that De Flores inspires in Beatrice-Joanna, which she expresses early in the play, ejecting the character 'beyond the scope of the possible, the tolerable, the thinkable'. Her first words to him amount to ejecting him by way of interruption (1.1.88) but at the same time the word 'welcome' she utters, be it ironically to say that De Flores is *not* welcome ('And how welcome for your part you are, / I'm sure you know' (1.1.94–5)), opens onto the ambivalent aspect that their relationship will have later on and anticipates the 'boomerang' effect that the play orchestrates. De Flores formulates the repulsion Beatrice-Joanna feels for him in terms that express the same kind of ambivalence in an aside: 'I know she had / Rather see me dead than living, and yet / She knows no cause for't but a peevish will' (1.1.101–2). The loathing being 'peevish', it may well change into its reverse. Beatrice-Joanna embodies this reversibility. The doubleness of her name may conjure both a figure of chastity and an embodiment of lust, 'part-virgin and part-whore'.[6] She formulates this reversibility herself when she explains to Alsemero why she 'seemed displeasèd, [. . .] on the sudden':

> Your pardon, sir, 'tis my infirmity;
> Nor can I other reason render you
> Than his or hers of some particular thing
> They must abandon as a deadly poison,
> Which to a thousand other tastes were wholesome:
> Such to mine eyes is that same fellow there,
> The same that report speaks of the Basilisk.
>
> (1.1.103–10)

For Beatrice-Joanna, De Flores is a poison, while, she says, he could be 'wholesome' to another woman's taste. What is striking is that Beatrice-Joanna presents her sense of the abject as exceptional, compared to the 'thousand other tastes'. The very formulation suggests that the abject is both within and without herself, part of herself and outside herself. The metaphor of poison indicates that De Flores is the thing that makes her sick, the thing she has to 'throw out' (*ab-jacere*). Alsemero declines the phenomenon of abjection through other metaphors and by mentioning both smell and taste:

> This is a frequent frailty in our nature;
> There's scarce a man amongst a thousand sound,
> But hath his imperfection: one distastes
> The scent of roses, which to infinites
> Most pleasing is, and odoriferous;
> One oil, the enemy of poison;
> Another wine, the cheerer of the heart
> And lively refresher of the countenance.
> Indeed this fault – if so it be – is general:
> There's scarce a thing but is both loved and loathed;
> Myself, I must confess, have the same frailty.
>
> BEATRICE-JOANNA
> And what may be your poison, sir? I'm bold with you.
> ALSEMERO
> What might be your desire perhaps – a cherry.
> BEATRICE-JOANNA
> I am no enemy to any creature

My memory has, but yon gentleman.
ALSEMERO
He does ill to tempt your sight, if he knew it.
BEATRICE-JOANNA
He cannot be ignorant of that, sir:
I have not spared to tell him so; and I want
To help my self, since he's a gentleman
In good respect with my father, and follows him.
ALSEMERO
He's out of his place then, now.

(1.1.111–31)

The dialogue expresses the ambivalence that is emblematic of abjection: although he is poison to her, the 'gentleman', De Flores, is the only creature in Beatrice-Joanna's memory ('My memory has but yon gentleman'), he 'tempts' her sight even if he is 'out of his place'. The scent of roses mentioned by Alsemero ironically refers to the name 'De Flores'. Abjection is here defined as a fault, a frailty that no one can escape, that is both personal and general, that one 'cannot help' having. Considering this ambivalence, the formulation 'and I want / To help my self, since he's a gentleman' may contain some ironic bawdy innuendo, all the more so since the scene parallels a sequence of bawdy bantering between Jasperino and Diaphanta. The dialogue in which Alsemero and Beatrice-Joanna describe their feeling of abjection as 'an infirmity' or a 'frailty' expresses a mixture of fascination and repulsion, obsession and rejection. Beatrice-Joanna's 'I shall change my saint, I fear me' (1.1.148) refers to her change in affection, which will also be a change in abjection and ironically suggests that she will become the object of her own fears ('I fear me').

In *Sex and Terror*, Pascal Quignard meditates on the Roman word *fascinatio*:

What the Greeks called *phallos* was called *fascinus* in Latin. The songs surrounding it are termed 'fescennine'. The *fascinus* arrests the gaze, to the point that it cannot detach itself from it. . . . Fascination is the perception of the dead angle of language. And that is why the fascinated gaze is always a sideways one.[7]

In *The Changeling*, De Flores obviously cannot detach his gaze from Beatrice-Joanna: 'I'll please my self with sight / Of her, at all opportunities' (1.1.98–9); 'I can as well be hanged as refrain seeing her' (2.1.28). After the episode of the glove, he formulates his sexual fantasy in terms of 'thrust[ing his] fingers / Into her sockets here' (1.1.226–7), an image[8] that will find an ironic, horrible echo when he cuts off Alonzo's finger, in a sequence of symbolic castration.[9] 'I'll haunt her still' (1.1.229), he decides, which implies that Beatrice-Joanna paradoxically cannot detach her gaze from De Flores either, even if he is a source of repulsion. De Flores, in an aside, describes the repulsive effect he has on Beatrice-Joanna:

> Some twenty times a day – nay not so little –
> Do I force errands, frame ways and excuses
> To come into her sight; and I have small reason for't,
> And less encouragement, for she baits me still
> Every time worse than other, does profess herself
> The cruellest enemy to my face in town,
> At no hand can abide the sight of me,
> As if danger, or ill luck hung in my looks.
> I must confess my face is bad enough,
> But I know far worse has better fortune –
> And not endured alone, but doted on
>
> (2.1.29–39)

Beatrice-Joanna confirms the effect this has on her in a soliloquy, once De Flores has exited the stage:

> I never see this fellow, but I think
> Of some harm towards me, danger's in my mind still,
> I scarce leave trembling of an hour after.

The next good mood I find my father in,
I'll get him quite discarded.

(2.1.89–93)

This description of the effect of abjection De Flores has on Beatrice-Joanna is to be related to the image of the basilisk[10] with which Beatrice-Joanna associates him, which is evocative of a mixture of fascination and repulsion, a mixture Beatrice-Joanna herself formulates when she says to herself (and to us): 'This ominous, ill-faced fellow more disturbs me / Than all my other passions' (2.1.53–4). John Bullokar, in *An English Expositor*, describes the basilisk as follows:

> Basiliske. Otherwise called a Cockatrice: the most venemous serpent that is. It breaketh stones and blasteth all plants with the breath thereof, burning euery thing that it goeth ouer; neither can any herbe growe neere the place where it lyeth. It is poyson to poyson, and driueth away all other serpents, with only hissing. If a man touch it but with a sticke, it will kill him, and if it see a man a farre off, it destroyeth him with his lookes.

The basilisk is a source of terror and at the same time it can be seen as a phallic image. The 'trembling' (2.1.91) that Beatrice-Joanna refers to may be considered in an ambivalent way, as a mixture of fear and pleasure.

In *The Changeling*, sex is definitely 'linked to terror'.[11] Beatrice-Joanna feels horror at the sight of De Flores, but also terror at the prospect of losing her 'dear companion', virginity (1.1.186–7) to Alonzo, which she describes as a form of violence imposed upon her by her father. '[B]e not so violent' (1.1.184), she tells him, when he announces that Alonzo is 'hot preparing for his day of triumph' (1.1.182). Then, when her father tells her to prepare for her wedding with Alonzo, the words he uses foreshadow the rape carried out by De Flores:[12] 'The day will steal upon thee suddenly' (2.1.103). This formulation ('steal upon thee') already points to the ravishment, the abduction she will have to suffer, and it is evocative of rape as property crime, as analysed by Frances E. Dolan.[13] 'I will be sure to keep the night' (2.1.104), she says in an aside, showing that the idea of this union with Alonzo is so odious and terrifying to her that she will avoid that day by all means. Alsemero offers to remove, to 'strike off', her 'fears' (2.2.22), by challenging Alonzo, which she refuses, exclaiming: 'Call you that extinguishing of fear / When 'tis the only way to keep it flaming?' (2.2.29–30). She prefers to use one 'poison' (De Flores) to 'expel another' (Alonzo) (2.2.46–7). The parallel between the two sources of abjection appears when Beatrice-Joanna tells her thoughts to De Flores, wishing 'creation' had 'formed [her] a man' (2.2.107–8), in a scene that is reminiscent of Beatrice's exclamation in *Much Ado About Nothing*, 'O God that I were a man' (4.1.304ff).[14] If I were a man, she says, 'I should have power / Then to oppose my loathings – nay, remove 'em' (2.2.111–12). A few lines later, she makes clear that De Flores and Alonzo are the same to her, in an aside: 'I shall rid / Myself of two inveterate loathings at one time: / Piracquo and his dog-face' (2.2.144–6). The text cultivates intimations of the violence the character is about to undergo, especially when De Flores exclaims that the mere thought of his reward 'ravishes' (2.2.132), a term that combines images of pleasure and violence. The play prepares the spectator for the absent-present act of rape that occurs at the end of Act 3 but that is not performed on stage (which a modern production can choose to represent or not). The explicit marker of the 'act' is Beatrice-Joanna's line at the beginning of Act 4: 'This fellow has undone me endlessly' (4.1.1). After the terror of losing her virginity, the play dramatizes the terror at the thought that Beatrice-Joanna's defloration may be discovered 'upon th'ensuing night' (4.1.3), so that her 'joys' become her 'fears' (4.1.67). The play obsessively refers to Beatrice-Joanna's fears, until she exclaims, 'Hark, by my horrors, / Another clock strikes two!' (5.1.10–11) and then, 'List! O my terrors, / Three struck by Saint Sebastian's!' (5.1.67–8), which creates a thriller-like suspense that is enhanced by the appearance of Alonzo's ghost:

'Some ill thing haunts the house, 't has left behind it / A shivering sweat upon me' (4.1.63–4). In this nightmarish atmosphere, terror and horror – which contemporary critics tend to differentiate – overlap, and loving and loathing become one and the same thing: 'His face loathes one, / But look upon his care, who would not love him?' (5.1.70–1).

Horror is finally displayed at the end of the play at the moment of *anagnorisis* when Alsemero understands the deeds that have been committed. Ironically, Beatrice-Joanna lays the burden of horror on his shoulders:

ALSEMERO
    [. . .] You are a whore.
BEATRICE-JOANNA
    What a horrid sound it hath!
    It blasts a beauty to deformity;
    Upon what face soever that breath falls,
    It strikes it ugly. O you have ruined
    What you can ne'er repair again!

(5.3.32–6)

This passage reveals the power of words over deeds. It is the name 'whore' that transforms Beatrice-Joanna into a whore, not her deeds, which she sees as deeds of love. Alsemero's words express his puzzlement:

    How comes this tender reconcilement else
    'Twixt you and your despite, your rancorous loathing,
    De Flores? He that your eye was sore at sight of,
    He's now become your arms' supporter, your
    Lips' saint.

(5.3.50–4)

When he ponders the fate of Diaphanta, Beatrice-Joanna wants him to 'hear a story of not much less horror' (5.3.61) when she admits to having become a murderess, again putting the burden of guilt on him: 'your love has made me / A cruel murd'ress' (5.3.65–6). She denies her adultery, thus distinguishing between the end and the means and suggesting that there is a difference between being unfaithful and being raped. When Alsemero exclaims 'O, thou art all deformed!' (5.3.78), she becomes an abjection to him, which he decides to put into a closet, together with De Flores. Alsemero himself creates a hellish sequence when he imagines what happens off-stage, in that closet, between the two 'cunning devils' (5.3.109):

> I'll be your pander now: rehearse again
> Your scene of lust, that you may be perfect
> When you shall come to act it to the black audience
> Where howls and gnashings shall be music to you.
> Clip your adult'ress freely – 'tis the pilot
> Will guide you to the Mare mortuum,
> Where you shall sink to fathoms bottomless.
>
> (5.3.115–21)

What happens in the closet is described in theatrical terms, which puts at a distance the horror that the scene can inspire without erasing it. The play uses sound effects to create the horror, as appears when Vermandero comments on his daughter's exclamations 'Oh, Oh, Oh!' and 'Oh, oh!' (5.3.140, 141), asking 'What horrid sounds are these?' (5.3.142). As Deborah Burks and others note, these sounds are 'ambiguous sounds, perhaps of passion, perhaps of agony'.[15] Sex and terror are tightly connected in this play, even in the secondary plot that takes place at Alibius's madhouse which reveals a husband's comic terror at the thought of being cuckolded and Isabella's being subjected to pressing sexual advances.

One can measure the play's world of abjection by counting the number of speeches delivered as asides by the characters, especially by De Flores and Beatrice-Joanna.[16] The 1974 BBC version starring Helen Mirren as Beatrice-Joanna[17] and Brian Cox as Alsemero, for example, usefully renders the omnipresence of these asides through the recurrent use of sequences in voice-over, which reveals to the spectators thoughts that are too vile and horrible to be shared with the other characters. (For a later use of the voice-over technique, see Sarah Dustagheer's essay in this volume.) It would appear that abjection is to be kept to oneself before being eventually displayed to the world.

The Jacobean theatre chooses to show this abjection through words, leaving many scenes unseen, whether it be Beatrice-Joanna's rape, the bed-trick or the closet scene, three episodes that are literally 'ob-scene', that is 'off-stage'. But the 1998 film shows these 'unscenes' (to use Marjorie Garber's expression),[18] visually and aurally creating in the spectators a mixture of fascination and repulsion.

## Marcus Thompson's horror film

In her 2009 book, *Horror*, Brigid Cherry focuses on 'Horror genre's sheer diversity'. According to her, the horror genre has

> endured for so long, from the earliest years of cinema to the present day, and derives from so many different sources that it has fragmented into an extremely diverse set of sub-genres. [...] The genre has evolved and developed many branches and offshoots. [...] What one person considers to be the defining features of a horror film may be in total disagreement with another's classification.[19]

The reception of horror films, she adds, can vary a lot from one person to another: 'In terms of the modes of emotional affect of horror cinema, what is actually horrifying, scary or terrifying can be extremely personal and what will scare one person may leave another indifferent.'[20] When it comes to horror, it seems that reception is even more a key matter than with any other type of film. Beyond these possible differences in appreciation of horror, Peter Hutchings has shown, in an article entitled 'Theatres of Blood. Shakespeare and the horror film',[21] that there is 'interaction between Shakespeare and horror films',[22] noting that

> in their own ways, Roman Polanski's *Macbeth* (1971), Kenneth Branagh's *Hamlet* (1996) and Julie Taymor's *Titus* (1999) align themselves (or can be aligned with) [*sic*] the horror genre. [...] Horror cinema since the 1930s has appropriated particular themes and ideas, to the extent that any pre-existing works containing these themes can be, and sometimes are, retrospectively classified as part of the horror genre.[23]

There is indeed a dialogue and possible interchange between Elizabethan and especially Jacobean plays and horror movies, and the case of *The Changeling* illustrates this filiation. In the *Critical Dictionary of Film and Television Theory*, Moya Luckett defines 'horror' as follows:

> Horror's association with perverse desire, abjection and the body have made it central to film studies. A long-established but controversial genre, horror has generally been critically maligned. Most classical horrors were B-features, while many of their 1980s high-budget counterparts were dismissed as low brow, appealing to mostly youthful audiences. Rather than blaming horror for individual disturbances, its critics see its excesses as symptomatic of repressed social desires.[24]

Desire, abjection and the body are at the centre of *The Changeling*, so perhaps it is not surprising that the play's screen adaptation should be influenced by the horror genre.

In her article on hospitality in *The Changeling* on film, Courtney Lehmann studies three film versions of the play that were part of what she defines elsewhere as 'the unprecedented burst of Middleton films that appeared in the late 1990s and early twenty-first century':[25] Thompson's *Middleton's Changeling*; Jay Stern's 2007 low-budget version; and Sarah

Harding's TV adaptation, *Compulsion* (2008–9). She describes Thompson's film as a 'horror film' that in the end verges on 'hard-core porn',[26] which is in keeping with the fact that the film was considered suitable only for persons of eighteen years and over. Contrasting Thompson's film with Stern's adaptation, which 'gives Beatrice-Joanna the freedom to choose Deflores rather than being victimized by him'[27] and with *Compulsion*, which 'offers a complex vision of female agency in twenty-first-century society',[28] Lehmann emphasizes the ambivalence of a film in which loathing and loving seem to progressively merge through visual and sound effects. The more recent adaptation *Compulsion* reveals, according to Pascale Aebischer, how the violent Jacobean tragedy can be integrated into mainstream culture.[29] Sarah Harding's analysis of her own film,[30] whose working title was *Undone*, both in reference to Beatrice-Joanna's statement after her 'rape' and to Lady Macbeth's nightmarish 'What's done cannot be undone' (*Macbeth*, 5.1.67–8),[31] reveals how her film 'had to work for a primetime ITV audience who had probably never heard of Middleton or Rowley'.[32] For Harding, Don Flowers (*Compulsion*'s version of De Flores, played by Ray Winstone), who is a chauffeur in the film, 'is at home with criminal activities' but also 'represents an almost courtly ideal of service'[33] up to the very end of the film when he nobly sacrifices himself. In this *Godfather*-like mafia context, the relationships between Anjika (*Compulsion*'s version of Beatrice-Joanna, played by Parminder Nagra) and Flowers are not repulsive and the monstrous De Flores obviously becomes lovable as 'she is expecting rape but receives love'.[34] The target audience clearly had an influence on the way the adaptation was designed. The director especially wanted to avoid the 'seedy dirty-old-man's film'[35] trap and carefully ensured the 'rape' scene was watchable by a wide spectrum of viewers. Sarah Harding tried to preserve the contradictions that, she thinks, are inherent in the play, which did not prevent some critics from finding the film disgusting, showing that there are degrees in acceptability and in what one may consider as abject or not.

In contrast to *Compulsion*, Thompson's film fills in the gaps left open by the text by explicitly and spectacularly representing abjection in various ways. The film displays features of the horror film and of several sub-genres, notably the monster scare, the psychological thriller and the splatter film, a mixture which leads Aebischer to write that '[t]his is the tragedy of a director who could not make up his mind',[36] and McMullan to note that the film 'deploys consciously postmodern spectacle, wilfully blending genres and periods'.[37]

De Flores (Ian Dury) is a monster in the film. In the play, he confesses that his face is 'bad enough' but that he knows 'far worse' faces (2.1.37–8) that have been successful in love. Thompson enhances the repulsiveness of the character by this casting decision, seeming to recycle the motif of beauty and the beast and playing on the codes of the monster scare. Dury, lead singer of punk band The Blockheads, contracted polio at the age of seven in the 1949 epidemic, the disease having left him with 'impaired movement in his left arm and right leg, prompting the need for his trademark walking stick.'[38] In this film, the deformity of the character is conveyed through images of physical disability, which are emphasized by shots of De Flores's figure that are distorted by its reflection in the water of a 'toad-pool'. The numerous close-up shots on De Flores's conspicuously 'scurvy', repulsive face, pickled with warts and scales that are evocative of the toad he is associated with in the play, the metal-tipped fingers that Thompson chooses to show him with at several crucial moments in the film, and the disabled body which follows Beatrice-Joanna (Amanda Ray-King) everywhere, albeit with difficulty – all these elements constitute De Flores as a monstrous figure reminiscent of Richard III. De Flores haltingly chases Beatrice-Joanna from place to place, down stairs at the beginning, in a labyrinthine garden later on, up to the final chase which will show him, in a western-like fashion, jumping down onto the top of a horse-drawn carriage to finally assault Beatrice-Joanna in a gory revision of the closet scene. As Lehmann notes, in Thompson's film, 'De Flores *is* everywhere',[39] which translates De Flores's aside: 'Some twenty times a day – nay not so little – / Do I force errands, frame ways and excuses / To come into her sight' (2.1.29–31). He keeps haunting the film, watching everything and often being in the position of the voyeur. The first sequence that focuses on him is evocative of this scopophilia: it does not reveal his ugliness yet, but it shows him from afar, alone in a kind of arena or stadium, as if he were preparing for and looking forward to the horrible show that is to come. One can see and hear him beating rhythm on a metal railing with his metal-tipped fingers to the sound of some operatic music. Beyond this meta-dramatic effect, the scene is probably a wink at the singer-actor behind the character,[40] but it also introduces the finger as a key element of abjection in the bloody and sexual imagery of the play and film and in the psychological thriller that ensues. The film indeed later cultivates this initial focus on fingers: it shows the glove episode (1.1.218–27) and we hear De Flores's fingers play on his private 'instrument' during a masturbation scene which demonstrates how much he enjoys Beatrice-Joanna's touching his face ('Her fingers touched me –', 2.2.81) and calling him 'my De Flores!' (2.2.98). The film explicitly translates what De Flores lives as 'half an act of pleasure / To hear her talk thus to [him]' (2.2.86–7). Having established the fingers as organs of pleasure, through these scenes and in the madhouse where Lollio (Campbell Morrison) repeatedly plays with them with bawdy suggestiveness, the horror of Alonzo's murder cannot but take on a sexual meaning when De Flores is shown cutting off his finger, symbolically castrating his rival post-mortem to retrieve Beatrice-Joanna's precious ring. The film makes it very clear that killing Alonzo amounts to dismembering him, and to replacing his finger with De Flores's metal digits. The substitution is made obvious when Thompson introduces flashback images of Alonzo's murder within the scene where De Flores demands his reward. Alonzo's amputated finger falls to the floor; De Flores's rises, to 'silence' (3.3.167) Beatrice. By interweaving a flashback of Alonzo's mutilation with the scene in which De Flores appears as a triumphant 'viper' (3.3.165), the film symbolically connects the two episodes. The murder of Alonzo is tightly linked visually with the rape of Beatrice-Joanna, as is shown by Courtney Lehmann who notes that Thompson 'employs a tableau from the horror-film genre, pairing De Flores's brutal sexual thrusts with flashbacks to a shadow profile of his knife as it stabs Piraquo [sic]'.[41] One act of violence haunts the other, creating a parallel between the two. Thompson even adds to this multi-layered design by inserting images in black and white which show Beatrice-Joanna in the middle of what looks like a civil war – whether a flashback, or a flash forward, is unclear. The traumatic effect of the play's bloody acts is translated by Thompson by the frequent use of flashbacks that reveal this devastating effect and by interpolated love sequences that seem to be a shield to the violence endured by Beatrice-Joanna.

In her re-reading of rape in *The Changeling*, Frances E. Dolan argues that the play 'depicts coercion and consent in socially and morally complex ways that describing it as a "rape-play" flattens'.[42] According to Pascale Aebischer, however, '[i]f there is one consistent interpretation of the play in this film, it is the unequivocal representation it offers of the sexual relationship of Beatrice-Joanna and De Flores as a rape'.[43] Yet, if it is the case that Thompson erases all of Beatrice-Joanna's lines that refer to her gradually loving De Flores, it can be argued that the haunting images and sounds he introduces in the film put pleasure in the picture, the film blending lust and violence.

The first rape scene, which is a major source of horror, is represented as a reduplication of Alonzo's murder: in the two cases, De Flores appears to be leading the characters to the scaffold to open the same hellish trap for them. The two scenes take place in the same gloomy Gothic-like tower. In each case the almost subliminal figure of a black panther seems to testify to the predatory nature of the act. The murder first and then the rape take place on the same trunk, a macabre symbol of secrecy into which De Flores has put Alonzo's bleeding corpse. When, during the rape scene, one can see blood oozing out from the coffer, the blood of murder and the blood of rape become one and the same, which announces the final sequence that will combine the two deeds.

In a second rape sequence, which, through its fragmented aesthetics, suggests that the act has become recurrent and that Beatrice-Joanna is leading two parallel lives (one with Alsemero [Colm O'Maonlai], the other with De Flores), Thompson again plays on several layers of images. We see De Flores chasing Beatrice into a bed and violently assaulting her. But the director chooses to combine these images of sexual violence with shots of tender chaste love scenes between Alsemero and Beatrice-Joanna. This has a double effect: it suggests that to make the rape bearable, Beatrice-Joanna mentally moves into another dimension, but it also seems to suggest that now Alsemero and De Flores merge so that one can no longer distinguish between torture and pleasure. The ambivalence is most disturbing for viewers and critics, as is shown by Stevie Simkin, who, in his *Early Modern Tragedy and the Cinema of Violence*, examines the articulation of sex and violence both in *The Changeling* and in the controversial film *Straw Dogs* (1971, dir. Sam Peckinpah). For Lehmann, 'Thompson's approach to rape from the viewpoint of "blaming the victim"' suggests Beatrice-Joanna is her 'own femme fatale'.[44] However, Aebischer notes that '[t]he objectification of the female upper-class body [...] is central to Thompson's vision'.[45] The play and the film's numerous suggestions that loathing turns into loving generates considerable discomfort and unease in the audience. During the wedding scene, flashes of the rape appear in the middle of what should be a festive dance, showing that the trauma of rape is here. But the groans of pleasure that accompany these flashbacks suggest that the affair with De Flores has become enjoyable. While Beatrice-Joanna is dancing with Alsemero, De Flores is shown greedily devouring a white carnation, which clearly demonstrates that he has already enjoyed what Alsemero has not. The wedding sequence also includes shots of Vermandero (Richard Mayes) throwing a look of concern and disapproval, which suggest that he knows everything and that his daughter has already become an abject figure for him. The flashbacks thus both maintain and question the horror of the rape in the spectators' minds and feed discomfort in the audience by combining horror and pleasure.

The same ambivalence appears in the rather unexpected and excessive final rape and murder scene which turns the film into a sort of splatter movie that shows the gory slaughter of Beatrice-Joanna in 'an erotic frenzy that leaves her panting and covered in blood from head to toe'.[46] The scene makes visible what remains unseen in the play, the sequence within the closet between Beatrice-Joanna and De Flores, which Middleton and Rowley and Alsemero leave to our imagination, although the text mentions the 'horrid sounds' coming from behind the door. The BBC 1974 film shows the inside of the closet or bedroom and the final deadly embrace between De Flores (Stanley Baker) and Beatrice-Joanna (Helen Mirren). The BBC film reverses the perspective as we thus hear Alsemero's voice from outside. In Thompson's film, the scene is completely delocalized into a private though outdoor space, a symbol of unleashed forces and bestial urges: an unbridled horse-drawn carriage. The motif of the horse was already present when spectators witnessed a tender scene in a stable between Alsemero and Beatrice-Joanna, the stable being evocative of a space of animal desires. In the film, Peeping Tom De Flores witnesses the whole sequence, at the end of which we see him in a carriage waiting for Beatrice-Joanna. In that scene, the stable is associated with unbridled sexuality that finds its expression in the taboo evocation of De Flores's masturbation. Thompson reuses the motif of the horse as a symbol of uncontrolled lust in this final carriage-carnage sequence. In this chaotic sequence, the spectators see Beatrice-Joanna being fiercely stabbed by De Flores, the frantic succession of extreme close-ups showing that stabbing and raping overlap and are in fact one and the same act. The sequence is intercut with an alternation of screams of agony and screams of pleasure, again suggesting that the victim could well be consenting to this outrageous act of violence. Creating horror is a hard task for a director. The excess of blood here verges on *Grand-Guignol* when the carriage door opens and reveals a flow of blood, De Flores dragging Beatrice-Joanna's agonizing body along the ground to her father's feet. Her whole body, from head to toe, is now the colour of her red dress, a bloody dress that contrasts with the white dress that she was wearing at the beginning of the film. The final scene explicitly merges sex and violence, again showing that this rape is a murder. Gordon McMullan rightly notes that the blood is not realistic, but 'rather obviously fake',[47] but one could argue that this is consonant with the theatricality that Alsemero mentions when he asks them to 'rehearse again' their 'scene of lust'.

The horror and discomfort created by the film also come from the treatment of the asylum scenes. Throughout the film, Thompson alternates scenes in various recurrent places: a garden where Beatrice-Joanna is seen frivolously walking, a courtyard which is the gathering point where male characters meet around a tree, the castle which turns into a hellish place, a church where Beatrice-Joanna and Alsemero first meet and then get married. McMullan rightly notes that '[t]he film follows the usual path of *Changeling* productions in chopping down the asylum subplot to the point of incomprehensibility'[48] However, what these scenes manage to create is a background of abjection for a story of abjection, as they depict a kind of museum of living horrors. Thompson creates a dark prison-like space that we recurrently see, where characters are seen raving. The visions we get of these anonymous characters constitute a tableau that conjures up even more horror in the film and echoes the horrors present in the main plot. The asylum is a world of sound and fury and looks like a manège where male and female creatures meaninglessly turn round and round. Although the cutting and scale of shots create a space where landmarks get lost, what appears very clearly is that these scenes are evocative of disturbing sex, violence and madness through the frantic gestures of the characters. Some characters mimic sexual abuse; a female character mimics child abuse by stabbing a doll she holds in her arms, so that one can clearly see that sex and violence are at the heart of this asylum, Thompson choosing to enhance the horror of the story by having the two plots mirror one another and especially by creating a sadomasochistic atmosphere. During the second rape sequence, the alternation of shots of Beatrice-Joanna and Alsemero, Beatrice-Joanna and De Flores and the madhouse merges the three stories into the same frantic whirl. Thompson's cinematic means also allows him to represent Diaphanta's being burnt alive in a graphic way, the director once again choosing to visualize what must happen off-stage in the Jacobean play while superimposing images of Alsemero and Beatrice-Joanna cuddling each other, their union thus being haunted by horrible images. The film is also suggestive of ghost films but in a very strange way. From the moment of the character's death, Alonzo's ghost is seen on several occasions, in various places – on top of a tree, on a castle tower – until the wedding scene, where he surrealistically appears hanged, almost stuck, on the closed church door. The effect is far from being horrible as the character is nothing like a zombie-like figure but appears in his former shape and costume, unaccompanied by any sensational sound effect. The images of a too 'normal' ghost hovering here and there contrast with the excess of sex and violence that the film cultivates. Alonzo, the film suggests, remains exterior to and untainted by the world of corruption and abjection that the film stages. Beyond death, Alonzo remains the outsider and thus escapes the world of defilement that characterizes the play.

In her article 'Film Bodies: Gender, Genre, and Excess', Linda Williams reminds the reader that 'the Latin *horrore* means to bristle', suggesting that scenes of horror have a physical impact on the viewer and may constitute 'moments of shivering excitement'. She also notices that in horror films 'women make the best victims'.[49] Focusing on three of what she calls the 'body genres', 'pornography, horror and melodrama', she asks questions about the reception of these films and the pleasure they can produce in spectators: 'Are the orgasmic women of pornography and the tortured woman of horror merely in the service of a sadistic male gaze?'[50] These questions can and must be asked about Thompson's film. According to Gordon McMullan, 'Middleton and Rowley's text is almost entirely cut, the bloody visuals obliterating the play's verbal and psychological subtleties.'[51] If the film emphasizes the horrors of the play, it nevertheless manages, beyond its excesses, to raise questions. The pleasure–torture ambivalence that is at the heart of the film, and that one can also find in the play itself, is all the more disturbing in the contemporary context of the #MeToo movement.

Thompson's film ends with a sequence that visualizes the happy life Beatrice might otherwise have lived. We see Alsemero overlooking a beach from the top of a fortress wall, and imagining Beatrice-Joanna wearing a white dress, running on a beach and playing with the waves in a dream-like sequence that seems to suggest that there was innocence before horror, that there was or could have been joy before pain. The sequence, which looks like a film within the film, is an adaptation of the epilogue of the play delivered by Alsemero:

> All we can do to comfort one another,
> To stay a brother's sorrow for a brother,
> To dry a child from the kind father's eyes,
> Is to no purpose, it rather multiplies:
> Your only smiles have power to cause re-live
> The dead again, or in their rooms to give
> Brother a new brother, father a child –
> If these appear, all griefs are reconciled.
>
> (5.3.219–26)

Thompson switches from the bloodiest of murder-rape scenes to a sequence of both purity and sensuality. Is this supposed to erase the horrors that we have seen? Is this sequence the smiles that allow the spectators to reconcile all griefs? Or does it rather make the horrors that we have just seen even more vivid? The end of the play dramatizes a rather unsettling conclusion by suggesting that once Beatrice-Joanna is dead, the male society is 'satisfied' and all injuries 'lie dead' (5.3.190–1). The end, through Alsemero's final speeches, summarizes the play into a series of changes: from 'servant-obedience' to 'murder' and from 'beauty' to 'whoredom' (5.1.197–9). Thompson's final sequence reconstitutes a world of beauty incarnated by 'Beatrice' but it also makes signs of 'Joanna's' sensuality visible, as if the seeds of danger and horror lay in beauty anyway. 'There's scarce a thing but is both loved and loathed.'

# 8

# Resources

## *Nora J. Williams*

### Introduction

*The Changeling* is an exciting choice for classroom study. Its two female protagonists – Beatrice-Joanna and Isabella – provide entry points to discussions of women's agency, morality and class in Jacobean England. Unlike Middleton and Rowley's other plays, it has a vibrant and varied performance history in the twentieth and twenty-first centuries, including a number of screen adaptations. For classes covering a range of early modern plays, it offers thematic parallels with, for example, *Measure for Measure*, *Twelfth Night*, *Macbeth*, *Othello*, *Richard III*, *The Duchess of Malfi*, *The White Devil* and *Women Beware Women*. Often anthologized with revenge tragedies, the play nevertheless resists generic categorization, testing the boundaries of both comedy and tragedy in the relationship between its two plots.

### Performance history

Despite the long gap in its professional performance history, its availability in print was perhaps a driving force in its selection for production by university dramatic societies in the 1940s and 1950s. Jennifer Panek and Sarah Dustagheer have traced this history; here, I will offer some of the most important secondary sources for those looking to study *The Changeling* through its performance history.

A key source for studying *The Changeling* and other early modern plays in performance is Pascale Aebischer and Kathryn Prince's edited collection, *Performing Early Modern Drama Today*.[1] Published in 2012, the collection takes stock of the cultural role of non-Shakespearean early modern drama on stage in the UK and USA in the twenty-first century, with chapters focusing on repertoire, the role of universities, programming at specific companies, film and digital productions and educational contexts. The volume ends with three enormously valuable appendices compiled by Jeremy Lopez and Karin Brown; these detail amateur, university and professional productions of early modern plays through to the date of publication.

In her chapter, Lucy Munro separates the current theatre repertory of early modern plays into 'three contrasting groups'.[2] The first group represents those plays that are part of the canon, see regular professional production, are on school and/or university curricula, and are generally better known than many of their contemporaries: in addition to *The Changeling,* her list includes Webster's *The Duchess of Malfi*, Middleton's *Women Beware Women* and Marlowe's *Doctor Faustus*. The second group consists of plays tangential to those in the first group, such as Marlowe's *Dido, Queen of Carthage* or Webster's *The White Devil,* which are slightly less well-known and do not generally appear on course reading lists, at least outside of specialist modules in higher education. The third group, which Munro labels the 'lost classics', includes plays that have not been professionally produced – or have been produced very infrequently – since the late seventeenth century. They comprise the largest of the three categories, which retains its size despite the efforts of programmes such as Globe Education's Read Not Dead initiative and the White Bear Theatre's 'Lost Classics' series. Munro notes that very few plays are able to break out of the 'lost classics' category because if they were to be revived on a regular basis, they would 'cease to be "lost classics"', and therefore their marketability as novelties would be diminished.[3] As such, Munro argues, implicitly or explicitly labelling certain plays as 'lost classics' can actually 'serve to reinforce the prominence of the central group of regularly performed plays' rather than to dethrone them.[4]

I would argue, however, that *The Changeling* is an exception: Munro's categories are differently relevant in different phases of its afterlife. *The Changeling* functioned, to some extent, as a 'lost classic' in the context of Richardson's 1961 production. Since that time, however, it has ascended Munro's pyramid to the very top and become a staple of the early modern canon and repertory. Margot Heinemann notes that, by 1980, Middleton's works could be seen 'freely staged in the theatre, viewed as Plays of the Month, or read aloud in the Sixth Form'; a footnote informs us that *The Changeling* had recently been set as an A-level text.[5] Inclusion in the educational system as a set text for national exams tends to solidify a play's canonical status and ensure that it is edited, printed, staged and experienced for generations to come. In the chapter that follows Munro's, Jeremy Lopez tracks a symbiotic relationship between professional theatre and educational institutions. Examining 106 individual plays, Lopez shows that only twenty-one have been performed 'more than ten times between 1887 and the present' at educational institutions; with one exception, these same plays have all been printed in the *Norton Anthology of Early Modern Drama*.[6] The conclusion to be drawn, Lopez argues, is that 'the most frequently anthologized plays of the twentieth century' – 'the plays that students read and write essays about in university classrooms' – are the same plays that see more frequent stagings in educational contexts over time. *The Changeling* is now among these often-anthologized, often performed plays.[7]

Particularly useful for educators wishing to teach *The Changeling* using performative exercises is Jonathan Heron, Nicholas Monk and Paul Prescott's chapter, 'Letting the Dead

Come Out to Dance: An Embodied Approach to Teaching Early Modern Drama'.[8] This detailed analysis of their pedagogy, which was developed through the Open-Space Learning Project, offers a rich account of a process employed for *The Changeling* specifically. 'Experiencing the text as a potential director or actor in rehearsal and carefully considering the multiple possibilities for a performance of the text', they argue, allows 'students [to] develop both their critical and their creative readings of the play'.[9] Such a clear and comprehensive set of exercises targeted for a particular early modern play is an unusual and therefore uniquely applicable resource; although the authors note that their methods could be adapted for almost any play, it will be especially helpful for teachers of *The Changeling* to take note of this existing work in their planning.

Interpretative exercises such as those recommended by Heron, Monk and Prescott resonate with the wider performance history of *The Changeling*, which is bursting with examples of innovative and adaptive staging. Michael Neill implies that innovation in a performance history occurs when a given play is well-known enough to feel tired: 'by the 1990s *The Changeling*'s reputation was sufficiently established to generate a series of experimental re-visionings evidently intended to breathe new life into an all-too-familiar classic'.[10] This is, perhaps, in line with the play's ascendance from 'lost classic' to top-tier status, according to Munro's classification system. M.J. Kidnie inverts the same principle in her study of Shakespeare and adaptation, arguing that '[t]he more canonical the author and dramatic work are, the more anxiety there is that one might inadvertently or carelessly accept false goods in place of the real thing'.[11] This tension between the desire for authenticity and authority in the production of canonical texts – in print as well as in performance – and the creative impulse to innovate within a tradition characterizes the theatrical life of *The Changeling* in the twenty-first century. (See Jennifer Panek's essay in this volume.) In working through these issues, students may wish to consider the implications of presenting the play in either modern or period dress. For example, how are the class tensions in the play differently expressed in Jacobean costume, modern dress or any period in between? Do changes to the setting or time period change the presentation of the play's sexual politics?

# Textual history

*The Changeling* comes down to us through a single early printed text: the 1653 quarto. This is available as a facsimile through Early English Books Online, as well as in a print copy by the Scolar Press, published in 1973. The 1668 quarto, apart from the title page, is identical to the 1653 printing. The early text of *The Changeling* is therefore remarkably stable, although it has received considerable emendation from editors in the twentieth and twenty-first centuries. In terms of scholarly work on that quarto text, N.W. Bawcutt remains the most detailed and reliable source, and subsequent work relies upon his strong foundation; students will find his account of the play's provenance accessible and enlightening.

It is an unfortunate truth that the editorial paradigm for early modern plays was developed for Shakespeare, to the exclusion of other playwrights, and that therefore his plays represent what we perceive as normative for drama of the period.[12] Principles that evolved through sustained attention to Shakespeare are often applied wholesale to other playwrights, including Middleton and – when his works are edited at all – Rowley. Gary Taylor acknowledges this problem in his introduction to the Oxford *Middleton*: he justifies the 'federal' approach to editing in the collection by arguing that

> editorial paradigms based on the unusual conditions of the Shakespeare canon are of limited relevance to Middleton (and many other writers). Rather than simply applying to Middleton modes of editorial practice developed to represent another author, we have sought to present

Middleton's works in the manner most appropriate to their nature.[13]

Whether Taylor and his editorial team achieved the goal of editing Middleton's works 'in the manner most appropriate to their nature' is a matter of debate, of course, and scholars such as Lukas Erne, Lars Engle and Eric Rasmussen have criticized the superficiality of some of the editorial risks taken in the Oxford *Middleton*.[14] When thinking about the textual history of *The Changeling*, it is perhaps worth discussing Erne, Engle and Rasmussen's views. Is creating Middleton in the image of Shakespeare productive? Should the first academically-rigorous collection of Middleton's plays adhere to editorial tradition, or is Taylor right to break with convention? How meaningful are the editorial 'risks' taken in the Oxford *Middleton*, especially when it comes to better-known plays such as *The Changeling*?

The consequences of the single-author model are particularly clear in the longstanding and widespread lack of appreciation for the intricate relationship between *The Changeling*'s two plots. Gordon McMullan notes that '[n]othing in the actual violence enacted on and off stage seems to offend as these tonal tensions' between the two plots 'in their refusal of aesthetic comfort'.[15] Sustained scholarly attention over the course of two centuries, and theatrical interventions since 1961, however, have resulted in a change of opinion, so that the 'subplot' is (quite rightly) now considered a crucial component of the play.

# Textual features

Although *The Changeling* has sometimes been faulted for its structure – and some productions have gone so far as to cut the subplot or even write new, additional scenes from scratch – close analysis of the play reveals a meticulously constructed and highly organized text, with multiple layers of meaning, metaphor and wordplay running across its length and breadth. Christopher Ricks, for example, is particularly fascinated by the use of *double entendre* in the play on words such as 'service', and he even attributes Beatrice-Joanna's downfall to her 'tragic failure to see puns'.[16] He argues that 'the verbal basis of the play is a group of words, each of which has two meanings, one of them sexual; at the beginning of the play, the two meanings are distinct; by the end, they have become inextricable'.[17] Ricks was the first to engage with Middleton and Rowley's playful but detailed approach to collaborative playwriting in *The Changeling*, pulling apart some of the complex layers of wordplay within the text. Ann Pasternak Slater extends Ricks's arguments in her article 'Hypallage, Barley-Brake, and *The Changeling*', where she argues that the play can be understood through a rarely-acknowledged *OED* definition of 'changeling': hypallage, a rhetorical device in which words change their usual places.[18] She identifies what she calls 'the play's exploitation of moral hypallage, whereby vice and virtue exchange places, so that vices are committed in the name of virtue, and virtues themselves become vicious'.[19] Slater argues that '*The Changeling*'s unforgettable intensity lies precisely in its fusion of the vicious and the virtuous', and that therefore '[t]he tone of the play [...] is one in which antithetical values continually change places, to create a kind of alternating current from negative to positive and back again'.[20] Slater also offers an extended reading of the metaphor of barley-brake in the play. The game involves two couples trying to cross a space occupied by a third couple, who must try to break up the others without losing hold of each other; Slater skilfully parses out this metaphor and identifies a series of couples that are changed, rearranged or destroyed throughout the course of the play. Ricks and Slater therefore offer intriguing starting points for exercises inviting students to 'map' features such as wordplay, coupling and moral ambiguity.

Their essays also provide jumping-off points for reading *The Changeling* through the number of inversions, variations and permutations of classic literary and dramatic devices and tropes – including the structuring of the plots, the revenger character and the 'bed trick' – that characterize its relationship to the wider canon of early modern drama. Students familiar with Shakespeare's plays and the broader canvas of early modern drama will recognize dramaturgical devices familiar from other plays appearing in different, unexpected configurations. *The Changeling* is a remarkably intertextual play that demonstrates Middleton's and Rowley's awareness of the broader context of early modern drama and literature. At the same time, the playwrights' manipulation of well-known structures demonstrates their creativity and the strength of their collaborative relationship. These permutations are evident throughout both plots of *The Changeling*. As Patricia Thomson puts it in her New Mermaids introduction, the subplot 'provides a through-the-looking-glass, madhouse reflection' of the castle plot.[21] This is a departure from the typical dual-plot structure in drama of this period, as Richard Levin notes: 'Although most double-plot plays utilizing the relationship of direct moral contrast place the virtuous line of action in the main plot', *The Changeling* is the 'most famous' example of a play in which 'that arrangement is reversed'.[22] He goes on to suggest that Rowley 'titillates' the audience with a standard comic set-up in the hospital plot, only to 'startl[e] (if not disappoin[t]) us by Isabella's chastity'.[23] In addition, the revenging character, Tomazo, is neither the protagonist – as in *The Spanish Tragedy*, *Hamlet* and *The Revenger's Tragedy* – nor a particularly effective avenger. He fails to correctly identify and kill his brother's actual murderers, being content instead with the untimely end they bring upon themselves. Similarly, the convention of the 'bed trick' – in which one proposed sexual partner (usually the woman in a heterosexual coupling) is substituted by a more willing person without the knowledge of the third party – is usually used to re-establish a legitimate or desirable relationship, particularly in Shakespeare (see, for example, *Measure for Measure* and *All's Well That Ends Well*). In *The Changeling*, however, the 'bed trick' undermines Beatrice-Joanna's marriage to Alsemero, obscures her complicity in the murder of Alonzo, and protects De Flores. Students reading *The Changeling* alongside other early modern drama should be able to identify the ways in which it manipulates dramatic conventions such as these.

## Historical perspectives

Middleton and Rowley completed *The Changeling* extraordinarily quickly in the spring of 1622. Whilst John Reynolds' *The Triumph of God's Revenge* was printed in 1621, other influences materialized just months before the play was licensed: Frances Howard, who seems to have inspired the virginity test episode, was released from the Tower in January 1622, and Leonard Digges's translation of G. de Céspedes y Meneses's prose fiction *Gerardo, The Unfortunate Spaniard* was licensed in March of the same year (see Berta Cano-Echevarría's chapter in this volume).[24] *The Changeling* was licensed for performance just two months later, in May of 1622. The celerity of its construction is often cited as evidence of the strong and successful professional relationship between the two playwrights.[25]

The years 1618 to 1624 have been identified as the climax of a 'crisis' for the English monarchy, and work by Margot Heinemann, Jerzy Limon, A.A. Bromham and Zara Bruzzi, Swapan Chakravorty, Adrian Streete, Mark Hutchings and many others have assessed Middleton's – but not Rowley's – perspective on that crisis.[26] It is important to acknowledge Streete's caution that the term 'crisis' exposes the scholar to 'an accusation of retrospective anachronism'; note, too, however, his judgement that 'many living at the time viewed contemporary events in a similar manner' – that is, as precisely that.[27] *The Changeling*'s place within that crisis is worth exploring, as the socio-political climate in which the play emerged is as much a source for its content and themes as any of its literary sources.

In terms of the playwrights' relationship to the crisis years of the 1620s, most critics have focused on Middleton's Calvinism without considering Rowley's role in creating the moral worlds of their collaborative drama. This is partly a reflection of the enduring perception of Rowley as the inferior playwright. David Nicol's work, however, has shown that Rowley was, in fact, the more senior playwright in the partnership. Nicol argues that Rowley's moral and religious feelings are at least as important to an understanding of *The Changeling* as Middleton's: 'phrases such as "Middleton and Rowley's Beatrice" or "Middleton and Rowley's degraded world" assume that Beatrice and the world view of the play are stable concepts, and that there is no difference in the way the two authors represent them', when in fact the playwrights' different world views are very much reflected in their writings.[28] Structuring his analysis around each playwright's handling of 'decision points' in *All's Lost by Lust*, *The Spanish Gypsy* and *The Changeling*, Nicol suggests that Rowley's Pelagian worldview can be seen in his characters' 'struggle to control their passions' before 'knowingly making the wrong choice', whereas Middleton's Calvinism – and particularly the doctrine of predestination – is evident in his characters' apparently inherent goodness or evil.[29] In other words, whilst Middleton's reprobate characters cannot help but sin, Rowley's characters choose to sin. Nicol argues that the ramifications of that distinction in *The Changeling* are manifest in, appropriately, the changeability of its characters and the slipperiness of its genre: '[t]he collision of [. . .] different interpretations of truth is one reason why the conclusion of *The Changeling* remains both upbeat and disturbing' in the present day.[30]

Nicol's work is unique in its consideration of Rowley's biography and singly-authored works alongside Middleton's. Very little criticism that considers Rowley's history in any detail is available, and the scholar of Rowley must rely on a strong knowledge of (and access to) primary sources. A notable exception is Charles Wharton Stork's *William Rowley: His 'All's Lost by Lust' and 'A Shoemaker, A Gentleman'*, *with an Introduction on Rowley's Place in the Drama*, published by the University of Pennsylvania in 1910. Teachers looking to emphasize the collaborative authorship of the play have more resources now than even a decade ago, but information specific to Rowley is still a little tricky to track down; Nicol's book is therefore an invaluable resource.

# Two playwrights: Two plots

Gary Taylor has dubbed Thomas Middleton 'our other Shakespeare', a comment upon Middleton's growing popularity and permanence in the canon.[31] Taylor's epithet, however, encourages a mis-reading of *The Changeling*'s dramaturgical structure and of the relationship between Middleton and Rowley as playwrights. Firstly, it sets up Middleton as a solitary genius in the nineteenth-century mode, distancing him from the many playwrights with whom he collaborated on a regular basis, including Rowley, Dekker and Shakespeare himself.[32] In this, Taylor follows the tradition established by a number of nineteenth-century anthologies, including Havelock Ellis's *The Best Plays of the Old Dramatists: Thomas Middleton* (1887) and A.H. Bullen's *The Works of Thomas Middleton* (1885–6). Taylor's attempt to balance the field of early modern playwrights not only perpetuates a myth about Shakespeare's genius but also applies that myth to Middleton, discounting, for example, Rowley's contributions to his success.

As I have noted above, much scholarship on *The Changeling* and Middleton's professional relationship with Rowley concurs with Taylor's implied reading of Middleton as the superior, leading playwright, the artist who creates the play's pathos, and Rowley as the inferior collaborator who contributed little, if anything, to their collective success.[33] The erroneous tendency to read *The Changeling* as the work of a great auteur (Middleton) marred by the contributions of a second-rate clown (Rowley) stems primarily from the Romantics and their successors. '[I]ndividualistic notions of genius' developed during the eighteenth and nineteenth centuries have since become clichés, but they continue to wield power over current interpretations of literature and understandings of authorship.[34]

That this bias for singular talent continued after what is usually considered the end of Romanticism is evidenced in T.S. Eliot's essay on Middleton:

> And Middleton in the end – after criticism has subtracted all that Rowley, all that Dekker, all that others contributed – is a great example of great English drama. He has no message; he is merely a great recorder. Incidentally, in flashes and when the dramatic need comes, he is a great poet, a great master of versification:
>
> *I that am of your blood was taken from you*
> *For your better health; look no more upon't,*
> *But cast it to the ground regardlessly,*
> *Let the common sewer take it from distinction:*
> *Beneath the stars, upon yon meteor*
> *Ever hung my fate, 'mongst things corruptible;*
> *I ne'er could pluck it from him; my loathing*
> *Was prophet to the rest, but ne'er believed.*
>
> The man who wrote these lines remains inscrutable, solitary, unadmired[.][35]

Eliot speaks truer than he knows: the lines quoted here come from the final scene of *The Changeling*, which has been attributed to Rowley, not Middleton.[36] Eliot's 'master of versification' is, then, Middleton's collaborator.

Rowley truly remains 'unadmired', despite evidence suggesting that he may have occupied a higher hierarchical position than Middleton in the early modern playhouses where they worked. A 'famous clown' and shareholder in the Prince Charles's Men, Rowley's role in playwriting for that company may have included casting and repertory-building, as well as 'an organizational or directorial role during rehearsal'.[37] Although the currently accepted division of authorship has been the standard since at least 1975, Nicol points out that of the existing studies of the Middleton–Rowley canon, very few have 'grappled seriously with the fact that in each of these plays, a sizeable proportion of the text, often more than half of it, was written by an obscure playwright whose solo works [. . .] are rarely studied'.[38] Indeed, as demonstrated by Eliot's misattribution above, many critics either forget or ignore the division of labour between Middleton and Rowley across the two plots of *The Changeling*. David Lake and others have shown that Rowley was primarily responsible for the first and last scenes of the play, all of the hospital plot, and a handful of lines in Act 4.[39] That leaves the middle section of the castle plot, including the bulk of the Beatrice-Joanna/De Flores relationship, to Middleton, but it gives Rowley authority over the crucial first and last moments of the play.

The relationship between the two plots has presented difficulties for both academics and theatre practitioners from the nineteenth century to the present day. In the twentieth century, scholars such as Muriel Bradbrook, William Empson and N.W. Bawcutt argued for the merits of the hospital plot, whilst critics such as Una Ellis-Fermor, R.H. Barker and Samuel Schoenbaum insisted on its irrelevance and inferiority.[40] Certain scholars have even suggested that the madhouse plot as we now have it is incomplete: R.J. Holdsworth, for example, has argued that at least three scenes must be missing, and the 2004 Shakespeare at the Tobacco Factory production used this kind of scholarship as a rationale for commissioning Dominic Power to write a series of new scenes for the hospital plot.[41] As Douglas Bruster notes, however, Holdsworth himself has also provided a great deal of evidence *against* the missing scenes theory, and it seems unlikely that such scenes ever existed.[42] Robert Ornstein's tepid praise perhaps encapsulates the relationship between the two plots and the academic community: 'To understand the necessity of the subplot [. . .] we need only try to imagine *The Changeling* without it. Then we realize how narrow is Middleton's tragic focus and how thin is the texture of the main plot.'[43] To see how this sentiment has been carried over into twenty-first-century theatrical treatments of *The Changeling*, consider director Joe Hill-Gibbins' initial refusal to direct the play because he perceived its dual-plot structure as 'too fucking hard' to do.[44]

The textual and performance histories of *The Changeling* offer different ways of handling the problem of the two plots, however. Many of the perceived structural issues in the play resolve themselves through performance, where subtle thematic connections or dramaturgical echoes can be made more explicit through, for example, careful cutting, staging and casting choices. It is particularly telling that in the Royal Court production in 1961, the critical response generally praised the production but panned the play. Referring to the apparent disconnect between the plots, Richard Findlater called *The Changeling* a 'weird compost of farce and melodrama, poetry and fustian', and J.C. Trewin dubbed it a 'half-masterpiece'.[45] Commenting on the merits of Tony Richardson's production, however, Findlater conceded that he found it 'rich and strange and altogether absorbing'.[46] Perhaps T.C. Worsley of the *Financial Times* summed up the general critical response: 'The play has a pretty irrelevant but entertaining sub-plot.'[47] Richardson's staging established a theatrical tradition for *The Changeling* that creates visual links between the two plots; Dominic Dromgoole's 2015 Sam Wanamaker Playhouse production is a notable exception. Students might spend time imagining creative ways to bring the two plots together through performance, informed by the text.

# The 'psychoanalytical' reading

Performance is simultaneously an integral part of a play's afterlife and, often, an unacknowledged influence on the critical reception of and academic writing about a particular text. In the case of *The Changeling*, we can see this principle manifested in the longstanding tradition of reading Beatrice-Joanna's relationship with De Flores as a proto-Freudian love-hate relationship. This reading has a very weak basis in the text: it hinges on Alsemero's line, '[t]here's scarce a thing but is both loved and loathed'.[48] Read outside the wider context of the scene, the line appears to endorse a love-hate reading; understood in context, however, such a reading does not apply at all. Alsemero speaks this line as part of a speech responding to Beatrice's inability to explain her dislike of De Flores. The whole exchange reads as follows:

ALSEMERO
> This is a frequent frailty in our nature;
> There's scarce a man amongst a thousand sound,
> But hath his imperfection: one distastes
> The scent of roses, which to infinites
> Most pleasing is, and odoriferous;
> One oil, the enemy of poison;
> Another wine, the cheerer of the heart,
> And lively refresher of the countenance.
> Indeed this fault – if so it be – is general:
> There's scarce a thing but is both loved and loathed,
> Myself, I must confess, have the same frailty.

BEATRICE
> And what may be your poison, sir? I'm bold with you.

ALSEMERO
> What might be your desire perhaps – a cherry.[49]

Much of this long speech, as well as the exchange about Alsemero's dislike of cherries, tends to be cut in performance. Seen (or heard) in context, however, '[t]here's scarce a thing but is both loved and loathed' does not mean 'a person can feel both love and loathing towards the same thing' but, rather, 'different people have different tastes, and what I hate you might enjoy'. Read in this way, the line provides no justification for a Freudian reading of Beatrice's relationship with De Flores.

Nonetheless, that reading was perpetuated for decades by a cycle of performance, review and scholarship, such that this so-called 'psychoanalytical' interpretation of the play was inescapable by the mid-1980s and has only been dislodged very recently.[50] As Kate Lechler notes, this cycle joins up with education and popular culture as well, resulting in a trickle-through effect from performance to 'professors, students, and interested readers, and from there to Wikipedia, SparkNotes, film versions, and other popular cultural representations of and engagement[s] with literature'.[51] Typically, however, editions of the play do not acknowledge their symbiotic relationship with theatrical performance and wider culture. Joost Daalder, editor of *The Changeling* for the New Mermaids in 1990, states unequivocally that Beatrice-Joanna's unconscious attraction to De Flores is 'one of the main facts of the play'.[52] He does not acknowledge the role that productions and reviews of productions played in propping up and cementing this interpretation as fact. Jay O'Berski's 2012 Palgrave handbook on *The Changeling* declares that Beatrice-Joanna and De Flores are 'in tune with pop psychology after Freud'.[53] Such interpretations, reinforced by decades of support from *both* performance and scholarship, are not easily overturned. It is therefore important that teachers are attuned to the problems with this interpretation and that they contextualize any readings that espouse it for their students.

This psychoanalytic interpretation of Beatrice-Joanna reached its peak in the 1970s and 1980s. According to Michael Billington, Emma Piper's 1978 Beatrice perfectly 'conveys the sado-masochistic fantasies of a reclusive virgin' and 'reminds us of the play's psychological modernity'.[54] Sally Hedges in Kate Crutchley's 1979 production gives a 'fine performance' of 'sexual self-deceit', whilst Sue Jenkins and John Branwell are 'inextricably linked in a love-hate relationship of great psychological complexity', the same year in Manchester.[55] As Roberta Barker and David Nicol remind us, however, this interpretation of the play also 'risks affirming that Middleton and Rowley's heroine actually desires a rape she pleads against in the lines they wrote for her'; the text undermines the dominant critical and theatrical interpretation of the play.[56] So, they argue,

> As critics' descriptions of the laughter that greeted Beatrice's line, 'This fellow hath undone me endlessly' (IV.i.1) in

[Terry] Hands' sexually graphic production suggest, this reading allows the audience to remain content that Beatrice really wants De Flores even if the director stages the characters' climactic confrontation as a brutal rape scene. Although the victim seems unwilling, in fact it's all a bit of saucy fun: no means yes, and one need not feel pity for a heroine whose corruption is also her awakening to her true nature.[57]

This reading of Beatrice-Joanna as a repressed virgin requiring De Flores to bring about her 'awakening' has very little basis in the text of the play; nonetheless, it was a major component of academic criticism throughout the twentieth century, as evidenced by Daalder's 1990 introduction and Douglas Bruster's placement of asides in the Oxford Middleton edition.[58] Even more recent critical texts, like O'Berski's, maintain that 'In a play like *The Changeling* it often seems like "no" means "yes" means "maybe". With an opaque character like Beatrice-Johanna [*sic*], intentions can no longer always be taken at face value.'[59] Beyond its lack of textual grounding, such an approach to the play – bizarrely, being espoused in 'student-friendly introductory guides' written eight years *after* Barker and Nicol's landmark essay – cannot be tolerated 'in a world where rape victims are still subjected to humiliating cross-examination about their sexual pasts on the witness stand' and world leaders brag about grabbing women 'by the pussy' without consent.[60] Nonetheless, the professional theatre – including Shakespeare's Globe and the Stratford Festival in Ontario, Canada – continues to flirt with this debunked understanding of the play as an exploration of Beatrice-Joanna's unconscious desire for De Flores, and the consequent trivializing of her rape. Dismantling this interpretation of the play is not just good scholarship – it's an urgent feminist issue. Students might spend time thinking about how different performances, editions and scholarly outputs frame Beatrice-Joanna's relationship to De Flores differently, and how those differences affect our perceptions of the issues raised in the play around gender and sexuality.

# Gender, sexuality and human rights issues

How, then, to discuss Beatrice-Joanna's sexual relationship with De Flores in a classroom setting without either trivializing (*à la* Freud) or sensationalizing her rape? This is a crucial question for Kim Solga: 'How do we square this work's enormous cultural capital with its profound distance from contemporary attitudes toward social justice and human rights?'[61] Solga provides a detailed and accessible overview of the history of violence against women in legal as well as theatrical terms. She reminds us that, in the early modern period, '[r]ape was a crime against a household, a husband or a father, his goods, property and honour; domestic violence was "reasonable correction", a form of household-ordering essential to the proper functioning of parish, county, and state'.[62] In terms of *The Changeling*, Solga offers a detailed analysis of the 2006 Cheek by Jowl production and emphasizes the 'paradox' of Beatrice-Joanna as simultaneously a 'classic Jacobean "bad girl"' and a 'rape victim' – a combination that makes her 'virtually incomprehensible' in both her own time and ours.[63] Pascale Aebischer addresses this same problem, making use of Lynda Nead's work on obscenity to consider violated bodies in *Titus Andronicus*, *Hamlet*, *Othello* and *King Lear*. For example, she contrasts the ways in which the mutilations of Lavinia and Titus himself in *Titus Andronicus* are represented by the play's text:

> In a striking contrast with Titus' on-stage hand-amputation, which stresses the act of cruelty and immediate physical suffering of the victim, the tragedy's strategy of withholding the process of Lavinia's dismemberment from view focuses the audience's attention on the *result* of the amputation, the 'lopped' figure of Lavinia as a *fait accompli*. As a consequence, mutilated Lavinia is available for interpretation not so much as a suffering subject of violence, but as an object.[64]

Aebischer refers to the concealment of violence against women from the stage as the 'obscene' or 'ob-scene': drawing on Nead's *The Female Nude*, she describes the 'raped Lavinia' as 'literally "off, or to one side of the stage"'; 'her mangled, leaking, open body forces into our view "that which is just beyond representation"'.[65]

In thinking about the representation of women and sexual violence in *The Changeling*, it is important to note the paralleling of Isabella in the madhouse and Beatrice-Joanna in the castle; nowhere is this juxtaposition more evident than in their disparate handling of their various male aggressors. If Beatrice-Joanna can be seen as reprobate – in line with Middleton's apparent belief in predestination – Isabella can be read as both an alternative example of feminine resistance and a strident example of Rowley's Pelagian worldview. She has the option to sin and comments upon the possibility of having an affair with Antonio: 'Here the restrainèd current might make breach, / Spite of watchful bankers' (3.2.204–5). Indeed, the kiss that is implied between them in 3.2 is staged as implicitly consensual in many productions. Isabella's decision to rebuff not only Antonio but also Franciscus and Lollio can be read as an inversion – a 'through the looking-glass' version, in Patricia Thomson's words – of Beatrice-Joanna.[66]

In performance, these parallels are often preserved, and even explicitly highlighted. Peter Gill's 1978 production, for example, was widely praised for its skilful manipulation of the two plots, which, critics agreed, resulted in a subtle but powerful dialogue between the castle and the madhouse and especially between Beatrice-Joanna and Isabella. Gill created an unnerving connection between the two women: they walked by each other 'shoulder to shoulder' as one exited and the other entered the stage, with 'a chilled glance passing between them' – 'as like ships in the night as you could ever hope to see on dry land', according to Robert Cushman.[67]

Whilst Hill-Gibbins and Svendsen's 2012 reworking of the play's structure at the Young Vic sometimes illuminated parallels between the two plots or between particular characters, the rearranging sometimes obscured these links as well. Consider, for example, Martin White's analysis of the relationship between the virginity test scene in the castle plot (4.2) and the scene following in which Isabella feigns madness in the hospital plot (4.3): 'The scheme of the two scenes is clear: Beatrice-Joanna's feigning conceals the truth, Isabella's reveals it, and such counterpointing of scenes and smaller units of action is characteristic of the relationship of the plots throughout the play'.[68] In both Young Vic versions, these scenes were separated and their order reversed. Whereas the virginity test scene is followed immediately by Isabella's 'madness' scene in the quarto text, the Young Vic places the latter scene first; it is followed by the Madmen's Morris and the dumbshow before we come to the Wedding Night section, which opens with Beatrice-Joanna's soliloquy ('This fellow has undone me endlessly' [4.1.1]) and then continues into the virginity test sequence. This separation, which, allows for the raw juxtaposition of the madhouse dance and the wedding masque, obscures one of the more subtle juxtapositions of plot built into the quarto text.

Finally, it is worth giving some attention to *The Changeling*'s representation of disability and mental health. The feigning 'fool' Antonio and 'madman' Franciscus complicate the audience's relationship to disability and madness in the play: if they are only faking, does that not give the audience permission to laugh at their antics, without mocking genuine disability? And yet, their performances of disability are convincing to Alibius, Lollio and Isabella – all of whom work with actual patients on a daily basis – and therefore must represent at least a persistent stereotype of a disabled or mentally ill body. Lollio recognizes Antonio's trickery only after overhearing a covert conversation between Antonio and Isabella (3.2). Meanwhile, an ensemble of 'fools' and 'madmen' interject from 'within' or enter the playing space; what is the relationship between these 'inmates' and their feigning counterparts? The text provides no easy answers.

Although it is true, of course, that attitudes towards mental health and physical ability have changed significantly since the seventeenth century, recent productions have failed to address these issues adequately.⁶⁹ In the 2012 Young Vic production, for example, Antonio (played by Henry Lloyd-Hughes in the original production and Nick Lee in the revival) was portrayed as disabled: he used a wheelchair and was outfitted with a bib and crash helmet; he spoke with an affected voice that implied a learning disability. Both actors doubled as Tomazo in the castle plot, proving themselves to be able-bodied when they transitioned between characters. Lloyd-Hughes and Lee in this context were engaging in a practice known as 'cripping up' to play Antonio; although this practice is generally frowned upon, its role in *The Changeling* is particularly complex because the *character*, too, is 'cripping up' within the narrative. The Young Vic approach was especially problematic for its conflation of physical and mental disability. As Frances Ryan argues in reference to Eddie Redmayne's portrayal of Stephen Hawking, 'We wouldn't accept actors blacking up, so why applaud "cripping up"?'.⁷⁰ Teachers may therefore wish to frame a discussion of disability and mental illness in the play through a conversation about casting.

At the Sam Wanamaker Playhouse in 2015, similar problems presented themselves. Able-bodied actors Brian Ferguson and Adam Lawrence played Antonio and Franciscus, respectively. In this case, the production's resort to historical authenticity caused a number of issues, including in its approach to portrayals of disability and mental illness. Director Dominic Dromgoole was widely praised in the press for the uproariously funny hospital plot scenes, but his approach was to ask the audience to laugh at the named madhouse characters (Antonio, Franciscus, Lollio, Isabella, Alibius) as well as the ensemble of 'fools and madmen', who are depicted as genuine patients of Alibius's hospital. This lack of distinction between laughing at mistaken identities or comic pranks and laughing at portrayals of genuine disability and/or mental illness raised a number of ethical questions in this production. With this context in mind, it may be productive to ask students to imagine how they might stage the hospital scenes: should Antonio and Franciscus perform differently from the rest of the madhouse ensemble? How can we create humour in these scenes without mocking those suffering from mental illness or those navigating physical impairments? How can these scenes be performed sensitively?

It is worth noting, too, that De Flores has occasionally been interpreted as disabled, including in Marcus Thompson's 1998 film *Middleton's Changeling*, the subject of Nathalie Vienne-Guerrin's essay in this volume. Here, De Flores was played by rocker Ian Dury, who became disabled after contracting polio as a child. Since the film does not entirely cut the hospital plot, screening some scenes in class may offer opportunities to discuss representations of disability and mental illness in a filmic *Changeling*.

# Notable scholarly editions

Douglas Bruster (ed.), in G. Taylor and J. Lavagnino (eds), *Thomas Middleton: The Collected Works* (Oxford: Oxford University Press, 2007).
The Oxford *Middleton* was a major coup when it appeared on the market in 2007, but the long delay in its publication means that some of the interpretations it implies are out of date. Bruster's *Changeling* is notable for its redistribution of asides, particularly in Act 2, Scene 2, as compared to older editions.

Michael Neill (ed.), New Mermaids (London: Bloomsbury, 2006).
Neill's edition makes a noteworthy departure from editorial tradition in joining what are usually two scenes at the beginning of Act 3. This is especially important to note when students are working with different editions of the play.

Joost Daalder (ed.), New Mermaids (London: A&C Black, 1990).
Daalder's 1990 edition was the gold standard until Neill's update in 2006. This edition is notable for its insistence on a 'psychoanalytic' reading of the play.

Patricia Thomson (ed.), New Mermaids (London: Ernest Benn Limited, 1964).
Thomson is still the only woman to edit a major scholarly edition of *The Changeling*. Her description of the madhouse as a

'through the looking-glass' version of the castle is particularly memorable and noteworthy; very few critics took the hospital plot seriously at the time.

N.W. Bawcutt (ed.), Revels Plays (London: Methuen, 1958).
Bawcutt's is the first real scholarly edition of the play. It has been reprinted with an updated introduction many times, but Bawcutt's original work has stood the test of time remarkably well. He was one of the few advocates for a meaningful relationship between the two plots in the first half of the twentieth century.

# *The Changeling*, Middleton, and Rowley online

This is a fantastic time to be studying early modern drama beyond Shakespeare: new criticism is published on a regular basis and access to performances is improving rapidly. Some of these are in included in the 'Selected Bibliography' that follows this essay. There are also some online resources related to *The Changeling* that may be helpful to students and teachers approaching the play for the first time. Subscription services such as *Early English Books Online* (EEBO) and the World Shakespeare Bibliography are clear starting points, but there are a number of helpful free resources, too. These include:

- The University of Warwick's Centre for the Study of the Renaissance includes pages on Thomas Middleton, *The Changeling*, and performance history. See http://www2.warwick.ac.uk/fac/arts/ren/projects/elizabethan_jacobean_drama/
- Digital Renaissance Editions, inspired by the Internet Shakespeare Editions, offers scholarly editions of early modern plays that are published electronically. These also include old-spelling transcriptions, critical and textual introductions, and other supplementary materials. *The Changeling* is not yet part of its collection, but they do have a completed edition of *The Honest Whore, Part I*,

which is attributed to Middleton and Thomas Dekker. In addition, Rowley's *All's Lost By Lust* is currently in preparation.

- Shakespeare at the Tobacco Factory provides a number of resources for educators as part of the online archive for its 2004 production of *The Changeling,* which featured additional scenes written by a contemporary playwright. See http://stf-theatre.org.uk/the-changeling
- Shakespeare's Globe conducts podcast interviews with cast members, including Hattie Morahan and Trystan Gravelle of the 2015 *Changeling*. For Morahan's interviews, see http://www.shakespearesglobe.com/discovery-space/adopt-an-actor/archive/beatrice-joanna-played-by-hattie-morahan. For Gravelle, see http://www.shakespearesglobe.com/discovery-space/adopt-an-actor/archive/de-flores-played-by-trystan-gravelle
- Heather Neill conducted an interview with dramaturg Zoë Svendsen regarding the 2012 Young Vic production of *The Changeling* for *Theatre Voice,* which is accessible at http://www.theatrevoice.com/audio/dramaturg-zoe-svendsen-discusses-the-young-vic-production-of-the-changeling/
- Emma Smith of Hertford College, Oxford has a series of podcasts entitled *Not Shakespeare: Elizabethan and Jacobean Popular Theatre*. Although *The Changeling* is not a subject of her lectures, these highly accessible talks are a great introduction to the period and the playwrights. In addition, there are lectures dedicated to *The Witch of Edmonton,* on which Rowley was a collaborator with Thomas Dekker and John Ford, and Middleton's *A Chaste Maid in Cheapside, The Revenger's Tragedy* and *The Roaring Girl* (co-written with Dekker). See https://podcasts.ox.ac.uk/series/not-shakespeare-elizabethan-and-jacobean-popular-theatre

# NOTES

## Introduction

1 T.S. Eliot, 'Thomas Middleton', in *Elizabethan Dramatists* (London: Faber & Faber, 1963), 83–93; 88. Somewhat contradictorily, Eliot remarks that 'In poetry, in dramatic technique, *The Changeling* is inferior to the best plays of Webster'; ibid. The essay first appeared (unsigned) in the *TLS*, 30 June 1927, 445–6. All references to the play in the essays that follow are keyed to Michael Neill, ed., *The Changeling* (London: Bloomsbury, 2006). Neill departs from editorial tradition in marking thirteen rather than fourteen scenes, so that the opening sequence in Act 3 depicting the tour of the castle and Alonzo's murder constitutes a single scene.

2 *The Changeling* was licensed on 7 May 1622, by the Master of the Revels Sir John Astley, who had assumed the post (having had it in reversion) when Sir George Buc went mad; later in the year he sold it on to Sir Henry Herbert; see Richard Dutton, *Mastering the Revels: The Regulation and Censorship of English Renaissance Drama* (Iowa City: Iowa University Press, 1991), 222. The 1668 quarto text is a reprint of Q (1653), the copy-text for modern editions. Samuel Pepys saw a production of the play on his birthday in 1661; it was staged at court in 1668. Davenant had long been familiar with the play, judging from an allusion in a play he wrote in 1635; see Mark Hutchings, '*News from Plymouth* and *The Changeling*', *Notes and Queries* 64.3 (2017), 610–11.

3 Although the last known production in the seventeenth century is the court performance of 1668, we ought not to assume that the play did not feature subsequently, given the lack of surviving performance records.

4 Unless *A Match at Midnight*, included in Volume 6 and attributed there to Rowley, is accepted as being partly or wholly

by him (which scholars have considered doubtful), none of his plays were included.

5   *The Changeling* appears in Volume 4, together with two other plays ascribed in whole or in part to Middleton: *The Spanish Gypsy* (which also involved Rowley) and *More Dissemblers Besides Women*. From a critical perspective Dilke's choice of plays is marginally more in tune with modern scholarly evaluations of literary merit than is Dodsley's, the latter including a number of plays little regarded today.

6   Rowley's earliest sole-authored play, *A New Wonder*, may have been composed as early as 1611 or as late as 1615; see David Nicol, *Middleton and Rowley: Forms of Collaboration in the Jacobean Playhouse* (Toronto: University of Toronto Press, 2012), 150.

7   Mark Hutchings and A.A. Bromham, *Middleton and his Collaborators* (Plymouth: Northcote House, 2008), 74.

8   Nicol, *Middleton and Rowley*, 67.

9   Douglas Bruster, '*The Changeling*', in 'Works Included in this Edition: Canon and Chronology', Gary Taylor and John Lavagnino, gen. eds., *Thomas Middleton and Early Modern Textual Culture: A Companon to The Collected Works* (Oxford: Oxford University Press, 2007), 422–3; 423 (italics original).

10  See Michael E. Mooney, '"Framing" as Collaborative Technique: Two-Middleton-Rowley Plays', *Comparative Drama* 13 (1979), 127–41, and Richard L. Nochimson, '"Sharing" *The Changeling* by Playwrights and Professors: The Certainty of Uncertain Knowledge about Collaboration', *Early Theatre* 5 (2002), 37–57. The consensus that in addition to the opening and closing scenes and subplot scenes (1.1 and 5.3, 1.2, 3.2 and 4.3) Rowley also wrote the first sixteen lines of 4.2 (proposed by Cyrus Hoy), together with R.V. Holdsworth's contention that Middleton's hand may be detected in 5.3, perhaps the first 121 lines, and Douglas Bruster's suggestion that 1.1 shows some signs of Middleton, collectively underscore the views of scholars such as Nochimson that *The Changeling* was an exceptionally close collaboration. See Hoy, 'The Shares of Fletcher and his Collaborators in the Beaumont and Fletcher Canon (V)', *Studies in Bibliography* 13 (1960), 77–108; Holdsworth, 'Notes on *The*

*Changeling*', *Notes and Queries* 234 (1989), 344–6; and Bruster, in 'Works Included in this Edition: Canon and Chronology', 423.

11 G.E. Bentley, *The Profession of Dramatist in Shakespeare's Time, 1590–1642* (Princeton: Princeton University Press, 1971), 199; see R.A. Foakes, ed., *Henslowe's Diary* 2nd edn (Cambridge: Cambridge University Press, 2002).

12 R. H. Barker, *Thomas Middleton* (1958), 177–80; cited in Michael Dobson, 'Works Included in this Edition: Canon and Chronology', 375–7; 376.

13 Hutchings and Bromham, *Middleton and his Collaborators*, 87; Nicol, *Middleton and Rowley*, 6–7 and *passim*; see also John Jowett, ed., *Timon of Athens* (London: Thomas Nelson and Sons, 2004), 132–53.

14 Famously Hamlet tells the visiting players, 'let those that play your clowns speak no more than is set down for them' (3.2.38–9); Harold Jenkins, ed., *Hamlet* (London: Methuen, 1982).

15 See Mooney, '"Framing" as Collaborative Technique'.

16 For these attributions, see Gary Taylor, 'Works Included in this Edition: Canon and Chronology', 331–443.

17 The key works of criticism in this field are Margot Heinemann, *Puritanism and Theatre: Thomas Middleton and Opposition Drama under the Early Stuarts* (Cambridge: Cambridge University Press, 1980); Jerzy Limon, *Dangerous Matter: English Drama and Politics in 1623/24* (Cambridge: Cambridge University Press, 1986); and A.A. Bromham and Zara Bruzzi, *'The Changeling' and the Years of Crisis, 1619–1624: A Hieroglyph of Britain* (London: Pinter Publishers, 1990). On the topicality of the 1623 collaboration, see Gary Taylor, 'Historicism, Presentism, and Time: Middleton's *The Spanish Gypsy* and *A Game at Chess*', *Sederi* 18 (2008), 147–70. As relations between England and Spain deteriorated further into 1625 – in September war broke out – the satire in *A Game at Chess* took on a patriotic hue; it was printed three times in 1625.

18 For example, while the glove-dropping at the end of 1.1 may recall *The Spanish Tragedy*, where Bel-Imperia drops her glove for Horatio to pick up, it has also been read as alluding to a moment years earlier at court, when Prince Henry publicly

refused to accept Frances Howard's, on the grounds that it had already been 'stretched by another' – which the business that presumably accompanied De Flores' 'I should thrust my fingers / Into her sockets here' (1.1.226–7) would have reinforced: see Swapan Chakravorty, *Society and Politics in the Plays of Thomas Middleton* (Oxford: Clarendon Press, 1996), 147; cited in Neill, ed., 1.1.227n. Lisa Hopkins has argued that De Flores' closing lines in 3.3 allude to Ben Jonson's *Hymenaei*, composed for Howard's first marriage; see her 'Beguiling the Master of the Mystery', *Medieval and Renaissance Drama in England* 9 (1997), 149–61. Diaphanta's fear, 'She will not search me? Will she? / Like the forewoman of a female jury' (4.1.99–100), is accepted as referring unambiguously to the controversy over the physical examination Howard underwent.

19 See J.L. Simmons, 'Diabolical Realism in Middleton and Rowley's *The Changeling*', *Renaissance Drama* n.s. 11 (1980), 135–70; David Lindley, *The Trials of Francis Howard: Fact and Fiction at the Court of King James* (London: Routledge, 1993); Alastair Bellany, *The Politics of Court Scandal in Early Modern England: News Culture and the Overbury Affair, 1603–1660* (Cambridge: Cambridge University Press, 2002); Bromham and Bruzzi, *'The Changeling' and the Years of Crisis*, especially Ch.1; and Sara D. Luttfring, 'Bodily Narratives and the Politics of Virginity in *The Changeling* and the Essex Divorce', *Renaissance Drama* n.s. 39 (2011), 97–128.

20 For recent discussions of play structure and the structuring of space generally, see Tim Fitzpatrick, *Playwright, Space, and Place in Early Modern Performance: Shakespeare and Company* (Farnham: Ashgate, 2011). See also Peter Womack, 'Off-Stage', and Bruce C. Smith, 'Scene', in Henry S. Turner, ed., *Early Modern Theatricality* (Oxford: Oxford University Press, 2013), 71–92 and 93–122 respectively.

21 Scenes 1.2, 3.2 and 4.3 total 678 lines out of 2,151, or nearly 32 per cent; the line count is taken from Neill, ed., *The Changeling*.

22 However, since Alsemero's friend Jasperino might be expected to be present at the denouement, but features only briefly in 5.3, his final exit occuring at 5.3.11, the actor playing him is perhaps a more likely candidate for the role of Tomazo.

23 See Roberta Barker and David Nicol, 'Does Beatrice Joanna Have a Subtext?: *The Changeling* on the London Stage', *Early Modern Literary Studies* 10.1 (May 2004), 3.1–43.

24 See Mark Hutchings, 'The Interval and Indoor Playmaking', *Studies in Theatre & Performance* 33.3 (2013), 263–79.

25 That is not to say, however, that interpretation is closed off: Kim Solga discusses the role played – or *to be played* – by the audience in her *Violence Against Women in Early Modern Performance: Invisible Acts* (Basingstoke: Palgrave Macmillan, 2009), 141–75.

# Chapter 1

1 *The Marrow of Complements* (London, 1654), 124, 124–6, 126–7. Further evidence of the apparent popularity of Jasperino may be found in a William Davenant play dating from 1635; see Mark Hutchings, '*News from Plymouth* and *The Changeling*', *Notes and Queries* 64:3 (2017), 410–11.

2 See N.W. Bawcutt, 'Introduction', in Thomas Middleton and William Rowley, *The Changeling*, ed. N.W. Bawcutt (Cambridge: Harvard University Press, 1958), xxvi–xxx.

3 Ibid.

4 Walter Scott, ed., *Sir Tristrem*, 4th edn (Edinburgh: Archibald Constable and Co., 1819), 70.

5 Ibid., 320.

6 C.W. Dilke, ed., *Old English Plays*, vol. 4 (London: Whittingham and Rowland, 1815), 222.

7 Alexander Dyce, ed., *The Works of Thomas Middleton*, vol. 1 (London: Edward Lumley, 1840), lv.

8 James Russell Lowell, 'The Plays of Thomas Middleton', *The Pioneer* 1 (Jan. 1843): 35.

9 Ibid., 36.

10 Leigh Hunt, *Imagination and Fancy; or Selections from the English Poets* (New York: Wiley and Putnam, 1845), 160–1.

11 A.H. Bullen, ed., *The Works of Thomas Middleton*, vol. 1 (Boston: Houghton, Mifflin and Co., 1885), lx.

12 Ibid., lxvii.
13 Ibid.
14 A.H. Bullen, ed., *The Works of Thomas Middleton*, vol. 6 (London: John C. Nimmo, 1885), 73n.
15 Havelock Ellis, ed., *Thomas Middleton* (London: Vizetelly & Co., 1887), 85.
16 A.C. Swinburne, 'Introduction: Thomas Middleton', in *Thomas Middleton*, ed. Havelock Ellis (London: Vizetelly & Co., 1887), xxxv.
17 Ibid., xxxiv, xxxv–xxxvi.
18 Edmund Gosse, *The Jacobean Poets* (New York: C. Scribner's Sons, 1894), 127.
19 Pauline G. Wiggin, *An Inquiry into the Authorship of the Middleton-Rowley Plays* (Boston: Ginn, 1897), 43.
20 Ibid., 56.
21 Ibid., 58.
22 Gamaliel Bradford, 'The Women of Middleton and Webster', *The Sewanee Review* 29.1 (Jan. 1921): 17–18.
23 Ibid., 18, 19, 20.
24 Ibid., 20.
25 Ibid., 22.
26 William Archer, *The Old Drama and the New: An Essay in Re-valuation* (Boston: Small, Maynard and Company, 1923), 96.
27 Ibid., 100.
28 T.S. Eliot, *Selected Essays: New Edition* (New York: Harcourt, Brace & World, Inc., 1950), 141.
29 Ibid., 142.
30 M.C. Bradbrook, *Themes and Conventions of Elizabethan Tragedy* (Cambridge: Cambridge University Press, 1966), 212.
31 Ibid., 214, 212.
32 Ibid., 224.
33 William Empson, *Some Versions of Pastoral* (London: Chatto & Windus, 1935), 48.
34 Ibid., 52; Una Ellis-Fermor, *The Jacobean Drama: An Interpretation* (London: Methuen & Co. Ltd., 1965), 146–8, 149.

35 Ellis-Fermor, 144.
36 Samuel Schoenbaum, *Middleton's Tragedies: A Critical Study* (New York: Columbia University Press, 1955), 147.
37 Ibid., 147, 216.
38 Ibid., 103.
39 Ibid., 138, 216, 142, 139.
40 Richard Hindry Barker, *Thomas Middleton* (New York: Columbia University Press, 1958), 124.
41 Ibid., 128.
42 Ibid., 129.
43 Ibid., 130.
44 Bawcutt, 'Introduction', lxii.
45 Ibid., lxvii.
46 Christopher Ricks, 'The Moral and Poetic Structure of *The Changeling*', *Essays in Criticism* 10 (1960), 290–306; 290.
47 Ibid., 303.
48 Ibid., 291.
49 Ibid., 302–3.
50 T.B. Tomlinson, *A Study of Elizabethan and Jacobean Tragedy* (Cambridge: Cambridge University Press, 1964), 186.
51 Ibid., 192.
52 Ibid.
53 Robert Jordan, 'Myth and Psychology in *The Changeling*', *Renaissance Drama* 3 (1970), 157–65; 157.
54 Ibid., 159.
55 Ibid., 165.
56 Richard Levin, *The Multiple Plot in English Renaissance Drama* (Chicago: University of Chicago Press, 1971), 43.
57 Ibid., 47.
58 Dorothy M. Farr, *Thomas Middleton and the Drama of Realism: A Study of Some Representative Plays* (Edinburgh: Oliver & Boyd, 1973), 67.
59 Ibid., 71.

60 Ibid.

61 Raymond J. Pentzell, '*The Changeling:* Notes on Mannerism in Dramatic Form', *Comparative Drama* 9.1 (Spring 1975), 3–28; 7.

62 Ibid., 6.

63 Ibid., 14.

64 Levin, 40; Farr, 59, 53.

65 Caroline Lockett Cherry, *The Most Unvaluedst Purchase: Women in the Plays of Thomas Middleton* (Salzburg: Institut fur Englische Sprache und Literatur, 1973), 161.

66 Ibid., 166.

67 Ibid., 174.

68 Roger Stilling, *Love and Death in Renaissance Tragedy* (Baton Rouge: Louisiana State University Press, 1976), 248.

69 Ibid., 254.

70 Ibid., 255.

71 Ibid., 256.

72 Paula Johnson, 'Dissimulation Anatomized: *The Changeling*', *Philological Quarterly* 56.3 (Summer 1977), 329–38; 334.

73 Ibid., 336.

74 Ibid.

75 Nicholas Brooke, *Horrid Laughter in Jacobean Tragedy* (New York: Harper & Row, 1979), 78.

76 J.L. Simmons, 'Diabolical Realism in Middleton and Rowley's *The Changeling*', *Renaissance Drama* 11 (1980), 135–70; 136.

77 Ibid., 138.

78 Ibid., 144, 146, 147.

79 Ibid., 159.

80 Margot Heinemann, *Puritanism and Theatre: Thomas Middleton and Opposition Drama under the Early Stuarts* (Cambridge: Cambridge University Press, 1980), 174, 173.

81 Ibid., 175, 176.

82 Michael Scott, *Renaissance Drama and a Modern Audience* (London: Macmillan Press, 1982), 77.

83 Ibid., 78.

84 Jonathan Dollimore, *Radical Tragedy: Religion, Ideology, and Power in the Drama of Shakespeare and His Contemporaries*, 2nd edn (Durham: Duke University Press, 1993), 178.

85 Peter Morrison, 'A Cangoun in Zombieland: Middleton's Teratological *Changeling*', in *'Accompaninge the players': Essays Celebrating Thomas Middleton, 1580–1980*, ed. Kenneth Friedenreich (New York: AMS Press, 1983), 219–41; 225.

86 Ibid., 227.

87 Ibid., 227, 230.

88 Sara Eaton, 'Beatrice-Joanna and the Rhetoric of Love in *The Changeling*', *Theatre Journal* 36.3 (Oct. 1984), 371–82; 372.

89 Ibid., 374.

90 Dale B.J. Randall, 'Some Observations on the Theme of Chastity in *The Changeling*', *English Literary Renaissance* 14.3 (Sept. 1984), 347–66.

91 T. McAlindon, *English Renaissance Tragedy* (Vancouver: University of British Columbia Press, 1986), 209.

92 Ibid., 198, 205.

93 Leo Salingar, *Dramatic Form in Shakespeare and the Jacobeans* (Cambridge: Cambridge University Press, 1986), 225.

94 Ibid., 225, 226.

95 Joost Daalder, 'Folly and Madness in *The Changeling*', *Essays in Criticism* 38.1 (Jan. 1988), 1–21; 10, 11.

96 Ibid., 1; McAlindon, 209; Salingar, 235.

97 A.A. Bromham and Zara Bruzzi, *'The Changeling' and the Years of Crisis, 1619–1624: A Hieroglyph of Britain* (London: Pinter Publishers, 1990), 2.

98 Cristina Malcolmson, '"As Tame as the Ladies": Politics and Gender in *The Changeling*', *English Literary Renaissance* 20.2 (Mar. 1990), 320–39; 320.

99 Sharon Stockton, '"The 'broken rib of mankind'": The Sociopolitical Function of the Scapegoat in *The Changeling*', *Papers on Language and Literature* 26.4 (Fall 1990), 459–77; 460.

100 Michael Neill, '"Hidden Malady": Death, Discovery, and Indistinction in *The Changeling*', *Renaissance Drama* 22 (1991), 95–121; 100.

101 Ibid., 102.

102 Ibid., 103.

103 Martin Wiggins, *Journeymen in Murder: The Assassin in English Renaissance Drama* (Oxford: Clarendon Press, 1991), 185, 188.

104 Arthur L. Little, Jr., '"Transshaped" Women: Virginity and Hysteria in *The Changeling*', in *Madness in Drama*, ed. James Redmond (Cambridge: Cambridge University Press, 1993), 19–42: 34.

105 Marjorie Garber, 'The Insincerity of Women', in *Desire in the Renaissance: Psychoanalysis and Literature*, ed. Valeria Finucci and Regina Schwartz (Princeton: Princeton University Press, 1994), 19–38; 25.

106 Ibid., 26, 27.

107 Ibid., 27.

108 Joost Daalder and Antony Telford Moore, '"There's scarce a thing but is both loved and loathed": *The Changeling* I.i.91–129', *English Studies* 80.6 (1999), 499–508; 502, 507.

109 Deborah G. Burks, '"I'll Want My Will Else": *The Changeling* and Women's Complicity with Their Rapists', *English Literary History* 62.4 (Winter 1995), 759–90; 763.

110 Ibid., 774.

111 Ibid., 771.

112 Ibid., 776.

113 Swapan Chakravorty, *Society and Politics in the Plays of Thomas Middleton* (Oxford: Clarendon Press, 1996), 150.

114 Ibid., 158.

115 Ibid., 164.

116 Lisa Jardine, *Reading Shakespeare Historically* (London: Routledge, 1996), 119.

117 Ibid., 120.

118 Lisa Hopkins, 'Beguiling the Master of the Mystery: Form and Power in *The Changeling*', *Medieval and Renaissance Drama in England* 9 (1997), 149–61.

119 Ibid., 156.

# Chapter 2

A big thank-you to my wonderful research assistant, Abigail Holt, whose work saved me immense amounts of time.

1 N.W. Bawcutt, ed., *The Control and Censorship of Caroline Drama: The Records of Sir Henry Herbert, Master of the Revels 1623–73* (Oxford: Clarendon Press, 1996), 136, 148. On the fortunes of Beeston's Cockpit/Phoenix, see Andrew Gurr, *The Shakespearean Playing Companies* (Oxford: Clarendon Press, 1996), 123–7.

2 Lady Elizabeth's company was alternately known as the Queen of Bohemia's company after their patron assumed that title in 1619; Herbert's record of licensing *The Changeling* is the first evidence that this company had re-formed in London after several years of provincial touring. In 1626, some of its players became part of Christopher Beeston's newly-formed troupe, Queen Henrietta's Men, who continued to play at the Cockpit until Beeston dissolved them in 1636, to be replaced the following year by the King and Queen's Young Company, also known as Beeston's Boys (Gurr, *Playing Companies*, 419, 424). This was the company that William Beeston inherited in 1638 and for whom he legally protected *The Changeling* and other plays in 1639. The above summary is drawn from the detailed histories in Gurr, *Playing Companies*, 419–24, and Siobhan Keenan, *Acting Companies and their Plays in Shakespeare's London* (London: Bloomsbury, 2014), 43–6. For a succinct account of *The Changeling*'s progress through these companies, see the Introduction to N.W. Bawcutt's Revels edition of *The Changeling* (London: Methuen, 1961), xxiv–xxvi.

3 Gurr, *Playing Companies*, 424.

4 Douglas Bruster, 'The Changeling', in *Thomas Middleton and Early Modern Textual Culture: A Companion to the Collected Works* (Oxford: Oxford University Press, 2007), 1094–5.

5 E.M. Symonds, 'The Diary of John Greene (1635–57)', *English Historical Review* 43.171 (July 1928), 386.

6 Quoted in Bawcutt, 'Introduction', xxvii; Gurr, *Playing Companies*, 155, notes that the Praeludium was written for a 1638 Cockpit revival of *Shepherdess*.

7 Andrew Gurr, *The Shakespearean Stage 1574–1642*, 4th edn (Cambridge: Cambridge University Press, 2009), 107, 112–13.

8 Bawcutt, 'Introduction', xxvii. The passage is from *A Key to the Cabinet of the Parliament, By their Remembrancer* (London, 1648), 8.

9 John Downes, *Roscius Anglicanus, or An Historical Review of the Stage* (London, 1708), 17–19. Downes is cited in William Van Lennep, ed., *The London Stage 1660–1800: Part 1: 1660–1700* (Carbondale: Southern Illinois University Press, 1965), 7, 25. For Pepys' comments, see Sara Jayne Steen, *Ambrosia in an Earthern Vessel: Three Centuries of Audience and Reader Response to the Works of Thomas Middleton* (New York: AMS, 1993), 60–1.

10 Downes, 19.

11 Van Lennep, 148. At some point between Pepys' 1661 record and the court performance, *The Changeling* was in the repertory of the Duke of York's Company, owned by William Davenant, playing at his innovative new Lincoln's Inn Fields theatre, opened in June 1661. An edition of the play published in 1668 mentions this company and theatre on its title page; the court performance of the same year was also by this company. On the Lincoln's Inn Fields theatre, see Frances M. Kavenik, *British Drama, 1660–1779: A Critical History* (New York: Twayne, 1995), 4–5.

12 William Hayley, *Plays of Three Acts; Written for a Private Theatre* (London, 1784), 95–6. Hayley's account of how Richardson proposed an adaptation to Edward Young, but Hayley himself ended up writing it, would appear to be corroborated by Young's biographer and by a brief mention in a letter by Richardson. See Harold Forster, *Edward Young: The Poet of the Night Thoughts 1683–1765* (Alburgh, Harleston, Norfolk: Erskine, 1986), 331; Peter Sabor, ed., *Samuel Richardson: Correspondence with Lady Bradshaigh and Lady Echlin*, Vol. 3: 1758–1762 (Cambridge: Cambridge University Press, 2016), 778. My thanks to Peter Sabor for locating this reference. That Hayley was working from *The Changeling* and not just 'a concise sketch of the story as related by Richardson', as his introduction might imply, is detailed in James Hogg, 'William Hayley's Marcella and Thomas Middleton and William

Rowley's *The Changeling*: A Case of Literary Plagiarism?' in *Essays in Honour of Professor Tyrus Hillway*, ed. Erwin A. Sturzl (Salzburg: Universitat Salzburg, 1977), 74–128. Hogg quotes several reviews of *Marcella* and letters from Hayley on the Drury Lane fiasco.

13 Hayley, 111, 151.

14 Charles Wentworth Dilke, ed., *Old English Plays; Being a Selection from the Early Dramatic Writers*, Vol. 4 (London, 1815), 222. Even *Marcella*, however, was too much for one contemporary reviewer, who reacted to the heroine's 'crimes' of promise-breaking and accessory to murder with 'indignant horror' and 'disgust.' See 'Arts and Culture', *Prompter*, 9 November 1789.

15 'Arts and Culture', *English Chronicle*, 7–10 November 1789. While the published *Marcella* has the protagonist ask Hernandez to steal the ring, this review's plot summary implies that on stage the episode was amended to her being merely overheard by him: 'She was imprudent enough to express her wishes on this head in the hearing of *Hernandez*.'

16 'Arts and Culture', *The World*, 9 November 1789; 'News', *London Chronicle*, 7–10 November 1789.

17 On Lowell and Swinburne, see Jay O'Berski, *'The Changeling': A Guide to the Text and the Play in Performance* (Basingstoke: Palgrave Macmillan, 2012), 128–30.

18 William Archer, *The Old Drama and the New: An Essay in Re-Evaluation* (1923; rpt. New York: Benjamin Blom, 1972), 97, 100.

19 Martin Quinn, 'William Archer', in *Modern British Dramatists, 1900–1945*, ed. Stanley Weintraub, *Dictionary of Literary Biography* vol. 10 (Detroit: Gale, 1982), 9–10. *Beatriz Juana* was published three years after Archer's death.

20 Archer, 388.

21 Jonathan Croall, *Sybil Thorndike: A Star of Life* (London: Haus, 2008), 148–9. On the Phoenix Society and its mission to revive the plays of Shakespeare's contemporaries, see Anthony Cuda, 'Evenings at the Phoenix Society: Eliot and the Independent London Theater', in *The Edinburgh Companion to T. S. Eliot and the Arts*, ed. Frances Dickey and John D. Morgenstern

(Edinburgh: Edinburgh University Press, 2016), 202–24. Archer, 110–13, attacks the Society's admirers.

22 'The London Letter', *Gloucester Citizen*, 29 June 1925.

23 'The Theatres', *Times*, 6 July 1925.

24 'Plays and Players', *Sunday Times*, 4 December 1927, 6; Norman Marshall, *The Other Theatre* (London: John Lehman, 1947), 76. The performances of *White Devil* and *Arden* are documented in J.P. Wearing, *The London Stage 1920–1929* (Lanham, MD: Rowman and Littlefield, 2014), 391, 405.

25 Marilyn Roberts, 'A Preliminary Checklist of Productions of Thomas Middleton's Plays', *Research Opportunities in Renaissance Drama* 28 (1985), 37–61; 39. The original documents from this performance are held at the Billy Rose Theater Division of the New York Public Library. I am grateful to Marilyn Roberts and to John Calhoun at the Billy Rose for providing me with copies.

26 Records of this production, including the programme, several photographs, and the annual report for 1938–9, were kindly supplied by Birkbeck archivist Victoria Rea. An announcement appears in 'The Universities', *Observer*, 27 November 1938.

27 A.D., 'Play by Middleton and Rowley', *Manchester Guardian*, 10 December 1938.

28 *Tatler and Bystander*, 8 June 1949; *Times*, 19 May 1949. It is unclear whether this production included the subplot: the *Times* reviewer, who saw a dress-rehearsal, said it was omitted, but the *Tatler* identified a picture of 'Mr. Charles Pasternak, who played Alibius'.

29 'Pegasus Society', *Times*, 17 May 1954. See also Philip Hope-Wallace, 'A Lurid Piece from 1622: Middleton's "Changeling",' *Manchester Guardian*, 18 May 1954.

30 'Oxford Theatre Club', *Times*, 29 November 1956.

31 Five pre-1960 amateur English productions appear in the online list from the University of Warwick's Centre for the Study of the Renaissance; Birkbeck makes six. The first American production was at Yale in 1939, the first Canadian at the University of Western Ontario in 1946: these are listed in Roberts, 'A Preliminary Checklist'.

32 Tony Richardson, 'Why We Revived *The Changeling*', *Plays and Players* 8.7 (April 1961), 5; Nora Williams examines the 1961 promptbook in '"Cannot I keep that secret?": Editing and Performing Asides in *The Changeling*', *Shakespeare Bulletin* 34.1 (2016), 29–54, 35–9.

33 Philip Hope-Wallace, 'Too Little Care for the Words?', *Guardian*, 22 February 1961; T.C. Worsley, 'The Changeling', *Financial Times*, 23 February 1961; 'At The Play', *Punch*, 1 March 1961; W. J. Weatherby, 'The Durrell Brothers', *Guardian*, 6 May 1961.

34 Harold Hobson, 'Men are Not Born Equal', *Sunday Times*, 5 March 1961.

35 'Tragedy's Close Likeness to Macbeth', *Times*, 22 February 1961.

36 John Heilpern, *John Osborne: The Many Lives of the Angry Young Man* (New York: Knopf, 2006), 210; Roberta Barker and David Nicol, 'Does Beatrice Joanna Have a Subtext?: *The Changeling* on the London Stage', *Early Modern Literary Studies* 10.1 (2004), *passim*.

37 Kenneth Tynan, 'The Problem of Pain', *Observer*, 26 February 1961.

38 Richardson, 'Why We Revived *The Changeling*'.

39 Robert Muller, 'Mary Ure Takes the Plunge', *Daily Mail*, 22 February 1961; J. C. Trewin, 'Stiff News', *Illustrated London News*, 4 March 1961.

40 In 1938 the Westport County Playhouse had considered a production set in Francoist Spain, with 'Phalangists and mantillas', but it seems not to have materialized. See Richard Skinner, 'A Note on Interstate Commerce', *New York Times*, 19 June 1938; a list of Westport's 1930s productions is in Richard Somerset-Ward, *An American Theatre: The Story of the Westport County Playhouse* (New Haven: Yale University Press, 2005), 262–3.

41 John Beaufort, 'On and Off Broadway: East Riverside Shakespeare', *Christian Science Monitor*, 15 August 1956.

42 Jerry Tallmer, 'Theatre: The Changeling', *Village Voice*, 9 May 1956. This follows a description of 3.3 that could indicate cuts to the final speeches: 'De Flores says ... he wants *her*. She reels, gasps, slaps his face, and with that he grabs her. Music up. Blackout.' However, Papp's annotated script leaves the end of

the scene intact, with a prompt beside Beatrice-Joanna's 'Vengeance begins', stating 'no way out'. My thanks again to John Calhoun at the Billy Rose for describing the script to me.

43 N.J.A., 'Changeling Revived', *New York Times*, 4 May 1956. The early years of the Shakespearean Theater Workshop, including the details about costumes and pay, are recounted in Kenneth Turan and Joseph Papp, *Free For All: Joe Papp, the Public, and the Greatest Theater Story Ever Told* (New York: Doubleday, 2009), 56–78.

44 'Changeling Set to Open Repertory', *New York Amsterdam News*, 31 October 1964.

45 Howard Taubman, 'Theater: The Changeling is Revived', *New York Times*, 30 October 1964. Glenn Loney, 'Broadway in Review', *Educational Theatre Journal* 17.1 (March 1965), 58–7.

46 Elia Kazan, 'Elia Kazan Ad-Libs on '"The Changeling" and its Critics', *Show: The Magazine of the Performing Arts* 5.1 (January 1965), 38.

47 Sam Zolotow, 'The Changeling will Close December 23', *New York Times*, 12 November 1964; Albert J. Devlin and Marlene J. Devlin, eds, *The Selected Letters of Elia Kazan* (New York: Knopf, 2014), 522–3.

48 Elia Kazan, *Kazan on Directing* (New York: Knopf, 2009), 143. On Kazan's personal life, see his *Elia Kazan: A Life* (New York: Knopf, 1988), 6–7, 691, 722–4.

49 Elia Kazan, Richard Schechner and Theodore Hoffman, 'Look! There's the American Theater!' *Tulane Drama Review* 9.2 (1964), 81.

50 Loney, 59.

51 Kazan, *A Life*, 610–11.

52 Louis Chapin, 'Savage "Changeling",' *Christian Science Monitor*, 4 November 1964; Loney, 59; Taubman. See also Richard Cooke, 'The Theater: Strong Brew, Weak Acting', *Wall Street Journal*, 2 November 1964.

53 Kazan, 'Elia Kazan Ad-Libs', 40.

54 Patty Duke (1946–2016) starred in *The Patty Duke Show* (1963–6), an American sitcom about the misadventures of a high-spirited teenaged girl.

55 Chapin; Taubman.
56 Robert Brustein, 'We Are Two Cultural Nations', *Seasons of Discontent: Dramatic Opinions 1959–1965* (New York: Simon and Schuster, 1965), 254–5.
57 'Kazan Defeated by The Changeling', *Times*, 23 December 1964.
58 Richard Schechner, 'New York: Sentimentalist Kazan', *Tulane Drama Review* 9.3 (1965), 197.
59 Taubman; Chapin.
60 Elenore Lester, 'At Yale: Joy, Baby, Joy', *New York Times*, 9 October 1966. Papp had recently begun teaching directing at the Yale School of Drama, where Robert Brustein – whom Kazan lists as leading the pack of critics 'seeking to destroy' him after his *Changeling* – had just become Dean. See Kazan, *A Life*, 694. I can find no record of this production taking place.
61 As counted by the University of Warwick's list at http://www2.warwick.ac.uk/fac/arts/ren/projects/elizabethan_jacobean_drama/middleton/changeling/stage_history/
62 B.A. Young, 'Jeannetta Cochrane: The Changeling', *Financial Times*, 27 July 1966.
63 D.F.B., 'One Step from Madness', *Stage*, 28 July 1966.
64 'Marat/Sade method for Middleton play', *Times*, 6 May 1967; see also http://www.lucaronconi.it/scheda/teatro/i-lunatici.
65 F.W.D., 'The Changeling', *Stage*, 17 September 1970;
66 http://www.sltarchive.co.uk/wiki/index.php?title=The_Changeling_(1974).
67 Michael Coveney, 'Glasgow Citizens' The Changeling', *Financial Times*, 23 February 1976.
68 Sheridan Morley, 'Second Sight', *Punch*, 25 October 1978.
69 Peter Jenkins, 'Covering Up', *Spectator*, 9 September 1978; Irving Wardle, 'Towering Summit on Jacobean Theatre', *Times*, 6 September 1978; B.A. Young, 'Riverside Studios: The Changeling', *Financial Times*, 6 September 1978.
70 Michael Billington, 'The Changeling', *Guardian*, 6 September 1978. For these comments see Billington; Wardle; Young; Jenkins.
71 Wardle.

72 Robert Cushman, 'Passion and the Playwrights', *Observer*, 10 September 1978; Billington, 'The Changeling'. Both Cushman and Jenkins acknowledge that Beatrice-Joanna is an unusually difficult role.

73 See also J.L. Styan, 'High Tide in the London Theatre: Some Notes on the 1978–79 Season', *Comparative Drama* 13.3 (1979), 253; Benedict Nightingale, 'The Alexandrian Duet', *New Statesman*, 20 October 1978.

74 Nightingale, 'Alexandrian': 'Brookish' refers to Peter Brook, then directing a stripped-down *Antony and Cleopatra* at Stratford. J.C. Trewin, 'The High Noises', *Illustrated London News*, 1 December 1978; Morley, 'Second Sight.' A comparison of the two productions, uncomplimentary to Hands, is in *Research Opportunities in Renaissance Drama* 21 (1978), 68–9.

75 Wardle; Billington, 'The Changeling'.

76 Billington, 'The Changeling'; Nightingale.

77 Barker and Nicol, paragraph 12.

78 Nightingale; Wardle.

79 Dennis Kennedy, 'Theatre in Review', *Theatre Journal* 31.3 (1979), 423.

80 Costuming described by G.M.P., 'The Changeling', *Cahiers Élisabéthains* 15 (1979), 131; see also Kennedy, 423.

81 Quotation is from Irving Wardle, 'Towering Summit', who was also struck by this scene.

82 Billington, 'The Changeling'; G.M.P.

83 B.A. Young, 'Theatre Royal, Bristol: The Changeling', *Financial Times*, 6 November 1978.

84 Marilyn J. Plotkins, *The American Repertory Theatre Reference Book: The Brustein Years* (Westport, CT: Praeger, 2005), 1–5.

85 Richard Eder, 'Getting Its Act Together?' *Boston Review*, 1 April 1986, 8.

86 Steve Vineburg, 'The Changeling', *Theatre Journal* 38.2 (May 1986), 224–5. See also Ari Z. Posner, 'More of the Same Thing with ART's 'Changeling',' *Harvard Crimson*, 5 December 1985.

87 Carolyn Clay, 'Moon Over Mayhem', *Boston Phoenix*, 10 December 1985. The concubines are mentioned by Vineburg.

Objections to Bottoms' comedy include Arthur Friedman, *Boston Herald*, 26 November, 1985; Kevin Kelly, *Boston Globe*, 29 November 1985.

88 Vineburg, 226.
89 Clay, 'Moon.'
90 Deborah Weisgall, 'The ART of Robert Brustein', *Boston Review*, 1 April 1988, 24. See also Kevin Kelly, *Boston Globe*, 29 November 1985: 'Beatrice-Joanna and De Flores are Krafft-Ebbing case histories.'
91 Christopher Edwards, 'Damned Souls', *Spectator*, 2 July 1988; Jim Hiley, 'Waterloo Sunrise', *Listener*, 7 July 1988.
92 Sheridan Morley, 'National Change of Eyre', *Punch*, 8 July 1988; Edwards; Peter Porter, 'Pre-echoes and Paradoxes', *TLS*, 8 July 1988. See also Betty Caplan, 'Family Fortunes', *New Statesman*, 8 July 1988.
93 John Peter, 'Is this a Breath of Fresh Eyre?' *Sunday Times*, 26 June 1988; Alex Renton, 'Classics Poles Apart', *Illustrated London News*, August 1988, 64. See also Hiley.
94 Kate Kellaway, 'Lust Conquers All', *Observer*, 26 June 1988. Barker and Nicol, paragraph 17, quote another review that characterizes this De Flores as 'a man of primitive drives' whose 'alien background . . . has gouged itself into his personality.' The caricature of Harris's De Flores in *Punch*, bug-eyed and open-mouthed, borders on racist.
95 Hiley.
96 Renton, 'Classics Poles Apart.'
97 Ibid.
98 Edwards; Michael Billington, 'Fateful Attractions', *Guardian*, 25 June 1988.
99 Billington, 'Fateful Attractions.'
100 On *Tallgrass Gothic*, see O'Berski, 102–6; he discusses a 2009 Chicago production pairing the adaptation with the original. Susan Bennett analyses *The Ugly Man* in *Performing Nostalgia: Shifting Shakespeare and the Contemporary Past* (London: Routledge, 1996), 91–3. A third adaptation, Dan Jemmett's *Dog Face* (2003), keeps the language of *The Changeling*'s main plot, but makes the characters a company of modern-day travelling

players, raising the question of whether the audience is watching 'performance' or 'reality'; see O'Berski, 91–5.

101 Michael Neill makes this observation in the performance history section of his New Mermaids edition: see Thomas Middleton and William Rowley, *The Changeling*, ed. Michael Neill (London: A&C Black, 2006), xxxvi.

102 Lena Pissaro, *Time Out*, 23 January 1991; Malcolm Rutherford, *Financial Times*, 19 January 1991; Rick Jones, *Time Out*, 23 January 1991. All found in *Theatre Record* 11.2 (1991), 66–7. E-mail correspondence with Peter Cockett confirmed that the deflowering was portrayed as a rape, occurring offstage after a violent onstage struggle.

103 Irving Wardle, *Independent on Sunday,* 20 January 1991.

104 Quotations are from Wardle; Michael Billington, *Guardian*, 22 January 1991; Malcolm Rutherford, *Financial Times*, 19 January 1991. These and other reviews reprinted in *Theatre Record* 11.2 (1991), 65–6.

105 See, for instance, Sylvester Onwordi, *What's On*, 23 January 1991.

106 Quoted in O'Berski, 89, who provides a longer analysis of Woodruff's production than I have space for here.

107 Peter Marks, '17th-Century Foxes Voguing, Dancing and Killing', *New York Times*, 8 March 1997; Elyse Sommer, 'The Changeling', *CurtainUp* (www.curtainup.com/changel.html); Donald Lyons, 'Classi(e)st Jews in Atlanta: Updating the Classics', *Wall Street Journal*, 6 March 1997; Glenda Frank, www.backstage.com/reviews/reviews_22/.

108 Francine Russo, 'Dead Men's Walk', *Village Voice*, 18 March 1997.

109 Marks; Lyons; Sommer.

110 Michael Coveney, 'The Bit on the Side Takes Centre Stage', *Observer*, 8 November 1992; Andrew St. George, 'Horror and Farce in "The Changeling",' *Financial Times*, 5 November 1992.

111 Stephen Wall, 'The Slatted Trap', *Times Literary Supplement*, 20 November 1992.

112 Kate Kellaway, 'Lust Runs Hot and Cold', *Observer*, 30 May 1993.

113 Benedict Nightingale, 'Absurd, perhaps, but Irresistible', *Times*, 27 May 1993; Irving Wardle, 'No Room at the Inn in Thatcher's Britain', *Independent*, 29 May 1993.

114 Malcolm Rutherford, 'The Changeling', *Financial Times*, 27 May 1993; see also Nightingale, 'Absurd', who describes Beatrice-Joanna as 'slumm[ing] her way to the sort of dark ecstasy Freud is supposed to have discovered.'

115 Ann Fitzgerald, 'Mad About Malcolm and Cheryl', *The Stage*, 4 February 1993.

116 John Peter, 'Theatre Check', *Sunday Times*, 8 November 1992; Kellaway, 'Lust.'

117 The below-stage madhouse is discussed in Robert Wilcher, 'The Changeling', *Cahiers Élisabéthains* 44 (1993), 89–91; Wall, 'Slatted Trap.'

118 Karin Brown, 'Appendix I: Professional Productions of Early Modern Drama in the UK and USA, 1960–2010', in *Performing Early Modern Today*, ed. Pascale Aebischer and Kathryn Prince (Cambridge: Cambridge University Press, 2012), 178–217. The seven post-2010 productions I'm aware of include the four covered in Susan Dustagheer's chapter in this volume, plus Brent Griffin (Tallahassee, Florida, 2012); Jesse Berger (New York, 2015); and Jackie Maxwell (Stratford, Ontario, 2017). To Brown's list of productions up to 2010 can be added Stephen Unwin (Nottingham, then touring, 2007), and Lindy Davies (Ljubljana, 2009); information on the latter is found at http://www.en.drama.si/repertoar/delo?id=1596.

119 Libby Purves, 'The Changeling', *Times*, 28 November 2012; Penelope Geng, 'The Changeling', *Cahiers Élisabéthains* 81 (2012), 63–7. 'Brilliantly bonkers' is Maxie Szalwinska's recollection of Dromgoole's production, *Sunday Times*, 25 January 2015.

120 Natasha Tripney, 'Changing the Changeling', *Exeunt*, 13 November 2012. http://exeuntmagazine.com/features/changing-the-changeling/

121 Paul Menzer, 'The Changeling', *Shakespeare Bulletin* 25.1 (2007), 94–7; Michael Billington, 'The Changeling', *Guardian*, 16 May 2006.

122 The most detailed discussion of this humanization is Will Sharpe's review in *Cahiers Élisabéthains* 69 (2006), 68–70; on the complex portrayal of Beatrice-Joanna in this production, see Kim Solga, *Violence Against Women in Early Modern Performance* (New York: Palgrave, 2009), 159–70.

123 Three reviews are reprinted in *Theatre Record* 22.21 (2002), 1360, including Rachel Haliburton's for *Evening Standard*, 15 October 2002.

124 Jill Truman, 'The Changeling at Southwark Playhouse', *Islington Gazette*, 25 November 2011; nearly every review decries the voice-overs, including Maddy Costa's relatively balanced one in the *Guardian*, 8 November 2011.

125 J. Kelly Nestruck, 'The Changeling is a Well-acted Tale of Two Faces', *Globe and Mail*, 16 June 2017.

126 Michael Coveney, 'The Changeling', *What'sOnStage*, 8 November 2011. http://www.whatsonstage.com/west-end-theatre/reviews/11-2011/the-changeling_6326.html

127 Kate Lechler, 'The Changeling', *Shakespeare Bulletin* 31.3 (2013), 516–19.

128 Three reviews are reprinted in *Theatre Record* 21.12 (2001), 752; quotations are from Patrick Marmion, *Evening Standard*, 18 June 2001, and Lucy Powell, *Time Out*, 20 June 2001.

129 Personal interview with Maxwell on 24 June 2017; I saw the performance of 23 June.

130 Hilton's script is available at http://stf-theatre.org.uk/wp-content/uploads/2015/07/The-Changeling.pdf_; quotations from pages 20 and 65.

131 Robert Shore, *Time Out London*, 6 October 2004; this and several other reviews of the Bristol and London productions are in *Theatre Record* 24.6 (2004), 369–70 and *Theatre Record* 24.20 (2004), 1243–4, respectively.

132 My notes, after seeing performance of 27 December 2015.

133 Michael Billington, 'The Changeling'; Menzer, 'The Changeling'; Peter J. Smith, 'Review of Thomas Middleton and William Rowley's *The Changeling*', *Shakespeare* 2.2 (2006), 220–1.

134 Dominic Cavendish, 'The Changeling', *Telegraph*, 28 November 2012; Paul Taylor, 'The Changeling', *Independent*, 3 February

2012. Hill-Gibbins explains his madhouse-inspired seating plans in Tripney, 'Changing the Changeling.'

135 Susan Irvine, 'The Changeling', *Sunday Telegraph*, 21 May 2006.

136 Shore, *Time Out*; Lyn Gardner, *Guardian*, 30 September 2004.

137 John Thaxter, *What's On*, 6 October 2004.

138 Sarah Hemming, *Financial Times*, 8 October 2004; John Peter, *Sunday Times*, 28 March 2004; see also Sam Marlowe, *Times*, 30 September 2004.

139 Sharpe, *Cahiers Élisabéthains*, 69; Solga, 163.

140 Ibid; Menzer, *Shakespeare Bulletin*, 97.

141 David Benedict, 'The Changeling', *Variety*, 29 May 2006; John Peter, 'The Changeling', *Sunday Times*, 21 May 2006.

142 Billington, *Guardian*, 16 May 2006. Billington was 'a leading proponent of the Freudian reading of the role' as far back as 1988 (Barker and Nicol, para. 20); Claire Allfree's *Metro* review of 17 May 2006 laments an 'insufficient sense of [Beatrice-Joanna's] subconscious destructive sexual appetites', but in thirteen reviews, these were the only two references. However, both Donnellan and Williams, in separate interviews, state that Beatrice-Joanna's loathing does mask erotic fascination; for Donnellan, see Paul Taylor, 'Thomas Middleton's Dramas Return to the Stage', *Independent*, 23 February 2006; Williams' interview is at http://www.cheekbyjowl.com/the_changeling.php#audio.

143 Michael Billington, 'The Changeling', *Guardian*, 3 February 2012; Michael Billington, 'The Changeling Review' *Guardian*, 21 January 2015.

144 Kate Kellaway, 'Romeo and Juliet; The Changeling; Master Class – Review', *Guardian*, 12 February 2012; Geng, 66.

145 Andrzej Lukowski, *Time Out London*, 27 January 2015; Quentin Letts, *Daily Mail*, 23 January 2015. These are among twelve reviews reprinted in *Theatre Record* 35.1–2 (2015), 42–5.

146 Holly Williams, 'Hattie Morahan on The Changeling: An Unsavoury Role Played with Relish', *Independent*, 19 January 2015.

147 Nancy Durrant, 'Hattie Morahan on Why it's Fun to Behave Badly', *Times*, 20 January 2015.

# Chapter 3

1. For one of the most influential early articulations of this claim, see Jeffrey Masten, *Textual Intercourse: Collaboration, Authorship, and Sexualities in Renaissance Drama* (Cambridge: Cambridge University Press, 1997).
2. Richard L. Nochimson, '"Sharing" *The Changeling* by Playwrights and Professors: The Certainty of Uncertain Knowledge about Collaborations', *Early Theatre* 5 (2002), 37–57.
3. Ibid., 50.
4. Michael E. Mooney, "Framing' as Collaborative Technique: Two Middleton-Rowley Plays', in *Drama in the Renaissance: Comparative and Critical Essays*, ed. Clifford Davidson, C.J. Gianakaris and John H. Stroupe (New York: 1986), 300–14. For a classic statement of the play's unified linguistic structure, see Christopher Ricks, 'The Moral and Poetic Structure of *The Changeling*', *Essays in Criticism* 10.3 (1960), 290–306.
5. Heather Anne Hirschfeld, *Joint Enterprises: Collaborative Drama and the Institutionalization of the English Renaissance Theater* (Amherst, MA: University of Massachusetts Press, 2004).
6. Ibid., 117.
7. Mark Hutchings and A. A. Bromham, *Middleton and His Collaborators* (Plymouth: Northcote House, 2008).
8. Gordon McMullan, 'The Changeling and the Dynamics of Ugliness', in *The Cambridge Companion to English Renaissance Tragedy*, ed. Emma Smith and Garrett A. Sullivan, Jr. (Cambridge: Cambridge University Press, New York, 2011), 222–35.
9. Ibid., 224.
10. Douglas Bruster, 'Canon and Chronology: *The Changeling*', in Gary Taylor and John Lavagnino (gen. eds), *Thomas Middleton and Early Modern Textual Culture: A Companion to the Collected Works* (Oxford: Clarendon Press, 2007), 422–3.
11. David Nicol, *Middleton and Rowley: Forms of Collaboration in the Jacobean Playhouse* (Toronto: University of Toronto Press, 2012).
12. Ibid., 37.

13 Annabel Patterson, 'Introduction' to *The Changeling*, ed. Doulas Bruster, in *Thomas Middleton: The Collected Works*, ed. Gary Taylor and John Lavagnino (Oxford: Clarendon Press, 2007), 1632–78.

14 A.A. Bromham and Zara Bruzzi, *The Changeling and the Years of Crisis, 1619–1624: A Hieroglyph of Britain* (London: Pinter Publishers, 1990).

15 Patterson, 1635.

16 Mark Hutchings, '*The Changeling* at Court', *Cahiers Élisabéthains* 81.1. (2012),15–24.

17 Mark Hutchings, 'Deflores between the Acts', *Studies in Theatre and Performance* 31.1 (2011), 95–111.

18 Ibid., 109.

19 Barbara Fuchs, *The Poetics of Piracy: Emulating Spain in English Literature* (Philadelphia: University of Pennsylvania Press, 2013), 65–70.

20 Mark Hutchings, '"Those rebellious Hollanders": *The Changeling*'s Double Dutch', *SEDERI*: 24 (2014), 143–56.

21 Kenneth S. Jackson, *Separate Theaters: Bethlem ('Bedlam') Hospital and the Shakespearean Stage* (Newark: University of Delaware Press, 2005).

22 Carol Thomas Neely, *Distracted Subjects: Madness and Gender in Shakespeare and Early Modern Culture* (Ithaca and London: Cornell University Press, 2004), and '"Distracted Measures": Madness and Theatricality in Middleton', in *Thomas Middleton in Context*, ed. Suzanne Gossett (Cambridge: Cambridge University Press, 2011), 295–313.

23 Carol Thomas Neely, 'Hot Blood: Estranging Mediterranean Bodies in Early Modern Medical and Dramatic Texts', in *Disease, Diagnosis, and Cure on the Early Modern Stage*, ed. Stephanie Moss and Kaara L. Peterson (Aldershot; Burlington, VT: Ashgate, 2004), 55–68.

24 Donald Hedrick and Bryan Reynolds, 'I Might Like You Better If We Slept Together: The Historical Drift of Place in *The Changeling*', in Reynolds, *Transversal Enterprises in the Drama of Shakespeare and his Contemporaries* (London: Palgrave Macmillan, 2006), 112–23.

25 Kim Solga, 'Playing *The Changeling* Architecturally', in *Performing Environments: Site-Specificity in Medieval and Early Modern English Drama*, ed. Susan Bennett and Mary Polito (Basingstoke; New York: Palgrave Macmillan, 2014), 56–78.

26 Ibid., 57–8.

27 Una Chaudhuri, *Staging Place: The Geography of Modern Drama* (Ann Arbor, MI: University of Michigan Press, 1995).

28 Roberta Barker and David Nicol, 'Does Beatrice Joanna Have a Subtext?: *The Changeling* on the London Stage', *Early Modern Literary Studies* 10.1 (May 2004), 3.1–43.

29 Deborah G. Burks, '"I'll want my will else": *The Changeling* and Women's Complicity with Their Rapists', *English Literary History* 62 (1995), 759–90.

30 Judith Haber, '"I(t) Could Not Choose But Follow": Erotic Logic in *The Changeling*', *Representations* 81 (2003), 79–98.

31 Kim Solga, *Violence against Women in Early Modern Performance: Invisible Acts* (New York: Palgrave Macmillan, 2009).

32 Frances E. Dolan, 'Re-reading Rape in *The Changeling*', *Journal for Early Modern Cultural Studies* 11.1 (2011), 4–29.

33 Christine Varnado, '"Invisible Sex!": What Looks Like the Act in Early Modern Drama?' in *Sex Before Sex: Figuring the Act in Early Modern England*, ed. James M. Bromley and Will Stockton (Minneapolis, MN: University of Minnesota Press, 2013), 25–52.

34 Lisa Hopkins, *The Female Hero in English Renaissance Tragedy* (New York: Palgrave, 2002).

35 Mara Amster, 'Frances Howard and Middleton and Rowley's *The Changeling*: Trials, Tests, and the Legibility of the Virgin Body', in *The Single Woman in Medieval and Early Modern England: Her Life and Representation*, ed. Laurel Amtower and Dorothea Kehler (Tempe, AZ: Arizona Center for Medieval and Renaissance Studies, 2003), 211–32. Margot Heinemann, *Puritanism and Theatre: Thomas Middleton and Opposition Drama under the Early Stuarts* (Cambridge: Cambridge University Press, 1980), 178.

36 Marjorie Garber, 'The Insincerity of Women', in *Subject and Object in Renaissance Culture*, ed. Margreta de Grazia, Maureen Quilligan and Peter Stallybrass (Cambridge: Cambridge University Press, 1996), 349–68.

37 Sara D. Luttfring, *Bodies, Speech, and Reproductive Knowledge in Early Modern England* (New York: Routledge, 2016), and 'Bodily Narratives and the Politics of Virginity in *The Changeling* and the Essex Divorce', *Renaissance Drama* 39 (2011), 97–128.

38 Jennifer Panek, 'Shame and Pleasure in *The Changeling*', *Renaissance Drama* 42.2 (2014), 191–215.

39 Jay Zysk, 'Relics and Unreliable Bodies in *The Changeling*', *English Literary Renaissance* 45.3 (2015), 400–24.

40 Michael Neill, 'Servant Obedience and Master Sins: Shakespeare and the Bonds of Service', in *Putting History to the Question: Power, Politics and Society on English Renaissance Tragedy* (New York: Columbia University Press, 2000), 13–48.

41 Michael Neill, '"A Woman's Service": Gender, Subordination, and the Erotics of Rank in the Drama of Shakespeare and His Contemporaries', *Shakespearean International Yearbook* 5 (2005), 127–44.

42 Mark Thornton Burnett, '*The Changeling* and Masters and Servants', in *Early Modern English Drama: A Critical Companion*, ed. Garret A. Sullivan, Patrick Cheyney and Andrew Hadfield (Oxford: Oxford University Press, 2006), 298–308.

43 Michelle M. Dowd, 'Desiring Subjects: Staging the Female Servant in Early Modern Tragedy' in *Working Subjects in Early Modern English Drama*, ed. Dowd and Natasha Korda (Farnham: Ashgate, 2011), 131–43.

44 John Higgins, '"Servant Obedience Changed to Master Sin": Performance and the Public Transcript of Service in the Overbury Affair and *The Changeling*', *Journal of Early Modern Studies* 4 (2015), 231–58.

45 Ibid., 234.

46 Ibid., 233.

47 Bradley D. Ryner, 'Anxieties of Currency Exchange in Middleton and Rowley's The Changeling', in *Money, Morality, and Culture in Late Medieval and Early Modern Europe*, ed. Juliann Vitullo and Diane Wolfthal (Surrey, England: Ashgate, 2010), 109–25.

48 Lara Bovilsky, *Barbarous Play: Race on the English Renaissance Stage* (Minneapolis: University of Minnesota Press: 2008).

49 Ibid., 154.

50 Patricia Cahill, 'The Play of Skin in *The Changeling*', *Postmedieval: A Journal of Medieval Cultural Studies* 3.4 (2012), 391–406.

51 Gail Kern Paster, 'The Ecology of the Passions in *A Chaste Maid in Cheapside* and *The Changeling*', in *The Oxford Handbook of Thomas Middleton*, eds. Gary Taylor and Trish Thomas Henley (Oxford: Oxford University Press, 2012), 148–63.

52 Ibid., 163.

53 Ibid., 151.

54 Mary Floyd Wilson, *Occult Knowledge, Science, and Gender on the Shakespearean Stage* (Cambridge: Cambridge University Press, 2013), 91–109.

# Chapter 4

1 Directed by Dominic Dromgoole, the production opened on 20 January 2015.

2 The rather complicated scholarly basis for the design of the Wanamaker is explained in Andrew Gurr and Farah Karim-Cooper, eds, *Moving Shakespeare Indoors: Performance and Repertoire in the Jacobean Playhouse* (Cambridge: Cambridge University Press, 2014), especially the contributions by Jon Greenfield and Oliver Jones, 32–78.

3 I discuss the idea of the Renaissance stage as a forecourt in Peter Womack, 'Off-stage', in *Early Modern Theatricality*, ed. Henry S. Turner (Oxford: Oxford University Press, 2013), 71–92.

4 William Empson, *Some Versions of Pastoral* (London: Chatto and Windus, 1935), 48–52.

5   See the OED entry for 'unconscious', section B. The noun, and the concept, established themselves a good deal earlier in German.
6   T.S. Eliot, 'Thomas Middleton', in *Selected Essays*, 3rd edn (London: Faber and Faber, 1951), 161–70.
7   In *Plays and Players*, April 1961, summarized in Wendy Griswold, *Renaissance Revivals: City Comedy and Revenge Tragedy in the London Theatre 1576–1980* (Chicago: University of Chicago Press, 1986), 171.
8   This is the standard modern interpretation, as is shown by Roberta Barker and David Nicol, 'Does Beatrice Joanna Have a Subtext?: *The Changeling* on the London Stage', *Early Modern Literary Studies* 10.1 (May 2004), 3. 1–43. The authors dissent cogently from the orthodoxy they identify.
9   Published in 1621. See the section on sources in Thomas Middleton and William Rowley, *The Changeling*, ed. N.W. Bawcutt, Revels Plays (London: Methuen, 1958), xxxi–xxxviii.
10  That the play is about unconsciousness in a religious sense is powerfully argued in John Stachniewski, 'Calvinist Psychology in Middleton's Tragedies', in R.V. Holdsworth, ed., *Three Jacobean Revenge Tragedies: A Casebook* (Basingstoke: Macmillan, 1990), 226–46.
11  See for example Paul S. Seaver, *Wallington's World* (London: Methuen, 1985), 183–4, and Peter Iver Kaufman, *Prayer, Despair and Drama: Elizabethan Introspection* (Urbana: University of Illinois Press, 1996), 42.
12  Charles Lloyd Cohen, *God's Caress: The Psychology of Puritan Religious Experience* (Oxford: Oxford University Press, 1986), 11.
13  John Rogers of Dedham, 'Sixty memorials for a godly life', quoted in Tom Webster, 'Writing to Redundancy: Approaches to Spiritual Journals and Early Modern Spirituality', *The Historical Journal*, 39.1 (March 1996), 33–56; 37. For more such injunctions, see David Booy's introduction to his edition of *The Notebooks of Nehemiah Wallington, 1618–1654* (Aldershot: Ashgate, 2007), 16–17.
14  Helen Gardner, 'The Tragedy of Damnation', in R.J. Kaufmann, ed., *Elizabethan Drama: Modern Essays in Criticism* (London:

Oxford University Press, 1961), 320–41, and Margot Heinemann, *Puritanism and Theatre: Thomas Middleton and Opposition Drama under the Early Stuarts* (Cambridge: Cambridge University Press, 1980).

15 The text is that of the Authorised Version.

16 *A commentarie upon the Epistle of Saint Paul to the Romanes, written in Latine by M. John Calvin, and newely translated into English by Christopher Rosdell preacher*, London, 1583, 91.

17 The basic reading list is: Jonathan Sawday, *The Body Emblazoned: Dissection and the Human Body in Renaissance Culture* (London: Routledge, 1995); David Hillman and Carla Mazzio, eds, *The Body in Parts: Fantasies of Corporeality in Early Modern Europe* (London: Routledge, 1997); Michael C. Schoenfeldt, *Bodies and Selves in Early Modern England* (Cambridge: Cambridge University Press, 1999); Gail Kern Paster, *Humoring the Body: Emotions and the Shakespearean Stage* (Chicago: University of Chicago Press, 2004); and Gail Kern Paster, Katherine Rowe and Mary Floyd-Wilson, eds, *Reading the Early Modern Passions: Essays in the Cultural History of Emotion* (Philadelphia: University of Pennsylvania Press, 2004).

18 Gail Kern Paster, 'The Ecology of the Passions in *A Chaste Maid in Cheapside* and *The Changeling*', in Gary Taylor and Trish Thomas Henley, eds, *The Oxford Handbook of Thomas Middleton* (Oxford: Oxford University Press, 2012), 148–63 (150).

19 Angus Gowland, 'Melancholy, Passions and Identity in the Renaissance', in *Passions and Subjectivity in Early Modern Culture*, ed. Brian Cummings and Freya Sierhuis (Farnham: Ashgate, 2013), 75–93 (79). The quotation is from Robert Burton, *The Anatomy of Melancholy* (Oxford, 1621), 129.

20 Joseph R. Roach, *The Player's Passion: Studies in the Science of Acting* (Newark: University of Delaware Press, 1985), 40.

21 Katharine Park, 'The Organic Soul', in *The Cambridge History of Renaissance Philosophy*, ed. Charles B. Schmitt et al. (Cambridge: Cambridge University Press, 1988), 468.

22 Most famously in Hamlet's reflections on the Player's speech about Hecuba, which are discussed and contextualized in Roach, 43–53.

23 Thomas Wright, *The Passions of the Minde in Generall*, 'corrected and enlarged' edition (London, 1604), 300.

24 Ibid., 309.

25 *Women Beware Women*, 2.2.319–21, where the heroine has been betrayed into the power of the lecherous Duke, who is about to rape her, and *A Game at Chess*, 3.1.349–52, where the innocent White Queen's Pawn has been lured into a trap by her black opposite number. References are to Thomas Middleton, *The Collected Works*, ed. Gary Taylor and John Lavagnino (Oxford: Oxford University Press, 2007). The ornithological fact, it seems, is that 'a panting gasping sound' is the turtle-dove's distress-call: see Stanley Cramp, ed., *Handbook of the Birds of Europe, the Middle East and North Africa*, vol 4: *Terns to Woodpeckers* (Oxford: Oxford University Press, 1985), 360.

26 Christopher Ricks discusses innuendo and unconsciousness in 'The Moral and Poetic Structure of *The Changeling*', *Essays in Criticism* 10 (1960), 290–306.

27 Compare the scene (2.1) in John Webster's *The Duchess of Malfi* (1614) in which the pregnant Duchess gorges on apricots, watched by another cynical male servant, Bosola.

28 The supposed phenomenon is staged in William Shakespeare, *Richard III*, 1.2.55–9. It is also referred to as a generally known fact in James I's *Daemonologie* (1597). King James VI and I, *Selected Writings*, ed. Neil Rhodes, Jennifer Richards and Joseph Marshall (Aldershot: Ashgate, 2003), 197.

29 The Standard Edition of Freud appeared in twenty-four volumes starting in 1953. Lawrence's cultural apogee followed F.R. Leavis's *D.H. Lawrence, Novelist* (1955) and the obscenity trial of *Lady Chatterley's Lover* (1960). Artaud's *The Theatre and its Double* appeared in English in 1958, and Peter Brook's famous 'Theatre of Cruelty' season was in 1964. The final crisis of theatrical pre-censorship, finally abolished in 1968, was precipitated by the first performance of Edward Bond's *Saved* at the Royal Court in 1965.

30 Lewis Wager, *The Life and Repentaunce of Mary Magdalene* (London, 1566), lines 1102–222.

31 A year or two before the play was first performed, Nehemiah Wallington, a young London tradesman whose spiritual

notebooks have survived, prayed to be given 'sight of his sins'. His prayer was granted, and what he saw so appalled him that he came close to suicide. Seaver, 16.

32 Peter Happé, 'The Protestant Adaptation of the Saint Play', in Clifford Davidson, ed., *The Saint Play in Medieval Europe* (Kalamazoo: Medieval Institute Publications, 1986), 205–40.

33 *The Spanish Gypsy*, 3.1.1–8. Gary Taylor thinks the play was written by Middleton and Rowley with John Ford and Thomas Dekker; he sets out the case in Gary Taylor and John Lavagnino, eds, *Thomas Middleton and Early Modern Textual Culture: A Companion to the Collected Works* (Oxford: Oxford University Press, 2007), 433–8.

34 Nemesius, Bishop of Emesa, *The Nature of Man*, translated by George Wither (London, 1636), 125–6. The passage is cited and discussed in E. Ruth Harvey, *The Inward Wits: Psychological Theory in the Middle Ages and the Renaissance* (London: Warburg Institute, 1975), 32.

35 Willem Teellinck, *Paul's complaint against his naturall corruption . . . . Set forth in two sermons upon the 24 verse of the 7 chapter of his epistle to the Romans*, 2nd edition (London, 1621), 5.

36 Ibid., 12–13.

# Chapter 5

1 See Brean Hammond, ed., *Double Falsehood* (London: A. & C. Black, 2010). For a concise account of Shakespeare's lost play, see '*Cardenio*', in Stephen Greenblatt et al., eds, *The Norton Shakespeare* (New York: W.W. Norton & Co., 1997), 3109; see also the relevant entry in www.lostplays.org.

2 N.W. Bawcutt, ed., *The Changeling* (London: Methuen, 1958), xxxi–xxxviii.

3 As scholars have noted, the characters' double names are also suggestive of their doubleness – De Flores as 'of the flowers'/'deflowerer' – and the two names of Beatrice-Joanna stand in contrast to Vermandero, whose honest, single anthroponym clearly derives from 'verdadero', Spanish for

'truthful'. On names in *The Changeling*, see William Power, 'Middleton's Way with Names', *Notes and Queries* 205 (1960), 26–9; 56–60; 95–8; 136–40; 175–9. See also Ivan Cañadas, 'What is in a Heroine's Name: Beatrice-Joanna in *The Changeling*', *Medieval and Early Modern English Studies* 20 (2012), 129–54, and Dale B.J. Randall 'Some Observations on the Theme of Chastity in *The Changeling*', *English Literary Renaissance* 14.3 (Autumn 1984), 347–66; 351–2.

4  See Annabel Patterson's introduction to *The Changeling* in Gary Taylor and John Lavagnino, gen. eds, *Thomas Middleton: The Collected Works* (Oxford: Oxford University Press, 2007), 1632–6.

5  This embassy is notable for the role it played regarding the circulation of books. Gustav Ungerer has traced a copy of Cervantes' *Don Quixote* in the Bodleian collection to as early as 1605, coinciding with the return of the embassy; see his 'The Earl of Southampton's Donation to the Bodleian in 1605 and Its Spanish Books', *Bodleian Library Record* 16 (1997), 17–41. Dudley Carleton reported to John Chamberlain his investment in books while in Spain as a member of the embassy: see Ungerer, 'The Spanish and English Chronicles in King James's and Sir George Buc's Dossiers on the Anglo-Spanish Peace Negotiations', *Huntington Library Quarterly* 61.3/4 (1998), 309–24.

6  Barbara Fuchs, 'Middleton and Spain', in Gary Taylor and Trish Thomas Henley, eds, *The Oxford Handbook of Thomas Middleton* (Oxford: Oxford University Press, 2012), 404–17.

7  John Reynolds, *Vox Coeli or Newes from Heaven* (1624), 57.

8  Playhouse influences include *Othello* (1604) and *Macbeth* (1606), for example, as editors have noted; the second of these Middleton adapted for the King's Men.

9  John Reynolds, *The Triumphs of God's Revenge Against the Crying and Execrable Sin of Murther* (London, 1621), B3.

10  Reynolds, *The Triumphs*, B3.

11  For Reynolds' trading activities along the Mediterranean coast, see John D. Sanderson, ed. and trans., *El trueque (1622) de Thomas Middleton y William Rowley: Alicante como escenario del teatro jacobeo*. (Alicante: Instituto Alicantino de Cultura Juan Gil-Albert, 2002). Sanderson found an entry for a 'maestro

Jaques Reynaldo' in the archives of the Kingdom of Valencia, where he is registered as entering the port twice, 24.

12 Dale B.J. Randall has shown that Reynolds pays attention to historical and geographical detail, which the playwrights follow, the setting thus 'more firmly anchored to real earth than we once recognized'; see his 'Some new perspectives on the Spanish setting of *The Changeling* and its source', *Medieval and Renaissance Drama in England*, 3 (1986), 189–216; 207.

13 The same year the Moriscos (who constituted 40 per cent of the province of Alicante's population) were expelled from Spain.

14 Reynolds, *The Triumphs*, 114.

15 Ibid., 127.

16 Ibid., 132–3.

17 Bawcutt, xxxii.

18 The name Alibius, which appears in the next story in Reynolds, has been interpreted as referring to 'in some other place', from the Latin adverb *alibi*; see Randall, 352. But there is also a possible connection with the adjective *albus,* therefore signifying 'whiteness', which thus differentiates him from the dark Spanish inhabitants of the castle; Lollio may derive from the Italian noun *l'olio* (oil), or someone who receives bribes.

19 All references to *A Game at Chess* are to Taylor, ed., *A Game at Chess: A Later Form*, in Taylor and Lavagnino, gen. eds, *Thomas Middleton: The Collected Works*, 1825–85.

20 See Frank P. Casa, 'El tema de la violación sexual en la comedia', in *El escritor y la escena: Actas del I Congreso de la Asociación Internacional de Teatro Español y Novohispano de los Siglos de Oro* (Juárez: Universidad Autónoma de Ciudad Juárez, 1993), 203–12.

21 In these plays the fate of the victims is not death, as the Lucrece tradition would have it. Jacinta is not a central character in *Fuenteovejuna* and her gang rape functions as a warning of what could happen to Laurencia, the female protagonist. In Calderon's play Isabel initially wishes for death but decides instead to enter a convent and so restore her honour with God. These 'solutions' contrast with English plays that feature rape, where the death of the rapist is often mirrored by the death of the victim; see Suzanne Gossett, '"Best Men Are Moulded out of Faults":

Marrying the Rapist in Jacobean Drama', *English Literary Renaissance* 14 (1984), 305–27. It is significant, however, that these English plays tend to draw on classical sources, so the influence of the Lucrece narrative is not surprising.

22 See Victoria López Cordón y Montserrat Carbonell Esteller, eds, *Historia de la Mujer e Historia del Matrimonio* (Murcia: Universidad de Murcia, 1997), 99–138.

23 Pedro Calderón de la Barca, *The Mayor of Zalamea,* trans. Adrian Mitchell (Bristol: Salamander, 1981). 'Al rey la hacienda y la vida / se han de dar, pero el honor / es patrimonio del alma, / y el alma sólo es de Dios' (1.18.869–76).

24 Gustavo Correa, 'El doble aspecto de la honra en el teatro del siglo XVII', *Hispanic Review* 26.2 (1958), 99–107.

25 Juan Hernández Franco and Encarnación Meriñán Soriano, 'Notas sobre la sexualidad no permitida y honor en Lorca (1575-1615)', in López Cordón y Carbonell Esteller, 131–8.

26 This is the case with John Fletcher's *The Queen of Corinth* (*c.*1616–18) and *Los Torneos de Aragón* (*The Tournaments of Aragon,* 1597) by Lope de Vega, to cite but two examples.

27 Gary Taylor, ed., *The Spanish Gipsy,* in Taylor and Lavagnino, gen. eds, *Thomas Middleton: The Collected Works,* 1723–65; Taylor attributes the authorship of the play to a four-man team: John Ford, Thomas Dekker, Middleton and Rowley.

28 Suzanne Gossett arrives at the opposite conclusion when comparing the play and the novella: Cervantes' tale is 'more lighthearted' because 'it does not focus as intently on the characters of rapist and victim' (Gossett, 'Best Men', 321), but being less psychologically-orientated does not detract from the fact that Leocadia suffers humiliation after humiliation before her final marriage, which invites scepticism about the apparent solution.

29 On the play's contemporary resonance regarding the Spanish Match negotiations, see Gary Taylor, 'Historicism, Presentism and Time: Middleton's *The Spanish Gypsy* and *A Game at Chess*', *SEDERI* 18 (2008), 147–70.

30 Suzanne Gossett does not discuss *The Changeling,* though she does consider *The Spanish Gipsy* at length; Gossett, 'Best Men', 321–4.

31 Joost Daalder and Antony Telford Moore, '"There's scarce a thing but is both loved and loathed": *The Changeling*

I.i.91-129', *English Studies* 80.6 (1999), 499–508; 502. See also Daalder, 'Folly and Madness in *The Changeling*', *Essays in Criticism* 38.1 (1988), 1–21. On theatre critics' endorsement of Freudian readings, see Roberta Barker and David Nicol, 'Does Beatrice Joanna Have a Subtext? *The Changeling* on the London stage', *Early Modern Literary Studies* 10.1 (May 2004), and the accounts of recent productions in this volume by Jennifer Panek and Sarah Dustagheer.

32  Frances E. Dolan, 'Re-reading Rape in *The Changeling*', *Journal for Early Modern Cultural Studies* 11.1 (2011), 759–90; 7.

33  For this observation see Lisa Hopkins, 'Beguiling the Master of the Mystery: Form and Power in *The Changeling*', *Medieval and Renaissance Drama in England* 9 (1997), 149–61; 154–5.

34  Judith Haber, '"I(t) could not choose but follow": Erotic Logic in *The Changeling*', *Representations* 81.1 (2003), 79–98.

35  Deborah Burks, '"I'll want my will else": *The Changeling* and Women's Complicity with their Rapists', *English Literary History* 62.4 (1995), 759–90; 781.

36  In Gary Taylor's view Middleton had a more than passable knowledge of Spanish; if so he could have read the original *Gerardo* before the translation was published. Taylor bases his argument on Middleton's use of Cervantes for the plots in *The Lady's Tragedy* (1611, often known as *The Second Maiden's Tragedy*) and *The Spanish Gipsy*; and in *The Triumphs of Honour and Industry* (1617) an entire passage is in Spanish. This may be so, but the Spanish in *The Triumphs* is so elaborate that Middleton must have had help of some kind. See Taylor, 'Works Included in this Edition: Canon and Chronology', in Taylor and Lavagnino, gen. eds, *Thomas Middleton and Early Modern Textual Culture: A Companion to The Collected Works* (Oxford: Oxford University Press, 2007), 335–443; 437.

37  Bertram Lloyd, 'A New Source of *The Changeling*', *M.L.R.* XIX (January 1924), 101–2; Bawcutt, 127–9.

38  Joost Daalder, ed., *The Changeling* (London: A&C Black, 1990), xiv; Fuchs, 411.

39  Miguel de Cervantes, *El Ingenioso Hidalgo Don Quijote de la Mancha*, ed. Florencio Sevilla (Madrid: Lunwerg Editores, 2004), 126.

40 'Vizcaino por tierra, hidalgo por mar, hidalgo por el diablo'; Cervantes *El Ingenioso Hidalgo Don Quijote,* 129; *The Ingenious, Gentleman, Don Quixote of La Mancha.* By Miguel de Cervantes, Saavedra. A Translation, with Introduction and Notes by John Ormsby (Smith, Elder and Co., 1885), 185.

41 Gonzalo de Céspedes y Meneses, *Gerardo the Unfortunate Spaniard*, trans. Leonard Digges (London: 1622), 95.

42 Céspedes, 96.

43 Ibid.

44 Ibid., 103.

45 Ibid., 106.

46 Their characteristic jargon was parodied in plays and prose as ungrammatical; see Manuel Ferrer-Chivite, 'La figura del Vizcaíno en el Teatro del Siglo XVI', *Foro Hispánico: Revista Hispánica de Flandes y Holanda*, coord. Margot Vesteeg, 19 (2001), 23–39.

47 Céspedes, 95.

48 Ibid., 106.

49 Bawcutt, xxxii.

50 See Peggy Muñoz Simonds, 'Overlooked Sources of the Bed Trick', *Shakespeare Quarterly* 34.3 (1983), 433–4.

51 Julia Briggs, 'Shakespeare's Bed Tricks', *Essays in Criticism* 44.4 (1994), 293–314; 296.

52 Neill, ed., *The Changeling*, xiii; Christopher Ricks, 'The Moral and Poetic Structure of *The Changeling*', *Essays in Criticism* 10 (1960), 290–306.

# Chapter 6

1 I would like to thank Jennifer Panek and her Research Assistant Abigail Holt for sharing materials for this chapter.

2 Unless explicitly stated, the chapter focuses on Joe Hill-Gibbins's original production of *The Changeling* in the Maria Studio, rather than the re-cast revival in the Main Space.

3 Neill, 'Introduction', in *The Changeling* (London: Bloomsbury, 2006), vii–xlv; xiv–xv. See Jennifer Panek's chapter in this book

for the treatment of the subplot across the play's performance history.

4 Michael Billington, 'derup Changeling, Barbican, London', The Guardian, 16 May 2006.

5 Peter J. Smith, 'Review of Thomas Middleton and William Rowley's *The Changeling* (directed by Declan Donnellan for Cheek by Jowl), at the Barbican, London (May–June 2006)', *Shakespeare* 2.2 (2006), 220–1 (220).

6 David Benedict, 'Review: *The Changeling*', *Variety*, 28 May 2006; Billington, 'Barbican'; Paul Menzer, '*The Changeling /Twelfth Night*', *Shakespeare Bulletin* 25.1 (2007), 94–100 (96), respectively.

7 Matt Trueman, 'The Next Challenge', Interview with Joe Hill-Gibbins, *The Stage*, 2 February 2012.

8 Natasha Tripney, '*The Changeling*, Young Vic', *The Stage*, 9 February 2012; Sarah Hemming, '*The Changeling*, Young Vic, London', *Financial Times*, 5 February 2012, respectively.

9 Billington, '*The Changeling*, Young Vic, London', *The Guardian*, 3 February 2012.

10 Deborah G. Burks, '"I'll want my will else": *The Changeling* and Women's Complicity with their Rapists', *English Literary History* 62.4 (1995), 759–90; Sara Eaton, 'Beatrice-Joanna and the Rhetoric of Love in The Changeling', *Theatre Journal* 36.3 (1984), 371–83; Judith Haber, '"I(t) Could Not Choose but Follow": Erotic Logic in *The Changeling*', *Representations* 81 (2003), 79–98.

11 *The Changeling/Twelfth Night*, Cheek by Jowl Programme, Cheek by Jowl Archive, http://archive.cheekbyjowl.com/wp-content/uploads/2014/11/Changeling-Programme.pdf (accessed 1 August 2017).

12 'Inside *The Changeling*', Young Vic Schools' Resource Pack, www.youngvic.org/sites/default/files/packs/The_Changeling_Pack_FINAL.pdf (accessed 1 August 2017), 29.

13 'Inside *The Changeling*', 28.

14 Personal Interview, 29 August 2017. All quotations from Oakley are from this interview, unless otherwise stated.

15 Maddy Costa, 'The Changeling, Southwark Playhouse, London', The Guardian, 8 November 2011; Alisdair Hinton, 'The Changeling, Thomas Middleton and William Rowley, Southwark Playhouse', British Theatre Guide, http://www.britishtheatreguide.info/reviews/changelingsouthwark-rev (accessed 1 August 2017).

16 Neill, xv.

17 Tripney, 'The Changeling, Southwark Playhouse', Exeunt Magazine, http://exeuntmagazine.com/reviews/the-changeling/ (accessed 1 August 2017).

18 Michael Coveney, 'The Changeling, West End', What's On Stage, http://www.whatsonstage.com/west-end-theatre/reviews/02-2012/the-changeling_5517.html (accessed 1 August 2017).

19 Stephen Purcell has shown how this approach is especially at work in mainstream theatre reviews of Shakespeare in his 2010 article '"That's not Shakespeare": Policing the Boundaries of "Shakespeare" in Reviews', Shakespeare 6.3 (2010), 364–70; see also W.B. Worthen, Shakespeare and the Authority of Performance (Cambridge: Cambridge University Press, 1996).

20 The Changeling: Rehearsal Notes, Cheek by Jowl Archive, http://archive.cheekbyjowl.com/wp-content/uploads/2014/11/CHANGELING-REHEARSAL-NOTES-2.pdf (accessed 1 August 2017).

21 Nicholas Brooke, Horrid Laughter in Jacobean Tragedy (London: Open Books, 1979), 70–88; Thomas L. Berger, 'The Petrarchan Fortress in The Changeling', Renaissance Papers (1969), 37–46.

22 Penelope Woods, 'The Audience of the Indoor Theatre', in Moving Shakespeare Indoors: Performance and Repertoire in the Jacobean Playhouse, ed. Andrew Gurr and Farah Karim-Cooper (Cambridge: Cambridge University Press, 2014), 152–67 (156).

23 For more on the SWP as a 'reconstructed' theatre and its critical reception see Will Tosh, Playing Indoors: Staging Early Modern Drama in the Sam Wanamaker Playhouse (London: Bloomsbury, 2018).

24 Susannah Clapp, 'The Changeling Review – Middleton and Rowley's Tragedy has Never Been so Acutely Funny, Sam Wanamaker Playhouse, London', The Observer, 25 January 2015.

25 Billington, '*The Changeling* Review – Hattie Morahan is Chillingly Good in Grisly Masterpiece, Sam Wanamaker Playhouse, London', *The Guardian*, 21 January 2015; Tripney, '*The Changeling*, Sam Wanamaker Playhouse', *The Stage*, 29 January 2015.

26 Nora Williams, 'Editing and Performing Asides in *The Changeling*', *Shakespeare Bulletin* 34.1 (Spring 2016), 29–45.

27 Williams, 'Editing', 31.

28 Eaton, 375.

29 For example, see Bridget Escolme, *Talking to the Audience: Shakespeare, Performance, Self* (London: Routledge, 2005); Jeremy Lopez, 'Chapter 3: Managing the Aside', in *Theatrical Convention and Audience Response in Early Modern Drama* (Cambridge: Cambridge University Press, 2002), 56–77; Stephen Purcell, *Shakespeare and the Audience in Practice* (Basingstoke: Palgrave, 2013).

30 Hattie Morahan, 'Adopt an Actor Archive: *The Changeling*', http://www.shakespearesglobe.com/discovery-space/adopt-an-actor/archive/beatrice-joanna-played-by-hattie-morahan/performance (accessed 1 August 2017); and Morahan qtd in Holly Williams, 'Hattie Morahan on *The Changeling*: an unsavoury role played with relish', *The Independent,* 19 January 2015, respectively.

31 Tripney, '*The Changeling*, Sam Wanamaker Playhouse'.

32 Menzer, 96.

33 Benedict, 'Review: *The Changeling*'; Claire Allfree, 'Metrolife: *The Changeling*', *Metro*, 17 May 2006.

34 'Olivia Williams, Tom Hiddleston and Will Keen talk about their roles in *The Changeling*', Cheek by Jowl Archive, http://archive.cheekbyjowl.com/the-changeling/ (accessed 1 August 2017).

35 Declan Donnellan qtd in Jay O'Berski, *Middleton and Rowley: The Changeling*, The Shakespeare Handbooks: Shakespeare's Contemporaries (Basingstoke: Palgrave, 2012), 96.

36 Annegret Maerten, 'Dog Food, Penis Pumps and Jello: *The Changeling* at the Young Vic', *One Stop Arts*, http://onestoparts.com/review-the-changeling-young-vic (accessed 1 August 2017).

37 Billington, '*The Changeling*, Young Vic, London', *The Guardian*, 27 November 2012.
38 Peter Kirwan, '*The Changeling* @ the Young Vic', http://blogs.nottingham.ac.uk/bardathon/2012/11/26/the-changeling-the-young-vic/ (accessed 1 August 2017).
39 Diana Damian Martin, 'Q&A Interviews: Michael Oakley', *Exeunt Magazine*, http://exeuntmagazine.com/features/michael-oakley/ (accessed 1 August 2017).
40 Costa, '*The Changeling*, Southwark Playhouse, London'.
41 Hinton, '*The Changeling*, Thomas Middleton and William Rowley, Southwark Playhouse'.
42 Paul Taylor, '*The Changeling*, Southwark Playhouse, London', *The Independent*, 15 November 2011.
43 Coveney, '*The Changeling*, Off West-End', *What's On Stage*, http://www.whatsonstage.com/west-end-theatre/reviews/11-2011/the-changeling_6326.html (accessed 1 August 2017).
44 'Olivia Williams, Tom Hiddleston and Will Keen . . .', Cheek by Jowl Archive.
45 Ibid.
46 Roberta Barker and David Nicol, 'Does Beatrice Joanna Have a Subtext?: *The Changeling* on the London Stage', *Early Modern Literary Studies* 10.1 (May 2004), 3.1–43, http://purl.oclc.org/emls/10-1/barknico.htm (accessed 1 August 2017), paragraph. 3.
47 Billington, '*The Changeling*, Barbican, London'.
48 Taylor.
49 Peter Brown, 'Reviews: *The Changeling*, Young Vic, London', https://www.londontheatre.co.uk/reviews/the-changeling (accessed 1 August 2017).
50 Quentin Letts, 'A Bloody Brutal Tale (Even my Seat was Murder)!', *Daily Mail*, 23 January 2015.
51 Trueman, 'The Next Challenge', Interview with Joe Hill-Gibbins.
52 Kirwan.
53 Trueman, '*The Changeling* (Sam Wanamaker Playhouse)', http://www.whatsonstage.com/london-theatre/reviews/changeling-sam-wanamaker-playhouse_36954.html (accessed 1 August 2017).

54 Williams, 'Hattie Morahan on *The Changeling*'.
55 Smith, 221.
56 Barker and Nicol, para. 43.
57 Tripney, 'Q & A Interviews: Changing *The Changeling*', *Exeunt Magazine*, http://exeuntmagazine.com/features/changing-the-changeling/2/ (accessed 1 August 2017).
58 Laura Estill, 'Theatre Reviews: *The Changeling*', *Shakespeare Bulletin* 31.2 (2013), 311–19 (316).
59 Tripney, '*The Changeling*, Young Vic'.
60 Brown; Maxie Szalwinska, 'Also Showing... *The Changeling*', *The Sunday Times*, 25 January 2015.
61 Pascale Aebischer and Kathryn Prince, 'Introduction', in *Performing Early Modern Drama Today*, ed. Aebischer and Prince (Cambridge: Cambridge University Press, 2012), 1–16 (2–3).

# Chapter 7

1 On this 'loving and loathing' ambivalence as an erotic mechanism in the play, see Judith Haber, '"I(t) could not choose but follow": Erotic Logic in *The Changeling*', *Representations* 81.1 (Winter 2003), 79–98.

2 Courtney Lehmann, '"Taking back the night": Hospitality in *The Changeling* on Film', *Shakespeare Bulletin* 29.4 (Winter 2011), 591–604, 591.

3 For negative readings of this film, see for example Gordon McMullan's article '"Plenty of Blood. That's the Only Writing": (Mis)representing Jacobean Tragedy in Turn-of-the-century Cinema', *Shakespeare en devenir – Les Cahiers de La Licorne - Shakespeare en devenir* 2 (2008), published online in January 2010. http://shakespeare.edel.univ-poitiers.fr/index.php?id=146 (accessed 10 July 2018); and Jay O'Berski's chapter on the play on screen in *Middleton & Rowley The Changeling*, The Shakespeare Handbooks. Shakespeare's Contemporaries (Houndmills, Basingstoke: Palgrave Macmillan, 2012), 121–5.

4 Julia Kristeva, *Powers of Horror. An Essay on Abjection*, transl. S. Roudier (New York: Columbia University Press, 1982), 1. 'Il y

a, dans l'abjection, une de ces violentes et obscures révoltes de l'être contre ce qui le menace, et qui lui paraît venir d'un dehors ou d'un dedans exorbitant, jeté à côté du possible, du tolérable, du pensable. C'est là, tout près mais inassimilable. Ça sollicite, inquiète, fascine le désir qui pourtant ne se laisse pas séduire. [. . .]. Inlassablement, comme un boomerang indomptable, un pôle d'appel et de répulsion met celui qui en est habité littéralement hors de lui.' Julia Kristeva, *Pouvoirs de l'horreur* (Paris: Seuil, 1980), 9.

5   Arya Rina, *Abjection and Representation. An Exploration of Abjection in the Visual Arts, Film and Literature* (Houndmills, Basingstoke: Palgrave Macmillan, 2014), 5.

6   Courtney Lehmann, '"Old dad Dead?" The Rise of the Neo-Noir "Heritage Film", or, Middleton with a View', in Gary Taylor and Trish Thomas Henley, eds, *The Oxford Handbook of Thomas Middleton* (Oxford: Oxford University Press, 2012), 210–26 (215).

7   Pascal Quignard, *Sex and Terror*, trans. Chris Turner (Seagull books, 2011), introduction, x. 'Le mot grec de *phallos* se dit en latin le *fascinus*. Les chants qui l'entourent s'appellent "fescennins". Le *fascinus* arrête le regard au point qu'il ne peut s'en détacher. t. . . . . . La fascination est la perception de l'angle mort du langage. Et c'est pourquoi ce regard est toujours latéral.' Pascal Quignard, *Le Sexe et l'effroi* (Paris: Gallimard, 1994), 11.

8   The same sexual image is used by Alibius when he expresses his wish for his wife's fidelity: 'I would wear my ring on my own finger' (1.2.27).

9   See Farah Karim-Cooper, *The Hand on the Shakespearean Stage. Gesture, Touch and the Spectacle of Dismemberment* (London: Bloomsbury, 2016): 'the four-fingered hand haunts De Flores, whose violent act of amputation lingers in the minds of the audience as well as his own' (84).

10  On the basilisk, see Nathalie Vienne-Guerrin, *Shakespeare's Insults. A Pragmatic Dictionary* (London: Bloomsbury, 2016), 35–7.

11  Quignard, trans. Turner, 39. 'Le sexe est lié à l'effroi' (Quignard, 84).

12  On rape in *The Changeling* as being part of a Jacobean concern about property right, see Deborah G. Burks, *Horrid Spectacle*.

*Violation in the Theater of Early Modern England* (Pittsburgh: Dusquesne University Press, 2003), 145–89.

13 Frances E. Dolan, 'Re-reading Rape in *The Changeling*', *Journal for Early Modern Cultural Studies* 11.1 (Spring/Summer 2011), 4–29.

14 *Much Ado About Nothing*, ed. Claire McEachern (London and New York: Bloomsbury, 2007).

15 Burks, 174.

16 On the recurrence of asides in the play, see Nora Williams, '"Cannot I keep that secret?": Editing and Performing Asides in *The Changeling*', *Shakespeare Bulletin* 34.1 (Spring 2016), 29–45.

17 Available at: https://www.youtube.com/watch?v=nP5iKtlUWlw (accessed 17 June 2018).

18 Marjorie Garber, *Shakespeare After All* (New York: Pantheon Books, 2004), 839.

19 Brigid Cherry, *Horror. Routledge Film Guidebooks* (New York: Routledge, 2009), 2.

20 Cherry, 54.

21 Peter Hutchings, 'Theatres of Blood. Shakespeare and the horror film', in *Gothic Shakespeares*, ed. John Drakakis and Dale Townshend (New York: Routledge, 2008), 153–66. The article is built on two sections, entitled 'Shakespeare into horror' (156ff) and 'Horror into Shakespeare' (162ff).

22 Ibid., 155.

23 Ibid., 156.

24 *Critical Dictionary of Film and Television Theory*, ed. Roberta E. Pearson and Philip Simpson (New York: Routledge, 2001), 223.

25 Lehmann, 'Old dad Dead?', 210–26, 211.

26 Lehmann, 'Taking back the night', 591; 596.

27 Lehmann, 'Taking back the night', 598. Middleton and Rowley's second source for the play might well be cited in support of such a reading: see Berta Cano-Echevarría's essay in this volume.

28 Lehmann, 'Taking back the night', 599.

29 Pascale Aebischer, *Screening Early Modern Drama. Beyond Shakespeare* (Cambridge: Cambridge University Press, 2013), esp. Chap. 5: 'Bend it like Nagra: Mainstreaming *The Changeling* in Sarah Harding's *Compulsion*', 187–216.

30 Sarah Harding, '*Compulsion*: A View from the Director's Chair', *Shakespeare Bulletin* 29.4 (2011), 605–15.

31 *Macbeth*, ed. Sandra Clark and Pamela Mason (London: Bloomsbury, 2015); see Harding, 612–13.

32 Harding, 605.

33 Ibid., 608.

34 Ibid., 611.

35 Ibid., 609.

36 Pascale Aebischer, 'Middleton in the Cinema', in Suzanne Gossett, ed., *Thomas Middleton in Context* (Cambridge: Cambridge University Press, 2011), 336–45, 341.

37 McMullan, § 4.

38 See the Science Museum's History of Medicine website. Available at: http://broughttolife.sciencemuseum.org.uk/broughttolife/people/iandury (accessed 22 July 2018).

39 Lehmann, 'Old dad Dead?', 214.

40 Dury's best-known song, 'Hit Me with your Rhythm Stick' was a number one hit in 1979.

41 Lehmann, 'Old dad Dead?', 215.

42 Dolan, 5.

43 Aebischer, 'Middleton in the cinema', 431.

44 Lehmann, 'Old dad Dead?', 217.

45 Aebischer, 'Middleton in the cinema', 342.

46 Ibid.

47 McMullan, § 5.

48 Ibid.

49 Linda Williams, 'Film Bodies: Gender, Genre, and Excess', in Robert Stam and Toby Miller, eds, *Film and Theory, An Anthology* (Malden and Oxford: Blackwell Publishing, 2000), 207–21, 211.

50 Ibid., 212.
51 McMullan, § 5.

# Chapter 8

1 Pascale Aebischer and Kathryn Prince, eds, *Performing Early Modern Drama Today* (Cambridge: Cambridge University Press, 2012).
2 Lucy Munro, 'The Early Modern Repertory and Performance Today', in Aebischer and Prince, eds, *Performing Early Modern Drama Today*, 17–34 (33).
3 Ibid.
4 Ibid., 19.
5 Margot Heinemann, *Puritanism and Theatre: Thomas Middleton and Opposition Drama Under the Early Stuarts* (Cambridge: Cambridge University Press, 1980), 1.
6 J. Lopez, 'The Seeds of Time: Student Theatre and The Drama of Shakespeare's Contemporaries', in Aebischer and Prince, eds, *Performing Early Modern Drama Today*, 35–52 (40).
7 Ibid., 40.
8 Jonathan Heron, Nicholas Monk and Paul Prescott, 'Letting the Dead Come Out to Dance: An Embodied Approach to Teaching Early Modern Drama', in Aebischer and Prince, eds, *Performing Early Modern Drama Today*, 162–77.
9 Ibid., 165.
10 Michael Neill, 'Introduction', in Michael Neill, ed., *The Changeling* (London: Bloomsbury, 2006), vii–xlvi (xxxvi–xxxvii).
11 M.J. Kidnie, *Shakespeare and the Problem of Adaptation* (London: Taylor & Francis, 2009), 23.
12 See, for example, Sonia Massai, 'Invisible Middleton and the Bibliographical Context', in Suzanne Gossett, ed., *Thomas Middleton in Context* (Cambridge: Cambridge University Press, 2011), 317–24.
13 Gary Taylor, 'How To Use This Book', in Gary Taylor and John Lavagnino, eds, *Thomas Middleton: The Collected Works* (Oxford: Oxford University Press, 2007), 18.

14 Lukas Erne, '"Our Other Shakespeare": Thomas Middleton and the Canon', *Modern Philology* 107.3 (2010), 493–505; Lars Engle and Eric Rasmussen, 'Review Essay: The Oxford Middleton', *Shakespeare Quarterly* 61.2 (2010), 246–61.

15 Samuel Schoenbaum, *Middleton's Tragedies: A Critical Study* (New York: Columbia University Press, 1955), 147; Gordon McMullan, '*The Changeling* and the Dynamics of Ugliness', in Emma Smith and Garrett A. Sullivan, eds, *The Cambridge Companion to English Renaissance Tragedy* (Cambridge: Cambridge University Press, 2010), 222–35 (224).

16 Christopher Ricks, 'The Moral and Poetic Structure of *The Changeling*', *Essays in Criticism* 10.3 (1960), 290–306 (302).

17 Ibid., 38.

18 Anne Pasternak Slater, 'Hypallage, Barley-Break, and *The Changeling*', *The Review of English Studies*, new series, 34.136 (1983), 429–40 (429).

19 Ibid., 431.

20 Ibid., 432, 433.

21 Patricia Thomson, 'Introduction', in P. Thomson, ed., *The Changeling* (London: Ernest Benn Limited, 1964), xxvi.

22 Richard Levin, *The Multiple Plot in English Renaissance Drama* (Chicago: Chicago University Press, 1971), 34; see also Slater, 440.

23 Slater, 440; see also Levin, 37.

24 For a full discussion of Frances Howard's trial and imprisonment (and the attendant scandals), see David Lindley, *The Trials of Frances Howard: Fact and Fiction at the Court of King James* (London: Routledge, 1993).

25 See, e.g. David Nicol, *Middleton and Rowley: Forms of Collaboration in the Jacobean Playhouse* (Toronto: University of Toronto Press, 2012), 25.

26 Heinemann; Swapan Chakravorty, *Society and Politics in the Plays of Thomas Middleton* (Oxford: Oxford University Press, 1996); A.A. Bromham and Zara Bruzzi, '*The Changeling' and the Years of Crisis, 1619–1624: A Hieroglyph of England* (London: Pinter Publishers, 1993); Mark Hutchings, '*The*

*Changeling* at Court', *Cahiers Élisabéthains* 81 (2012), 15–24. See also D.H. Willson, *King James VI & I* (New York: Oxford University Press, 1967) for a more complete history of English politics during this period.

27 Adrian Streete, '"An Old Quarrel Between Us That Will Never Be At an End": *Women Beware Women* and Late Jacobean Religious Politics', *The Review of English Studies* 60.244 (April 2009), 230–54 (231).

28 Nicol, 10.

29 Ibid., 39, 41.

30 Ibid., 64.

31 *Thomas Middleton*, http://english.fsu.edu/middleton/ (accessed 1 January 2016). The phrase 'our other Shakespeare' also appears on the book jacket of the Oxford *Collected Works*.

32 Gary Taylor, 'Thomas Middleton: Lives and Afterlives', in Taylor and Lavagnino, eds, *Thomas Middleton: The Collected Works*, 25–58, 58.

33 The notable exception here is N.W. Bawcutt who, according to G.B. Evans, 'argues manfully' for the importance of the hospital plot in his introduction to the play. G.B. Evans, '*The Changeling* by Thomas Middleton and William Rowley; N.W. Bawcutt' (Review), *The Journal of English and Germanic Philology* 58.4 (1959), 693–4.

34 Rob Pope, *Creativity: Theory, History, Practice* (London: Routledge, 2005), 102.

35 T.S. Eliot, 'Thomas Middleton', in T.S. Eliot, *Selected Essays* (London: Faber & Faber, 1976 [1932]), 161–70 (169; italics original).

36 David J. Lake's study, *The Canon of Thomas Middleton's Plays: Internal Evidence for the Major Problems of Authorship* (Cambridge: Cambridge University Press, 1975), was the first.

37 Nicol, 66, 21.

38 Ibid., 5; see note on Lake above.

39 Lake, *The Canon of Thomas Middleton's Plays*, 87–8.

40 M.C. Bradbrook, *Themes and Conventions of Elizabethan Tragedy* (Cambridge: Cambridge University Press, 1935); William Empson, *Some Versions of Pastoral* [1935] (London: The Hogarth Press, 1986) ; N.W. Bawcutt, 'Introduction' in N.W. Bawcutt, ed., *The Changeling* (London: Methuen, 1958); Una Ellis-Fermor, *The Jacobean Drama: An Interpretation*, 2nd edn (London: Methuen & Co, 1947); Richard Hindry Barker, *Thomas Middleton*, (London: Greenwood Press, 1974); Schoenbaum.

41 R.V. Holdsworth, *Three Jacobean Revenge Tragedies: A Casebook* (London: Macmillan, 1990); Andrew Hilton, 'Director's Note: *The Changeling*', *Shakespeare at the Tobacco Factory*, 2004. Available at: www.stf-theatre.org.uk/the-changeling, (accessed 16 April 2016).

42 Douglas Bruster, 'The Changeling', in Gary Taylor and John Lavagnino, eds, *Thomas Middleton and Early Modern Textual Culture: A Companion to the Collected Works* (Oxford: Oxford University Press, 2007), 1094–1104 (1095).

43 Robert Ornstein, *The Moral Vision of Jacobean Tragedy* (Madison: University of Wisconsin Press, 1960), 180.

44 Joe Hill-Gibbins qtd in Natasha Tripney, 'Changing *The Changeling*', *Exeunt*, 13 November 2012.

45 Richard Findlater, *Time & Tide*, 9 March 1961; J.C. Trewin, *Birmingham Post*, 22 February 1961.

46 Findlater; Felix Barker, *Evening News*, 22 February 1961.

47 T.C. Worsley, *Financial Times*, 22 February 1961.

48 1.1.120

49 1.1.111–23

50 See Roberta Barker and David Nicol, 'Does Beatrice Joanna Have a Subtext?: *The Changeling* on the London Stage', *Early Modern Literary Studies* 10.1 (2004), 3.1–43. Note, too, the prominence of Ernest Jones' psychoanalytic reading of *Hamlet* during the same period.

51 Kate Lechler, 'Thomas Middleton in Performance 1960–2013: A History of Reception' (Unpublished PhD Thesis, Florida State University, 2014), 42.

52 Joost Daalder, 'Introduction', in Joost Daalder, ed., *The Changeling* (London: A&C Black, 1990), xi–xlvii (xxv).

53 Jay O'Berski, *Thomas Middleton and William Rowley, The Changeling* (Basingstoke: Palgrave Macmillan, 2012), 3.

54 Michael Billington, 'The Changeling', *Guardian*, 6 September 1978.

55 T.G.W, 16 March 1979; A. Hulme, 'The Changeling', *Manchester Evening News*, 27 October 1978.

56 Barker and Nicol, 3.3.

57 Ibid., 3.38.

58 Daalder, xxv. See also Nora Williams, '"Cannot I Keep That Secret?" Editing and Performing Asides in *The Changeling*', *Shakespeare Bulletin* 34.1 (2016), 29–45.

59 O'Berski, 7.

60 Barker and Nicol, 3.38; Ben Jacobs, Sabrina Siddiqui and Scott Bixby, '"You Can Do Anything": Trump Brags about Using Fame to get Women', *Guardian*, 8 October 2016.

61 Kim Solga, *Violence Against Women in Early Modern Performance: Invisible Acts* (New York: Palgrave Macmillan 2009), 2.

62 Ibid., 7–8.

63 Ibid., 27. See also Kim Solga, 'The Architecture of the Act: Renovating Beatrice Joanna's Closet', in Susan Bennett and Mary Polito, eds, *Performing Environments: Site-Specificity in Medieval and Early Modern English Drama* (Basingstoke: Palgrave Macmillan, 2014), 141–75.

64 Pascale Aebischer, *Shakespeare's Violated Bodies: Stage and Screen Performance* (Cambridge: Cambridge University Press, 2004), 27–8.

65 Ibid., 29–30.

66 Thomson, xxvi.

67 Michael Scott, *Middleton and Rowley: The Changeling* (London: Penguin, 1989), 58; Robert Cushman, 'Passion and the Playwrights', *The Observer*, 10 September 1978.

68 Martin White, '*The Changeling*', in Martin White, *Middleton and Tourneur* (Basingstoke, Macmillan, 1992), 93–110, 107.

69 For an historical perspective on madness and the diagnosis and treatment of mental illness in the early modern period, see Carol Thomas Neely, *Distracted Subjects: Madness and Gender in Shakespeare and Early Modern Culture* (Ithaca: Cornell University Press, 2004).
70 Frances Ryan, 'We Wouldn't Accept Actors Blacking Up, So Why Applaud "Cripping Up"?', *Guardian,* 13 January 2015.

# SELECT BIBLIOGRAPHY

Aebischer, Pascale. 'Middleton in the Cinema', in Suzanne Gossett, ed., *Thomas Middleton in Context* (Cambridge: Cambridge University Press, 2011), 336–45.

Aebischer, Pascale. *Screening Early Modern Drama: Beyond Shakespeare* (Cambridge: Cambridge University Press, 2013).

Aebischer, Pascale and Kathryn Prince, eds. *Performing Early Modern Drama Today* (Cambridge: Cambridge University Press, 2012).

Barker, Robert Hindry. *Thomas Middleton* (New York: Columbia University Press, 1958).

Barker, Roberta and David Nicol. 'Does Beatrice Joanna have a Subtext?: *The Changeling* on the London Stage', *Early Modern Literary Studies* 10.1 (2004), 1–43.

Bawcutt, N.W. ed., *The Changeling* (London: Methuen, 1958).

Bennett, Susan. *Performing Nostalgia: Shifting Shakespeare and the Contemporary Past* (London: Routledge, 1995).

Berger, Thomas L. 'The Petrarchan Fortress in *The Changeling*', *Renaissance Papers* (1969), 185–212.

Boehrer, Bruce. 'Alsemero's Closet: Privacy and Interiority in *The Changeling*', *Journal of English and Germanic Philology* 96 (1997), 349–68.

Bradbrook, Muriel. *Themes and Conventions of Elizabethan Tragedy* 2nd edn (Cambridge: Cambridge University Press, 1980).

Bromham, A.A. and Zara Bruzzi. *'The Changeling' and the Years of Crisis, 1619–1624: A Hieroglpyh of Britain* (London: Pinter Publishers, 1990).

Brooke, Nicholas. *Horrid Laughter in Jacobean Tragedy* (London: Open Books, 1979).

Bruster, Douglas, ed. *The Changeling*, in Gary Taylor and John Lavagnino, gen. eds, *Thomas Middleton: The Collected Works* (Oxford: Oxford University Press, 2007), 1637–78.

Burks, Deborah G. '"I'll Want My Will Else": *The Changeling* and Women's Complicity with their Rapists', *English Literary History* 62 (1995), 759–90.

Burnett, Mark Thornton. '*The Changeling* and Masters and Servants', in Garrett A. Sullivan et al., eds, *Early Modern English Drama: A Critical Companion* (Oxford: Oxford University Press, 2006), 298–308.

Cahill, Patricia A. 'The Play of Skin in *The Changeling*', *Postmedieval: A Journal of Medieval Cultural Studies* 3.4 (2012), 391–406.

Chakravorty, Swapan. *Society and Politics in the Plays of Thomas Middleton* (Oxford: Oxford University Press, 1996).

Cox, John D. and David Scott Kastan, eds. *A New History of Early English Drama* (New York: Columbia University Press, 1997).

Daalder, Joost, ed. *The Changeling* (London: A&C Black, 1990).

Dawson, Anthony B. 'Giving the Finger: Puns and Transgression in *The Changeling*', *The Elizabethan Theatre* XII (1993), 93–112.

Dolan, Frances E. 'Re-reading Rape in *The Changeling*', *Journal for Early Modern Cultural Studies* 11.1 (2011), 4–29.

Dowd, Michelle and Natasha Korda, eds. *Working Subjects in Early Modern English Drama* (Farnham: Ashgate, 2011).

Dutton, Richard, ed. *The Oxford Handbook of Early Modern Theatre* (Oxford: Oxford University Press, 2009).

Eliot, T.S. 'Thomas Middleton', in *Elizabethan Dramatists* (London: Faber & Faber, 1963), 83–93.

Empson, William. *Some Versions of Pastoral* [1935] (London: The Hogarth Press, 1986).

Friedenreich, Frederick, ed. *'Accompaninge the players': Essays Celebrating Thomas Middleton, 1580–1980* (New York: AMS Press, 1983).

Gossett, Suzanne. '"Best Men are Molded out of Faults": Marrying the Rapist in Jacobean Drama', *English Literary Renaissance* 14.3 (1984), 305–27.

Gossett, Suzanne, ed. *Thomas Middleton in Context* (Cambridge: Cambridge University Press, 2011).

Gurr, Andrew and Farah Karim-Cooper, eds. *Moving Shakespeare Indoors: Performance and Repertoire in the Jacobean Playhouse* (Cambridge: Cambridge University Press, 2014).

Haber, Judith. '"I(t) could not choose but follow": Erotic Logic in *The Changeling*', *Representations* 81.1 (2003), 79–98.

Heinemann, Margot. *Puritanism and Theatre: Thomas Middleton and Opposition Drama under the Early Stuarts* (Cambridge: Cambridge University Press, 1980).
Hirschfeld, Heather Anne. *Joint Enterprises: Collaborative Drama and the Institutionalization of the English Renaissance Theater* (Amherst, MA: University of Massachusetts Press, 2004).
Holdsworth, Roger, ed. *Three Jacobean Revenge Tragedies* (London: Macmillan, 1990).
Hopkins, Lisa. 'Beguiling the Master of the Mystery: Form and Power in *The Changeling*', *Medieval and Renaissance Drama in England* 9 (1997), 149–61.
Hoy, Cyrus. 'The Shares of Fletcher and his Collaborators in the Beaumont and Fletcher Canon (V)', *Studies in Bibliography* 13 (1960), 77–108.
Hutchings, Mark and A.A. Bromham. *Middleton and his Collaborators* (Plymouth: Northcote House, 2008).
Hutchings, Mark. 'De Flores between the Acts', *Studies in Theatre & Performance* 31.1 (2011), 95–111.
Hutchings, Mark. '*The Changeling* at Court', *Cahiers Élisabéthains* 81 (2012), 15–24.
Jackson, Kenneth S. *Separate Theaters: Bethlem ('Bedlam') Hospital and the Shakespearean Stage* (Newark: University of Delaware Press, 2005).
Lehmann, Courtney. '"Taking back the night": Hospitality in *The Changeling* on Film', *Shakespeare Bulletin* 29.4 (2011), 591–604.
Levin, Richard. *The Multiple Plot in English Renaissance Drama* (Chicago: Chicago University Press, 1971).
Lindley, David. *The Trials of Frances Howard: Fact and Fiction at the Court of King James* (London: Routledge, 1993).
Luttfring, Sara D. 'Bodily Narratives and the Politics of Virginity in *The Changeling* and the Essex Divorce', *Renaissance Drama* 39 (2011), 97–128.
Masten, Jeffrey. *Textual Intercourse: Collaboration, Authorship, and Sexualities in Renaissance Drama* (Cambridge: Cambridge University Press, 1997).
Malcomson, Cristina. '"As Tame as the Ladies": Politics and Gender in *The Changeling*', *English Literary Renaissance* 20 (1990), 320–39.
McMullan, Gordon. '*The Changeling* and the Dynamics of Ugliness', in E. Smith and G.A. Sullivan, eds, *The Cambridge Companion*

to *English Renaissance Tragedy* (Cambridge: Cambridge University Press, 2010), 222–35.

Mooney, Michael E. '"Framing" as Collaborative Technique: Two-Middleton-Rowley Plays', *Comparative Drama* 13 (1979), 127–41.

Neely, Carol. *Distracted Subjects: Madness and Gender in Shakespeare and Early Modern Culture* (Ithaca: Cornell University Press, 2004).

Neill, Michael. '"Hidden Malady": Death, Discovery, and Indistinction in *The Changeling*', *Renaissance Drama* 22 (1991), 95–121.

Neill, Michael, ed. *The Changeling* (London: Bloomsbury, 2006).

Nicol, David. *Middleton and Rowley: Forms of Collaboration in the Jacobean Playhouse* (Toronto: University of Toronto Press, 2012).

Nochimson, Richard L. '"Sharing" *The Changeling* by Playwrights and Professors: The Certainty about Uncertain Knowledge about Collaborations', *Early Theatre* 5 (2002), 37–57.

O'Berski, Jay. *'The Changeling': A Guide to the Text and the Play in Performance* (Basingstoke: Palgrave Macmillan, 2012).

O'Callaghan, Michelle. *Thomas Middleton, Renaissance Dramatist* (Edinburgh: Edinburgh University Press, 2009).

Panek, Jennifer. 'Shame and Pleasure in *The Changeling*', *Renaissance Drama* 42.2 (2014), 191–215.

Paster, Gail Kern. 'The Ecology of the Passions in *A Chaste Maid in Cheapside* and *The Changeling*' in Gary Taylor and Trish Thomas Henley, eds, *The Oxford Handbook of Thomas Middleton* (Oxford: Oxford University Press, 2012), 148–63.

Patterson, Annabel. 'Introduction' to *The Changeling*, in Gary Taylor and John Lavagnino, gen. eds, *Thomas Middleton: The Collected Works* (Oxford: Oxford University Press, 2007), 1632–6.

Roberts, Marilyn. 'A Preliminary Checklist of Productions of Thomas Middleton's Plays', *Research Opportunities in Renaissance Drama* 28 (1985), 37–61.

Ricks, Christopher. 'The Moral and Poetic Structure of *The Changeling*', *Essays in Criticism* 10 (1960), 290–306.

Salingar, Leo. *Dramatic Form in Shakespeare and the Jacobeans* (Cambridge: Cambridge University Press, 1986).

Schafer, Elizabeth. 'Performance Editions, Editing, and Editors', *Shakespeare Survey* 59 (2006), 198–212.

Schoenbaum, Samuel. *Middleton's Tragedies: A Critical Study* (New York: Columbia University Press, 1955).
Simmons, J.L. 'Diabolical Realism in Middleton and Rowley's *The Changeling*', *Renaissance Drama* 11 (1980), 135–70.
Slater, Ann Pasternak. 'Hypallage, Barley-brake, and *The Changeling*', *Review of English Studies* 34 (1983), 429–40.
Solga, Kim. *Violence Against Women in Early Modern Performance* (New York: Palgrave Macmillan, 2009).
Solga, Kim. 'Playing *The Changeling* Architecturally', in S. Bennett and M. Polito, eds, *Performing Environments: Site Specificity in Medieval and Early Modern English Drama* (Basingstoke: Palgrave Macmillan, 2014), 56–78.
Steen, Sara Jayne. *Ambrosia in an Earthern Vessel: Three Centuries of Audience and Reader Response to the Works of Thomas Middleton* (New York: AMS Press, 1993).
Sugimora, N.K. 'Changelings and *The Changeling*', *Essays in Criticism* 56.3 (2006), 241–65.
Taylor, Gary and John Lavagnino, gen. eds. *Thomas Middleton: The Collected Works* (Oxford: Oxford University Press, 2007).
Taylor, Gary and John Lavagnino, gen. eds. *Thomas Middleton and Early Modern Textual Culture: A Companion to The Collected Works* (Oxford: Oxford University Press, 2007).
Taylor, Gary and Trish Thomas Henley, eds. *The Oxford Handbook of Thomas Middleton* (Oxford: Oxford University Press, 2012).
Tosh, Will. *Playing Indoors: Staging Early Modern Drama in the Sam Wanamaker Playhouse* (London: Bloomsbury, 2018).
White, Martin. *Middleton and Tourneur* (Basingstoke: Macmillan, 1992).
White, Martin. *A Chamber of Discoveries* (Bristol: Ignition Films, n.d.).
Williams, Nora. '"Cannot I keep that secret?": Editing and Performing Asides in *The Changeling*', *Shakespeare Bulletin* 34.1 (2016), 29–45.
Womack, Peter. 'Off-stage', in *Early Modern Theatricality*, ed. Henry S. Turner (Oxford: Oxford University Press, 2013), 71–92.

# INDEX

Aebischer, Pascale 162, 166, 177, 178, 180, 181, 188, 204, 205, 231n, 252n, 255n, 256n, 260n
Albertus, Arch-Duke 125
Allfree, Claire 154, 233n, 250n
Aldwych Theatre 50, 52
Amboyna massacre 74
American Repertory Theatre 55, 228n
Amster, Mara 82, 83, 236n
Antwerp, Treaty of 125
Aquinas, Thomas 107
Archer, William 21, 22, 40, 41, 216n, 223n, 224n
*Arden of Faversham* 40, 224n
Artaud, Antonin 114, 241n
Arya, Rina 167, 253n
Astley, Sir John 211n
Attenborough, Michael 59

Baker, Stanley 182
Bakhtin, Mikhail 86
Barber, Paul 58
Barbican, The 62, 144, 145, 146, 154, 248n, 251n
Barbican Pit 59
Barker, R.H. 4, 23–4, 199, 213n, 217n, 259n
Barker, Roberta 10, 44, 61, 64, 77, 159, 160, 161, 202, 203, 215n, 225n, 228n, 229n, 233n, 236n, 239n, 246n, 252n, 259n, 260n
Bawcutt, N.W. 23–4, 134, 139, 191, 199, 209, 215n, 217n, 221n, 222n, 239n, 242n, 244n, 246n, 247n, 258n, 259n
Beaumont, Francis 1, 2, 212n
bed trick 5, 6, 8, 9, 12, 17, 18, 19, 40, 64, 86, 94, 110, 139–41, 175, 193–4, 247n
Bedlam 30, 64, 74–5, 127, 131, 235n
Beeston, Christopher 35–6, 221n
Beeston, William 35–6, 221n
Bellany, Alastair 214n
Benedict, David 154, 233n, 248n, 250n
Bennion, Peggy 46
Bentley, G.E. 213n
Berger, Jesse 64, 231n
Berger, Thomas L. 151, 249n
Betterton, Thomas 37–8
Billington, Michael 52, 54, 57, 66, 145, 147, 152, 155, 159, 202, 227n, 228n, 229n, 230n, 231n, 232n, 233n, 248n, 250n, 251n, 260n
Birkbeck College Literary Society 41, 42, 242n

*Blackadder* 57
Bond, Edward 114
Bourdieu, Pierre 68
Bovilsky, Lara 88–9, 90, 238n
Bradbrook, M.C. 9, 22, 23, 199, 216n, 259n
Bradford, Gameliel 21, 216n
Branagh, Kenneth 176
Branwell, John 202
Briggs, Julia 140, 247n
British Chinese Theatre Company 58–9
Bromham, A.A. 3, 31, 69, 72, 195, 212n, 213n, 214n, 219n, 234n, 235n, 257n
Brook, Peter 50, 52, 228n, 241n
Brooke, Nicholas 28, 151, 218n, 249n
Brown, James 58
 'It's a Mad World' 58
Brown, Karin 61, 188, 231n, 252n
Brown, Peter 159, 251n
Brustein, Robert 48, 49, 55–6, 59, 227n, 228n, 229n
Bruster, Douglas 4, 70, 199, 203, 208, 212n, 213n, 212n, 234n, 235n, 259n
Bruzzi, Zara 31, 72, 195, 213n, 214n, 219n, 235n, 257n
Buc, Sir George 211n, 243n
Bullen, A.H. 19, 28, 197, 215n, 216n
Bullokar, John 171
 *An English Expositor* 171
Burks, Deborah G. 33, 78, 79, 133, 147, 174, 220n, 236n, 246n, 248n, 253n, 254n
Burnett, Mark Thornton 85–6, 87, 237n

Burton, Robert 106, 240n
 *The Anatomy of Melancholy* 106, 240n

Cahill, Patricia A. 10, 11, 89–90, 127, 238n
Calderon de la Barca, Pedro 128, 244n, 245n
 *El Alcalde de Zalamea* 128, 244n, 245n
Calvinism 71, 101, 104–5, 118, 195–6, 239n, 240n
Campbell, Cheryl 59–60
Cannon, J.D. 46
Carr (*née* Howard), Frances, countess of Somerset 5–7, 10, 19, 28, 31, 82–3, 133, 141, 195, 214n, 236n, 257n,
Carr, Robert, Earl of Somerset 5–7, 10, 82
Catholic Monarchs, The 129
Caves, David 158
Cerqueira, Daniel 66
Cervantes, Miguel de 121, 132, 135, 137, 139, 243n, 245n, 246n, 247n
 *Don Quixote de la Mancha* 135, 137, 243n, 247n
 *La Fuerza de la Sangre* 132
 *Novelas Ejemplares* 131
Chakravorty, Swapan 33, 195, 214n, 220n, 257n
Charles II 1
Charles, Prince of Wales 71–2, 124
Chaudhuri, Una 77, 236n
Cheek by Jowl 62, 145, 147, 150, 154, 158, 159, 161, 204, 248n, 249n, 250n, 251n

Cherry, Brigid 175, 254n
Cherry, Caroline Lockett 26–7, 218n
Clap, Susannah 152, 249n
Clark, Jill 51
Clay, Caroline 55, 228n, 229n
Clown role 3, 4–5, 8, 110, 197–8, 213n
Cockett, Peter 58, 230n
Cohen, Charles Lloyd 101, 239n
collaborative authorship 1–5, 10, 18, 20–1, 24, 26, 30, 67–71, 193–4, 196–200
*Compulsion* (TV drama) 13, 177, 255n
Cornwall, Charlotte 54
Correa, Gustavo 130, 245n
Costa, Maddy 148, 156, 232n, 249n, 251n
Coveney, Michael 51, 63, 149, 157, 158, 227n, 230n, 232n, 249n, 251n
Cox, Alex 13
Cox, Brian 52, 174
Crook, Helkiah 75
Crutchley, Kate 202
Cusack, Sinead 50
Cushman, Robert 52, 205, 228n, 260n

D'Aquila, Diane 55
Daalder, Joost 30, 32, 133, 134, 202, 203, 208, 219n, 220n, 245n, 246n, 260n
Davenant, Sir William 1, 211n, 215n, 222n
Davies, Lindy 61, 231n

De Céspedes y Meneses, Gonzalo 122, 134–5, 137, 139, 140, 195, 247n
  *Poema Trágico del Español Gerardo* 11, 134–41, 246n, 247n
De Molina, Tirso 130
  *El Celoso Prudente* 130
de Vega, Lope 128, 245n
  *Fuenteovejuna*, 128
Dekker, Thomas 5, 73, 86, 131, 197, 198, 210, 242n, 245n
Dekker, Thomas, and John Ford and William Rowley
  *The Witch of Edmonton* 86, 210
Devereux, Robert, Earl of Essex 82
Digges, Leonard 5, 134, 141, 195, 247n
  *Gerardo the Unfortunate Spaniard* 5, 11, 134–41, 246n, 247n
Dilke, C.W. 2, 17, 19, 212n, 215n, 223n
Dimou, Fotini 150
Disability studies 14, 91, 148, 178, 206–8, 261n
Dobson, Michael 213n
Dodsley, Robert 2, 212n
Dolan, Frances E. 79–80, 133, 172, 180, 236n, 248n, 254n, 255n
Dollimore, Jonathan 29, 219n
Donnellan, Declan 64, 65, 144, 145, 146, 147, 154, 233n, 248n, 250n
doubling of roles 7, 23–4, 146
Dowd, Michelle 86, 237n

Downes, John 37, 222n
Duce, Sharon 54
Dudley, William 57
Duke of York's Company 1, 222n
Duke, Patty 48, 226n
Durrell, Lawrence 43, 44, 225n
Dury, Ian 178, 208, 255n
Dutton, Richard 211n
Dyce, Alexander 18, 215n

Eaton, Sara 29, 147, 153, 219n, 248n, 250n
Eder, Richard 55, 228n
Edinburgh Theatre Festival 50
Edwards, Christopher 57, 229n
Eliot, T.S. 1, 2, 4, 21–2, 100, 198–9, 211n, 216n, 223n, 239n, 258n
Ellis, Havelock 19, 197, 216n
Ellis-Fermor, Una 22, 60, 199, 216n, 217n, 259n
Empson, William 9, 22, 23, 199, 216n, 238n, 259n
Engle, Lars 192, 257n
Erne, Lukas 192, 257n
Essex divorce case 19, 28, 82, 83, 133, 141
Estill, Laura 162, 252n
Evans, Frank 50
Eyre, Richard 50, 56, 57, 229n

Faith, Adam 45
Farr, Dorothy M. 25–6, 217n, 218n
Fensom, Jonathan 152, 153
Ferguson, Brian 207
Findlater, Richard 200, 259n
Fitzpatrick, Tim 214n

Fletcher, John 1, 2, 40, 75, 121, 212n, 245n
*The Loyal Subject* 37
*The Mad Lover* 37
*The Pilgrim* 75
*The Wild Goose Chase* 40
Floyd-Wilson, Mary 90, 240n
Foakes, R.A. 213n
Ford, John 5, 73, 86, 131, 210, 242n, 245n
Fraser, Brad 58
*The Ugly Man* 58, 229n
Freudian approaches 10, 24, 32, 44, 52, 64, 78, 100, 114, 133, 159, 200–3, 204, 231n, 233n, 241n, 246n
Fuchs, Barbara 73, 124, 134, 235n, 243n, 246n

Galenic theory 106, 117
Garber, Marjorie 32, 82, 175, 220n, 237n, 254n
Gardner Arts Centre, Brighton 50
Gardner, Lyn 65, 233n
Geidt Jeremy 55
Gibraltar, Battle of 74, 125
Gill, Peter 50–4, 57, 205
Goffe, Thomas 36
*The Careless Shepherdess* 36
Gondomar, Count of. See Sarmiento de Acuña, Don Diego de
Gosse, Edmund 20, 216n
Gossett, Suzanne 235n, 244–5n, 255n, 256n
Goya 44, 45, 50, 60, 122
Gravelle, Trystan 66, 154, 210
Gray, Pat 42
Greene, John 36, 221n

# INDEX

Gurr, Andrew 221n, 222n, 238n, 249n

Haber, Judith 78, 133, 147, 236n, 245n, 248n, 252n
Haliburton, Rachel 62, 232n
Halley, Janet 79
Hands, Terry 50, 52–4, 203, 228n
Harding, Sarah 176–7, 255n
Harris, George 56–7, 229n
Hawking, Stephen 207
Hayley, William 16, 17, 38–9, 222–3n
　*Marcella* 16, 17, 38–9, 222–3n
Hays, David 47
Hedges, Sally 202
Hedrick, Donald 76–7, 235n
Heilpern, John 225n
Heinemann, Margot 28–9, 82, 189, 195, 213n, 218n, 236n, 240n, 256n, 258n
Henry, Prince 124, 213n
Henslowe, Philip 4, 213n
Herbert, Sir Henry 35, 211n, 221n
Heron, Jonathan 189–90, 256n
Heywood, Thomas 4, 41
Higgins, John 87, 237
Hill-Gibbins, Joe 61, 66, 144, 146, 149, 155, 157, 159–60, 161–2, 199, 205, 233n, 247n, 248n, 251n, 259n
Hilton, Andrew 63, 65, 232n, 259n
Hinton, Alisdair 148, 157, 249n, 251n
Hirschfeld, Heather Anne 68, 234n

Hitchcock, Alfred 43
Hobson, Harold 44, 225n
Hoffman, Theodore 226n
Hogg, James 222–3n
Holdsworth, R.J. 199, 212n, 239n, 259
Hope-Wallace, Philip 43, 225n
Hopkins, Lisa 34, 81, 82, 214n, 220n, 236n, 246n
Howard, Frances, Countess of Somerset. *See* Carr, Frances
Hoy, Cyrus 212n
humours, theory of 88, 106–7
Hunt, Leigh 18–19, 20, 215n
Hutchings, Mark 69, 72–4, 195, 211n, 212n, 213n, 215n, 235n, 257–8n
Hutchings, Peter 175, 254n

*I Lunatici* 50
Ibsen, Henrik 40
interval 12, 72, 133

Jackson, Kenneth 74–5, 235n
James I & VI 5, 31, 71, 74, 75, 123–4, 214n, 241n, 243n, 257n, 258n
James, Emrys 53
Jardine, Lisa 33, 220n
Jenkins, Peter 51, 52, 53, 227n, 228n
Jenkins, Sue 202
jig, the 8
Johnson, Paula 27–8, 218n
Jones, Inigo 77
Jonson, Ben 1, 78, 133, 214n
　*Hymenaei* 133, 214n
　*Volpone* 61

Jordan, Robert 25, 217n
Jowett, John 213n

Kazan, Elia 46–9, 55–6, 226n, 227n
Keen, Will 65, 158, 250n, 251n
Keenan, Siobhan 221n
Keith, Ian 41
Kellaway, Kate 56, 60, 66, 229n, 230n, 231n, 233n
Kennedy, Dennis 228n
Kidnie, M.J. 190, 256n
King's Men 3, 37, 243n
Kirwan, Peter 155, 160, 251n
Kristeva, Julia 166–7, 252–3n
Kyd, Thomas
  *The Spanish Tragedy* 194, 213
Kynaston, Edward 38

Lady Elizabeth's Men 35, 221n
Lake, David 199, 258n, 259n
Lavagnino, John 70, 208, 212n, 234n, 235n, 241n, 242n, 243n, 244n, 245n, 246n, 257n, 258n, 259n
Law, John Philip 46
Lawrence, Adam 207
Lawrence, D.H. 114, 241n
Lechler, Kate 201, 232n, 260n
Lee, Nick 207
Lehmann, Courtney 166, 176–7, 178, 180, 181, 252n, 253n, 254n, 255n
Leong, Susan 58
Lerma, Duke of 125
Letts, Quentin 159, 233n, 251n
Levin, Richard 25, 26, 194, 217n, 218n, 257n
Limon, Jerzy 195, 213n

Lincoln Center Repertory Theater 46, 48–9
Lindley, David 214n, 257n
Little, Arthur L., Jr. 32, 220n
Lloyd, Bertram 134, 246n
Lloyd-Hughes, Henry 207
Loden, Barbara 46–7
Loney, Glenn 46, 48, 226n
Lowell, James Russell 18–19, 21, 39, 215n, 223n
Lopez, Jeremy 188, 189, 250n, 256n
Luckett, Moya 176
Luttfring, Sara D. 9, 82–3, 214n, 237n
Lyly, John 41
Lyon, Julian 58

McAlindon, T. 30, 219n
McDougall, Gordon 50
MacDowell Club, New York 41
McMullan, Gordon 69–70, 178, 183, 185, 192, 234n, 252n, 255n, 256n, 257n
Machiavel figure 73, 124, 137, 138
Madame Tussaud's 44
Maerten, Annegret 155, 250n
Magdalen Players, Oxford 42
Marlowe, Christopher 188
  *Dido, Queen of Carthage* 188
  *Doctor Faustus* 188
Marnich, Melanie 58
  *Tallgrass Gothic* 58
Marshall, Norman 224n
*Marrow of Complements, The* 15–16, 215n
Mary Tudor 124

## INDEX

Massinger, Philip 41
  *The Bondman* 37
Master of the Revels 5, 35, 211
Maxwell, Jackie 62, 63, 231n, 232n
Mayes, Richard 181
#MeToo movement 78, 185
Menzer, Paul 154, 231n, 232n, 233n, 248n, 250n
*Middleton's Changeling* (film) 13
Middleton, Thomas
  *A Chaste Maid in Cheapside* 210
  *A Game at Chess* 3, 5, 73, 116, 127, 131, 138, 213n, 241n
  *The Inner Temple Masque* 3
  *The Lady's Tragedy* 73, 246n
  *A Mad World, My Masters* 3, 4
  *Michaelmas Term* 3
  *More Dissemblers Besides Women* 212n
  *The Revenger's Tragedy* 3, 194, 210
  *A Trick to Catch the Old One* 3, 4
  *The Widow* 37
  *Women Beware Women* 81, 116, 187, 188, 241n
Middleton, Thomas, John Ford, William Rowley and Thomas Dekker
  *The Spanish Gypsy* 5, 37, 73, 116, 131–2, 196, 212n, 242n
Middleton, Thomas, and Thomas Dekker
  *The Roaring Girl* 210
Middleton, Thomas, and William Rowley
  *A Fair Quarrel* 4, 5
  *The Old Law* 4
  *Wit at Several Weapons* 4
Miller, Arthur 47
  *After the Fall* 47
Mirren, Helen 174, 182
Mooney, Michael E. 5, 68, 212n, 213n, 234n
Moore, Anthony Telford 32, 220n, 245n
Monk, Nicholas 189–90, 256n
Monroe, Marilyn 47
Morahan, Hattie 66, 153–4, 60, 210, 233n, 250n, 252n
Morley, Sheridan 53, 227n, 228n, 229n
Morrison, Campbell 179
Morrison, Peter 29, 219n
Moseley, Humphrey 36
Muller, Robert 45, 225
multiple plot 7
Munro, Lucy 188–90, 256n

Nagra, Parminder 177, 255n
National Theatre 50, 56, 157
National Theatre Company 50
Nead, Lynda 204–5
Neely, Carol Thomas 74–6, 235n, 261n
Neill, Heather 210
Neill, Michael 31, 85, 87, 140–1, 145, 190, 208, 211n, 214n, 219n, 230n, 237n, 247n, 249n, 256n
Nemesius, Bishop of Emesa 117, 242n
  *On the Nature of Man* 117, 242n

New York Shakespeare Festival 45
Nicol, David 3, 10, 44, 61, 64, 70–1, 77–8, 159, 161, 196–9, 203, 212n, 213n, 215n, 225n, 228n, 229n, 233n, 234n, 236n, 239n, 246n, 251n, 252n, 257n, 258n, 259n, 260n
Nightingale, Benedict 52–3, 228n, 231n
Nochimson, Richard L. 67–8, 70, 212n, 234n
North Africa 89

Oakley, Michael 62–3, 144, 148–51, 155–9, 248n, 251n
O'Berski, Jay 202, 203, 223n, 229–30n, 250n, 252n, 260n
offstage 7, 11, 12, 63, 83, 94–9, 140, 146, 148, 152, 158, 204–5, 230n
Ogura, Toshie 59
O'Maonlai, Colm 181
Ormerod, Nick 145, 154
Ornstein, Robert 199, 259n
Osborne, John 100
Overbury, Sir Thomas 6, 28, 82, 87
Oxford Experimental Theatre Club 42
Oxford Stage Company 50

Panek, Jennifer 9–10, 12, 83–4, 100, 122, 188, 190, 237n, 246n, 247n
Papp, Joseph 45–6, 49, 226n, 227n

Park, Katharine 107, 240n
Paster, Gail Kern 88–90, 238n, 240n
Patterson, Annabel 71–2, 235n, 243n
Paul, St 104–5, 108, 117
 *Epistle to the Romans* 104, 115, 118, 240n, 242n
Pegasus Society 42, 43, 224n
Peckinpah, Sam 181
Pentzell, Raymond J. 26, 218n
Pepys, Samuel 37, 211n, 222n
Peter, John 60, 65, 229n, 231n, 233n
Philip II 129
Phoenix (Cockpit) playhouse 35, 77, 116, 151, 221n
Phoenix Society, The 40, 41, 223n
Pinter, Harold 100
Piper, Emma 52–3, 202
Plotkins, Marilyn J. 228n
Polanski, Roman 176
Portway, Saskia 65
Power, Dominic 63, 199
Power, William 243
Prescott, Paul 189–90, 256n
Presley, Elvis 58
 'Love Me Tender' 58
Primus, Barry 48
Prince Charles's Men 71, 198
Prince, Kathryn 162–3, 188, 231n, 252n, 256n
Prowse, Philip 51
psychoanalytic theory 11, 69–70, 78–9, 200–3, 208, 259n
Purcell, Stephen 149, 249n, 250n

Queen of Bohemia's Men. *See* Lady Elizabeth's Men
Queen Henrietta's Men 36, 221n
Quick, Diana 53
Quignard, Pascal 169–70, 253n
Quinn, Martin 223n

Raine, Jessica 66
Randall, Dale B.J. 30, 32, 219n, 243n, 244n
Rasmussen, Eric 192, 257n
Ray, Robin 45
Ray-King, Amanda 178
Reade, Timothy 36–7
Red Bull Theater, New York 64
Redmayne, Eddie 207
Reed, Sophia 58
Reisch, Gregor 107
Renaissance Theatre (company) 40
Renton, Alex 57, 229n
Resurgens theatre company 63
Reynolds, Bruce 76, 77, 235n
Reynolds, John 11, 72, 101, 122, 123–8, 134–5, 137–9, 141, 195, 243–4n
 *The Triumphs of Gods Revenge* 11, 72, 101, 122, 123–8, 134–5, 137–9, 141, 195, 243–4n
 *Vox Coeli* 123, 243n
*Revengers Tragedy* (film) 13
Rhodes, John 37–8
Richardson, Samuel 38, 222n
Richardson, Miranda 56–7
Richardson, Tony 42–5, 47, 100, 189, 200, 225n
Ricks, Christopher 24, 141, 192–3, 217n, 234n, 241n, 247n, 257n

Riverside Studios, London 50–4, 227n
Robbins, William 37
Roberts, Marilyn 224n
Romans 104, 115, 118, 242n
Ronconi, Luca 50, 227n
Rowley, William
 *All's Lost by Lust* 210
 *A New Wonder* 212n
Royal Court Theatre, The 43, 45, 114, 200, 241n
Royal Shakespeare Company, The
Russo, Francine 59, 230n
Rutherford, Malcolm 58, 60, 230n, 231n
Ryan, Frances 207, 261n
Rylance, Mark 58
Ryner, Bradley 88, 238n

Sabor, Peter 222n
Salingar, Leo 30, 219n
Sam Wanamaker Playhouse 12, 93, 144, 151–2, 200, 207, 249n, 250n, 251n
Sarmiento de Acuña, Don Diego de (Count of Gondomar) 123–4, 131
Schechner, Richard 49, 226n, 227n
Schoenbaum, Samuel 22–3, 200, 217n, 257n, 259n
Scott, Michael 29, 218n, 260n
Scott, Sir Walter 16–18, 19, 34, 215n
 *Sir Tristrem* 16–17, 215n
Shakespeare, William
 *All's Well that Ends Well* 140, 194

*Hamlet* 176, 194, 204, 213n, 240n, 259n
*King Lear* 85, 204
*Macbeth* 176, 177, 187, 243n
*Measure for Measure* 140, 187, 194
*Much Ado About Nothing* 172
*Othello* 56, 85, 187, 204, 243n
*Pericles* 37
*Richard III* 178, 187, 241n
*Titus Andronicus* 204–5
*Twelfth Night* 85, 187
Shakespeare, William, and John Fletcher
  *Cardenio* 121, 242n
Shakespeare's Globe 12, 93, 188, 203, 210, 250n
Shakespearean Theater Workshop 45, 226n
Shaw, George Bernard 40
Shaw, Robert 44
Simkin, Stevie 181
Simmons, J.L. 28, 214n, 218n
Slater, Ann Pasternak 193, 257n
Smith, Bruce C. 214n
Smith, Emma 210, 234n, 257n
Smith, Peter J. 161, 232n, 248n, 252n
Solga, Kim 65, 77, 79, 204, 215n, 232n, 233n, 236n, 260n
South London Theatre Centre 51
Southwark Playhouse 62, 144, 148–50, 155–61, 232n, 249n, 251n
Spain (English attitudes to) 11, 71–4, 141
Spanish Civil War 62–3

Spanish Golden Age 130–1, 139, 141
Spanish Infanta, Ana María 124
Spanish Infanta, María Ana 124
Spanish Match 72–3, 76, 124, 245n
Spenser, Edmund 78
Stanislavski, Konstantin 47
Stern, Jay 176–7
Stockholm Syndrome 66
Stockton, Sharon 31, 219n
Stationers' Register 5
Steele, Tommy 45
Steen, Sara Jayne 222n
Stilling, Roger 27, 218n
Storry, Malcolm 59–60
Stratford Festival, Ontario 62, 203
Stratford-upon-Avon 59, 228n
Streete, Adrian 195, 258n
Strindberg, August 43, 44, 100
  *Miss Julie* 44
subplot 3–4, 7–10, 14, 15–26, 30, 34, 36, 38, 42, 45–6, 49–51, 54–5, 57–61, 63–4, 67–70, 94, 97, 123, 127–8, 144–9, 151–2, 157, 160, 183–4, 192–4, 197–200, 205–7, 209, 212–13n, 224n, 247–8n
Summers, W. 41
Svendsen, Zoe 205, 210
Swan, The (Stratford) 59
Swinburne, A.C. 19–20, 39, 216n, 223n
Symon, David 42
Symonds, E.M. 221n

Tallmer, Jerry 46, 225n
Taubman, Harold 49, 226n, 227n

Taylor, Gary 70, 191–2, 197, 208, 212n, 213n, 234n, 235n, 238n, 240n, 241n, 242n, 243n, 244n, 245n, 246n, 253n, 256n, 258n, 259n
Taylor, Paul 157, 158, 159, 232n, 233n, 251n
Taymor, Julie 176
*Titus* (film) 176
Teellinck, Willem 118, 242n
Thaxter, John 65, 233n
Theater for a New Audience 59
Theobald, Lewis 121
  *Double Falsehood* 121
Third Party theatre company 63
Thomas, Matthew 65
Thompson, Marcus 13, 175–86, 208
Thomson, Patricia 194, 205, 208, 257n, 260n
Thorpe, Jeremy 51
Tobacco Factory, Bristol 63, 199, 210, 259n
Tomkins, Silvan 83
Tomlinson, T.B. 24–5, 217n
Trewin, J.C. 45, 53, 200, 225n, 228n, 259n
Tripney, Natasha 149, 152, 154, 161, 162, 231n, 233n, 248n, 249n, 250n, 252n, 259n
Trueman, Matt 160, 248n, 251n
Turks 125
Turner, Anne 87
Tynan, Kenneth 44, 45, 225n

Ultz 146
unconscious, the 9–11, 23, 32–3, 65–6, 77–81, 97–104, 106, 109–13, 132–3, 159–62, 200–3, 239n, 241n
Ure, Mary 44, 225n

Valladolid 123–5
Van Lennep, William 222n
Varnado, Christine 80–1, 89, 236n
Velasquez 52, 122
Villiers, George, Duke of Buckingham 5, 131
Vineburg, Steve 228n, 229n
virginity test 5–7, 9, 18–19, 21, 29–30, 32, 40, 53, 69, 82–4, 88, 109–10, 123, 137, 158, 109, 206

Wager, Lewis 115–16, 241n
  *The Life and Repentance of Mary Magdalene* 115–16, 241n
Wall, Stephen 60, 230n, 231n
Walton, Dawn 62
Wardle, Irving 53, 227n, 228n, 230n, 231n
Wearing, J.P. 224n
Webster, John 41, 188, 211n, 241n
  *The Duchess of Malfi* 187, 188, 241n
  *The White Devil* 187, 188, 224n
Weatherby, W.J. 225n
Weintraub, Stanley 223n
Weisgall, Deborah 229n
Weiss, Peter 50
  *Marat/Sade* 50
Weston, Richard 87
White Bear Theatre 58, 188

White, Martin 206, 260n
Wiggin, Pauline C. 20–1, 216n
Wiggins, Martin 31–2, 220n
Williams, Holly 66, 160–1, 233n, 250n, 252n
Williams, Linda 184, 255n
Williams, Nora 13–14, 52, 91, 148, 153, 225n, 250n, 254n, 260n
Williams, Olivia 65–6, 154, 159, 233n, 250n, 252n
Williams, Tennessee
  *Cat on a Hot Tin Roof* 48
Winstone, Ray 177
Wither, George 117, 242n
Womack, Peter 11, 214n, 238n
Woodruff, Robert 59, 230n

Woods, Penelope 151, 249n
Worsley T.C. 43, 45, 200, 225n, 259n
Worthen, W.B. 149, 249n
Wright, Thomas 108, 241n
  *The Passions of the Minde in Generall* 108, 241n

Young, B.A. 50, 54, 227n, 228n
Young, Edward 222n
Young Vic, The 61, 64, 66, 144, 146–7, 149, 155, 157, 159, 205–7, 210
Yurka, Blanche 41

Zysk, Jay 84, 237n

www.ingramcontent.com/pod-product-compliance
Lightning Source LLC
Chambersburg PA
CBHW052154300426
44115CB00011B/1660